THE AUTOBIOGRAPHY OF FEDERICO SANCHEZ

JORGE SEMPRUN

THE AUTOBIOGRAPHY OF FEDERICO SANCHEZ AND THE COMMUNIST UNDERGROUND IN SPAIN

TRANSLATED BY HELEN R. LANE

KARZ PUBLISHERS · NEW YORK

Translation copyright © 1979 by Karz Publishers and
Harvester Press Limited

Published in French as *Autobiographie de Federico Sanchez*
by Editions du Seuil

Original title: *Autobiografia de Federico Sanchez*
© Jorge Semprún, 1977

Library of Congress Cataloging in Publication Data

Semprún, Jorge, 1923-
    The Autobiography of Federico Sanchez
    and the Communist underground in Spain.

    Translation of Autobiografía de Federico Sánchez.
    1. Semprún, Jorge—Biography—Political career.
2. Author, Spanish—20th century—Biography.
3. Communists—Spain—Biography.   4. Spain—
Politics and government—1939-1975.   I. Title.
PQ6669.E5117Z46313ʹ   843ʹ.9ʹ14   79-19605
ISBN 0-918294-05-3

Published in the United States
by KARZ PUBLISHERS
320 West 105th Street
New York, N.Y. 10025

CONTENTS

To
JAVIER PRADERA
AND
DOMINGO GONZÁLEZ LUCAS

1 LA PASIONARIA HAS ASKED FOR THE FLOOR

You raise your eyes from the papers in front of you on the table and look at La Pasionaria. She is plainly nervous. She smooths back a lock of white hair. Then she puts her hands together, separates them, and unfolds the piece of paper she has ready. The paper that she is about to read to Fernando and you. Because she has written out what she has to say. This does not surprise you. You have always known her to write out beforehand what she has to say at so-called crucial moments.

In the summer of 1959, for example, at Ouspenskoia, near Moscow, five years ago, when she resigned from her post as secretary-general of the party—and that decision, announced as irrevocable, exploded like a bomb at the meeting—she had also written out what she had to say beforehand, remember

(indeed I remember, you think now, many years later, in 1976, as you write these memoirs, I remember it very well: it was in the summer of 1959: seventeen years ago, that is: that's easily said, seventeen years: the space of an entire generation now separates us from that moment: in the summer, then, toward the middle of July—or perhaps at the end of the month—I was a member of the delegation that had been named to go to Moscow to talk with La Pasionaria: with Santiago Carrillo at the head of it, naturally, and with members Enrique Líster, Santiago Álvarez, Juan Gómez: perhaps others I no longer remember: maybe Romero Marín: and myself: or rather not myself: I scarcely existed at the time: so not myself but you: Federico Sánchez: it was a matter of going to persuade Dolores that the recent, resounding failure of the peaceful national strike, the HNP of June 18, hadn't been a failure at all but in reality a success: in the phantasmagorial reality of ideas, of the ideological, that is: I: all right then, you, Sánchez: had come from Madrid where I had been directing the work of the party in preparation for this Huelga Nacional Pacífica: I had been directing it with Francisco Romero Marín and Simón Sánchez Montero, but Simón couldn't get away to attend the meetings that summer: Simón had been arrested again on the very eve of our failure: on the afternoon of June 17: in the late afternoon: and it turned out that La Pasionaria had tried to oppose calling for a strike, had tried to persuade Carrillo in repeated letters of the need to refrain from sending out a call for a strike: Romero

Marín and I discovered this when we arrived abroad, and these letters of La Pasionaria's must be in the party archives I suppose: hence the failure of the strike had created a delicate situation among the party leadership, in which La Pasionaria still continued to occupy formally— and by that I do not mean observing the proper forms but purely as a matter of form—the post of secretary-general: a delicate situation that had grown even worse because before Romero Marín and I arrived from Madrid a strong critical current led by Fernando Claudín had already manifested itself in the first meetings of the party leadership devoted to examining the results of the action on June 18: a situation that Carrillo intended to resolve by convincing Dolores that that failure had not really been one at all: but instead, on reflection, analyzing it more dialectically, it had been a political success in general and more particularly his success: Carrillo's: and at the beginning of that meeting in Ouspenskoia that had been the situation between the delegation that had arrived from the West and La Pasionaria, around whom were seated the members of the Central Committee residing in Moscow at the time—Saiz, Balaguer, Sandvoal, Azcárate—if memory serves me: and that was when Dolores suddenly and unexpectedly read us the paper announcing her irrevocable resignation as secretary-general)

well anyway, what you wanted to say was that La Pasionaria was nervous at that moment as well, remember. At that moment as well she smoothed back a rebellious lock of white hair. So you are not surprised. Every time Dolores is about to make an important speech, she prepares it in writing. You already know this.

You have raised your eyes from your papers. You look at La Pasionaria.

Her speech is going to be decisive, doubtless, but it will be very brief. You are sitting across from her, on the other side of the long table. You can see perfectly well that she has written only a few lines, in her large sprawling hand, on the paper that she is about to read to you. A decisive speech, then, but a brief one. A thunderbolt perhaps.

Or so one might be led to suppose.

If you were in a novel, if you were a fictional character, you would now remember other meetings with Dolores Ibárruri as you looked at her. In skillfully constructed novels, lightning flashes of memory come at just the right time and are very impressive. What is more, they allow the author to give his story a density that cannot be achieved by way of a mere linear narrative line. If you were in a novel, instead of being at a meeting of the Executive Committee of the Communist Party, you would now remember your first meeting with La Pasionaria. That is only normal: at crucial moments memory always goes back to the origins, however remote, of the lived experience that one finds oneself immersed in. Or at any rate that is what happens in cleverly constructed, well-carpentered novels.

You would remember your first meeting with La Pasionaria.

It was in Paris, in 1947.

In the spring? Perhaps; such a thing is not impossible. You think you remember that it was one of those Paris days when it was raining, a sudden shower of the sort described in César Vallejo's verses. In any case it was in the building used by the party leadership, on the Avenue Kléber. The place was closed in September of 1950 when the French government forbade activities by the Spanish Communist Party in France and outlawed your organizations. But even before party activities became illegal, before contacts with comrades took place in a park, at a metro exit, in a safe apartment—or on the sidewalk of the Place de la République, in front of the shop windows of "La Toile d'Avion" when the contact was with the leaders of the PSUC, the Catalonian Communists, who did not seem to know any other place in Paris to meet—even before party activities became illegal, as you were saying, in the year 1950, that name Kléber was surrounded with a rather mysterious aura.

"They've said at Kléber." "We'll have to discuss it at Kléber." "Let's wait and see what Kléber decides." You frequently heard phrases such as these, at once straightforward and charged with multiple meanings, in those years. And the name "Kléber" eventually came to be something like a symbol for an indisputable power—at once immediate and remote —of a patriarchal type. Or a religious one, if you prefer.

Doubtless this symbolic function of the word "Kléber" stemmed in part from its concrete historical connotation: owing to the fact that Kléber had been the name of a general of the French Revolution, a fantastic figure and a fantastically conceited one, and the fact that this same name had served more recently as a *nom de guerre* for one of the military leaders of the International Brigades during your Civil War

(yours of course, Federico, not mine: let us be clear on that score: but go on, go on: I won't interrupt you again).

But this was not the most important thing. The phenomenon of symbolization based on topology that you are speaking of was not something unique to the Spanish Communist Party, nor did it occur only in connection with the now-forgotten building on the Avenue Kléber. In one form or another it was a universal phenomenon. For years, for example, French Communists—until the headquarters of their Central Committee was moved to the modernistic, technocratic building on the Place Colonel Fabien—used to talk of "44," this being the number on the Rue de Châteaudun where their party headquarters was located. And they spoke of "44" with the same fervor, and on occasion the same religious-like fear, with which you used to speak of Kléber. In other words the romantic aura surrounding the fantastic general of the French Revolution was perhaps not the primary factor in this case. The topological charisma would have operated in precisely the same way without the name Kléber. Charisma is something intrinsic to this type of relation with Superior Powers, and something universal: it functioned in the same way whether it was Kléber or Châteaudun, whether it was the French party or the Spanish.

If you were discussing this in some seminar or symposium on semiology, or simply having a few glasses of red wine with Rafael Sanchez Ferlosio and Javier Pradera, as in the old days, in some bar along Doctor Esquerdo, if you were with Ferlosio and Pradera, you would then improvise here, as you used to do with them, some sort of digression or discourse, half theoretical and half joking, on the arcana of party language, the ritualized, hierarchized, esoteric, operative jargon that constitutes Communist language. But you are not yet on Doctor Esquerdo with Rafael and Javier as in the old days. The old days are still to come in this story. You will still have time later to speak of your semantic divagations in the bars along Doctor Esquerdo.

For the present you are at Kléber, in 1947, and it is obvious that the Avenue Kléber is much less amusing than Doctor Esquerdo, but then that's the way things are and we are now going to be present at your first casual meeting with La Pasionaria.

But what are you doing at Kléber anyway?

You were only a rank-and-file militant in 1947. And even the business of your being a militant might be regarded as debatable. Let's say, rather, a dues-paying member of the party who occasionally attended neighborhood cell meetings, none too assiduously. Frankly, you do not believe you can truthfully say that in 1947 you fulfilled Lenin's criteria for membership in the vanguard of the party. And now that you're being frank, admit it frankly: the sort of daily, bureaucratic normality that sums up the legal existence of the militant has never interested you very much. You do not say that this normality, this patient, routine work on the social fabric, is useless. You simply say that it has never interested you. No more than that.

At the age of eighteen you immersed yourself, gladly and gaily, in the clandestine activity of the anti-Nazi Resistance. You endured, without major problems, with inexhaustible intellectual curiosity, the concentration-camp experience, at Buchenwald. You plunged once again, with a sort of wild *joie de vivre,* into the Spanish underground, after 1953. But between 1945, when you came back from Buchenwald, and June 1953, the date of your first clandestine trip to Spain, it cannot be said, in all truth, that you were an exemplary militant. You have always been bored by the nostalgic, victory-shall-be-ours platitudes of exile; the beatific murmurs of meetings completely out of touch with any sort of social reality; the manipulation of a ritualistic Marxist language, as though the essential task were to keep a prayer wheel turning. When all is said and done, the day-to-day aspect of politics has always bored you; politics has interested you only as risk and as total commitment. In other words, admit it once and for all and be damned: you have never been a proper militant.

In 1947 in any case, you occasionally attended meetings of the Communist cell in your neighborhood, none too assiduously. The cell met in a little rented room in the Learned Societies building, near the Place Saint-Michel. Of the militants who came to these meetings, there are a few you remember.

Old Vicente Arroyo, for example.

At the end of the twenties, Arroyo had been one of the principal leaders of the party. It is true that at that time the Spanish Communist Party was a tiny sect, torn apart by internal conflicts, most often ones of a personal nature, and neutralized as a possible vanguard force by the capricious, authoritarian, and manipulative leadership of the all-powerful delegates of the Comintern, who forced the party into constant contradictory shifts of policy and changes of the party line. In the last days of Primo de Rivera's dictatorship, when the nucleus of leaders of the Spanish Communist Party—grouped around Bullejos, Adame, and Trilla—was arrested in Spain, Vicente Arroyo was put in charge of reorganizing the work of the party from Paris, a task in which he was aided by two foreign advisers. It goes without saying that nothing better symbolizes the extrinsic nature of the relations of the Spanish Communist Party with the working class and the exploited masses in Spain than this leadership from exile, in which there was also to be heard the singsong voice of the *missi dominici* of Moscow, for whom Spain was simply a field for maneuvers in the complicated war of intrigues and compromises that was unfolding within the upper ranks of the Comintern following the abrupt shift to the left that took place as a result of the Sixth Congress of the Communist International.

During all these years, Arroyo had been the editor-in-chief of the Spanish edition of *Inprekor,* the weekly bulletin of the Communist International, the title of which in Spanish was *Correspondencia Internacional.* Arroyo's work as editor was merely to translate into Spanish the articles that the leaders of the Comintern had decided to publish in their weekly periodicals. As Arroyo knew neither Russian nor German, the usual working languages of the international secretariat, he translated the texts from the French. For this reason, his versions of the political literature of the Comintern, which was already more or less a hopeless farrago, were full of gallicisms that eventually contaminated the Spanish Communist Party's own press organs. Even the language of the Spanish Communist Party of that era was divorced from Spanish reality. Anyone who has the time and the inclination to nose around in collections of periodicals of those days can verify this.

In any event, you were not particularly interested in listening to old Arroyo in the meetings. His speeches were rhetorical celebrations of inevitable triumph to come, mere glosses on the latest editorial in *Mundo Obrero*. On the other hand, every time the occasion presented itself, you accompanied Vicente Arroyo to one of the neighborhood cafés after the cell meeting and got him to tell you tales of the old days. Arroyo was an indefatigable story-teller, and you never tired of listening to him reminisce about the early days of the party in Spain. As is well known, collective memory has always interested you, even when, as in this case, what was being recounted was a story that was mediatized, distorted, by the incredible sectarianism of the narrator.

But let us go on; you are not going to list here all those party members who used to hold somnolent weekly meetings in premises in the Rue Danton belonging to the Learned Societies. In the first place, because you can't remember them all. There will always be someone too insignificant or too ephemeral, who will necessarily escape your memory. Furthermore, you run the risk of confusing these meetings with others you attended in Paris neighborhoods down through the years until 1954, in the days when you were a rank-and-file Communist. You discussed the same things in all of them. In all of them there predominated that language symbolized in your memory by the exordium of that comrade who inevitably began his remarks, year after year, whatever the subject under discussion, with the words: "Comrades, it is obvious. . . . We are going on from triumph to triumph, from victory to victory. . . ." And then he would proceed to develop this thought, in the same fashion as the editor-in-chief of a liberal periodical in the days of Silvela, according to the story told you by Eugenio Xammar in The Hague in 1937, which you yourself will perhaps have time to retell before the end of this book.

You are not going to list the names of all the comrades, but you do want to call up the memory of Tano. As a matter of fact, you don't know whether Tano was his real name or a nickname: didn't all of you call him "el Tano" when you spoke of him? In any case, with or without quote marks, Tano was a comrade who was a metal worker. A man of few words, because words are difficult tools to handle. A very active militant

8

nonetheless. At meetings he would listen to what others had to say with prodigious concentration, especially the remarks of comrades who expressed themselves well. It was plain to see that he was fascinated by their free-flowing language, by their ability to handle words.

You remember that one time, when you took the floor, you spoke of the flux and reflux of the movement of the masses. You don't remember this expression because of its striking originality, of course. You remember it because when you used the words flux and reflux, your eyes happened to meet Tano's and you noticed in his a look of utter surprise, half admiring and half anxious, at these words, which he had, no doubt, never heard before.

Then after the meeting Tano came over to you to ask you to explain. The business about the flux and reflux of the movement of the masses had struck him as extraordinary, and he wanted to know precisely what the expression meant. You explained to him. He shook his head in amazement. He wrote down, with some difficulty, these new words in a notebook that he always carried with him. "Flux and reflux," Tano kept repeating, shaking his head. These two innocent seafaring words took on a mysterious force on Tano's lips. It was as though they reflected the complexities of social life, the mysterious but predictable and majestic element in historical movement, as though these two words were keys that had suddenly enabled him to understand this movement, given him access to its meaning.

"Flux and reflux," Tano kept saying, shaking his head. And it was as though the tides of history were moving in rhythm with his gesture, in an inexorable ebb and flow. "It's easy for you of course—you're an intellectual," Tano said, concluding his long, bedazzled meditation.

At other times Tano's reaction was precisely the opposite. He would be furious when he wasn't able to understand exactly what was being said. Perhaps what you yourself were saying. One of these times, you remember, after you had had the floor, Tano flew into a rage. He hadn't understood something you had said—you don't remember what. He marched straight over to you, pointing his finger accusingly. "I'm going to make your self-criticism for you, comrade Semprun!" he shouted, beside himself. "You're nothing but an intellectual!"

Yes, here we are already: the words *self-criticism* and *intellectual* have entered the picture.

But you are not going to discuss this theme in depth here. La Pasionaria has asked for the floor and is not going to wait for you to finish your digressions and your ravings. If you go on in this fashion, absorbed in your memories, you run the risk of not hearing the philippic that she has prepared for you. And you do not want to miss a syllable of it. What is more, the relations of the intellectual with the party, and in a broader sense with the workers' movement in general, is one of the fundamental themes of this attempt at autobiographical reflection. You will have any number of chances to come back to the subject, to try to shed light on it. You merely want to mention here, very much in passing, and in connection with this minor little story you have just recounted, the ambiguous situation that has always been yours. The word "intellectual," as a matter of fact, can be used either to enhance your reputation or to blacken it, can be used as either praise or anathema. It says everything, depending on the circumstances, and what it says is contradictory.

In any case, if you are at Kléber in the spring of 1947, that day of your first casual meeting with La Pasionaria, it is not because you are a more or less assiduous militant in your neighborhood cell, but because you are an intellectual. Your status as an intellectual allows you at times to escape your miserable mortal envelope as a rank-and-file militant and hover, like a little angel in a Murillo painting, in the lofty sphere of the Avenue Kléber. This privilege, naturally, involves the risk of your being cast into the hell of outermost darkness at the slightest *faux pas* on your part, at the slightest suspicion of you. But it is a truism of course that wherever there is privilege there is risk.

That day at Kléber you were meeting with Francisco Antón.

You don't remember now what was being discussed, nor do you think it really worth the trouble to try to remember. Since the year was 1947 and the place Paris, in exile, the reason for that meeting of a group of Communist intellectuals with Francisco Antón, who at the time was still at the height of his power, could hardly have been exciting.

You remember, on the other hand, some of those who were present. There was Lalo Muñoz, the painter from Valencia who during the Civil War had been a staff officer of the division of Valentín González (the famous "El Campesino") and who had later been deported to Mauthausen for five years by the Nazis. Since his return he had been busy making up for all the time he'd lost and all the pleasures of life he'd missed out on, and doing so with the vitality of an adolescent. There was José María Quiroga Pla, Miguel de Unamuno's son-in-law the writer, who managed to defend himself against the Calvinist rigors of the famous "Party Spirit" thanks to a healthy and corrosive ability to bitch at anything and everything. There was Salvador Bacarisse, the musician, affable and silent, resigned to being obliged to lend an ear to this or that stupid remark about Socialist Realism and allowing himself to be the target of self-criticism, so long as he was permitted to cultivate his little garden of celestial harmonies in peace afterwards. There was Benigno

Rodríguez, a self-taught man and a fabulous figure from the picaresque realm of Spanish politics, the son of a coachman, a former anarcho-syndicalist from Madrid, who on party orders had been Juan Negrín's secretary during the Civil War and during part of the period in exile in London and knew everything about everything. There was Emilio Gómez Nadal, the historian from Valencia, a cultivated, ironic man, undoubtedly the most intelligent of all of you who were present that afternoon. And then there was you

                    (no, not you, Federico: me: you, Sánchez, didn't exist yet: and it would never have occurred to any of those present that day that you would someday exist: and who was I?: what was I?: nothing in particular: I had no steady job: I spent my days somersaulting from one thing to another as I waited for an imminent end to exile: I turned out just enough translations not to die of hunger: every once in a while I published, under the *nom de plume* of Falcó, some critical note or other in the weekly *Action,* run by Pierre Courtade and Pierre Hervé: I killed time in cafés, absorbed in interminable theorizing: something else?: yes: all the rest: everything important: everything that makes a person what he is: everything that flooded back into my memory an hour ago when I played a record by Joan Baez: when I heard the voice of Joan Baez singing Miguel Hernández's verse in Spanish: *Llego con tres heridas: la del amor: le de la muerte: la de la vida—I come with three wounds, that of love, that of death, that of life:* that says it all right: wounds)

and you were there, listening to what Francisco Antón perhaps had to say about the mission and the function of the Communist intellectual, and then, just as the meeting was about to end, the door of that office on Kléber opened and La Pasionaria came in, greeting all of you with cheery cordiality. And La Pasionaria congratulated you on an article that you had just published in *Independencia,* a review that the party had started in France under Benigo Rodríguez's direction.

If you were in a novel, I repeat, you would remember this first meeting with La Pasionaria.

Your smile, Dolores.

                    I remember.
It was a warm afternoon in March, far from the homeland.
The rustle of thousands of green leaves
was still sleeping in the sap
and in the depths of buds
flowers were preparing their graceful negation.

Earth the mother boiled with rebirths as old as time.
With the old and the new thus locked in combat,
a tree, frail presage of victory,
announced glorious tomorrows
amid the last gasps of winter in its final agony.

  And the sun on the windowpanes, between life and death.

The door opened. You came in. We rose
From our chairs. You shook each of our hands,
Smiling.
  And at that moment spring burst forth.

(You wrote that. Well, no, it wasn't you: I was the one. My very own self.

I wrote that, many years before I was Federico Sánchez, remembering this first meeting with La Pasionaria in the offices on Kléber. As a matter of fact, many years before being Federico Sánchez, in the years of a very far-distant youth, I wrote lots of political poems. Fortunately, almost none of them ever saw print. But in these last weeks, searching through my files for certain documents, I came across a folder containing dozens and dozens of poems. And I was dumbfounded. Something like the laughter of a dying man overcame me as I reread this poetry dripping with Stalinist-lyrical sincerity and alienated religiosity. But in the final analysis we must accept what we have been. Some people were in the Falangist Youth Front or attended courses on How to Be a Good Christian, let's say, before becoming Communists. I was a Stalinized intellectual. It is only right to reveal that I was one, and I must explain why I was one. It would be very easy to forget one's own past, to lose one's memory the way our local, indigenous Little Helmsmen do. But that would be too easy. I am unwilling to forget my own past.

I wish to speak to you now, Dolores,
in my most intimate voice, from the depths of myself.

The militant's place I occupy
in your party's ranks
is a modest one;
and my work is scarcely more exemplary.
I tell you simply and sincerely:
I am not a Bolshevik; I am trying to be one.
Nor am I, Dolores, from the working classes:

there is no class consciousness within me
to be a compass for my words and actions.
You understand, I know. My heart is yours,
it beats to the glorious rhythm of this time of ours;
but in my brain are stubborn old specters
of the world in ruins, a fog
of vague dreams: the comrades help me banish them.

I tell you, Dolores, I proclaim it
to chase away the shadow of the old man
in me, to raise myself to the heights
of the time of victory.
                    The marvelous heights of this century
when all roads lead to Communism. . . .

Like the preceding poem, this one is an extract from a very long, an endless and unfinished, *Canto to Dolores Ibárruri.* I began it shortly after that meeting on the Avenue Kléber, in Paris, at the height of the personality cult, doubtless for one of La Pasionaria's birthdays. In those days her birthdays were the occasion for great collective ceremonies in celebration of this cult, and cantos, odes, elegies, ballads, and other poetic abortions formed an obligatory part of the outpourings of religious fervor that were offered Dolores at such times.

I have on my work table, for example, an issue of *Cuadernos de Cultura* from the early fifties. It is one devoted entirely to poetry. I quote the following lines, very typical of the phraseology of the era, from the introduction to this issue: "We find ourselves in the face of a new resurgence of Spanish poetry, of a poetry of combat, of a poetry that celebrates the struggle for life. Today what is alive, what is growing, what has a tomorrow—and not only a yesterday—is the people, the working class, the Communist Party. And Dolores Ibárruri is the symbol and the incarnation of this better tomorrow. She is the clairvoyant guide leading the people to their appointed goal, to victory."

And in view of the fact that La Pasionaria is "the symbol and the incarnation" of tomorrow, "the clairvoyant guide" of the people, almost all the poems published in this issue number 4 of *Cuadernos de Cultura* are dedicated to her.

Thus we find, to begin with, some verses by Juan Panadero. Juan Panadero, as is well known, was the homespun proletarian spokesman for Rafael Alberti, the double or twin or alter ego to whom the exquisitely sensitive poet from Cádiz was in the habit of entrusting the lesser labors of agitprop poetry.

Banner raised along the path
La Pasionaria with the hands
of poor peasants

Great sun, polar star
Dolores of the workers
on land and sea

Soul of the reconquest
fire in the wind
of the Communist Party

Good mother, strong mother
mother who for life
gave a son to death.

This last verse alludes to a delicate but essential theme in the Communist mythology—I was about to say "Christology"—of those years. As is common knowledge, one of La Pasionaria's sons died in the ranks of the Red Army, during the battle of Stalingrad. His name was Rubén, and many sons of Communist militants were named Rubén after him in those days.

Rubén Ruiz died at Stalingrad. And this private and painful event in the life of Dolores Ibárruri came to form part of the obligatory figures of Communist rhetoric. The religious, Christ-like overtones that this event can be made to take on are obvious. The Son of God became a Man, to redeem us through his death—to redeem others, that is, since no one, thank God, can wreak *my* salvation. And the Son of La Pasionaria enlisted as a combatant in a regiment of the Red Guards in order to save us from Fascism. His death was an exemplary sacrifice. "Mother who for life/Gave a son to death," Alberti-Pandero says, with the conciseness of a poetic language that has been perfectly mastered. And put to perfectly alienated uses.

The Christ-like theme of the death of Rubén Ruiz thus became a kind of mandatory rhetorical device in all the odes, cantos, and elegies of that era. It also figures, naturally, in my verses. And no one needed to urge the theme upon me. I was subjected to no outward moral pressure. One of the specific characteristics of ideological Stalinism is precisely this self-repressive internalization of all the collective clichés of the ego-worshiping superego. Thus a sonnet of mine written in the year 1948 ends with these two tercets:

> The blood of your blood was shed
> for our freedom at Stalingrad.
> The death of Rubén is a wound, it's true
>
> burning in your heart. But hark you
> though a child from your side is torn
> In the fight a thousand sons each day are born.

This metaphor of the multiplication of sons allows the family epic of La Pasionaria to be linked with the popular epic of the struggle of the party. The essential thing, then, is to underline the dual familial and collective significance that the theme of the Mother as an epic figure takes on.

This theme, significantly, becomes more profound and more complex in the *Canto al Partido* by César Arconada, a writer in exile in the USSR. This *Canto to the Party* was published in the same issue of *Cuadernos de Cultura* that I have mentioned.

> Father of all things, you, the Spanish people,
> Mother of all things, you, my gentle Spain,
> your prisoner's life is a painful one,
> sad pain yours, bitter pain,
> but you can now say hail to joy
> and farewell forever to misfortune,
> for the red spark is already aglow,
> and this first spark is already fire,
> and soon the fire will be conflagration
> and your freedom will be won.
> Your breath through time has proved fecund,
> your soul creative and fruitful,
> but your greatest handiwork
> has a name: Dolores, *Pasionaria!*
> . . . .
> Father of all things, you, the Spanish people,
> Mother of all things, you, my gentle Spain,
> on creating Dolores
> you have created your own wings. . . .

César Arconada here turns himself and us into children in a very significant way: he makes us witnesses to the primal scene. Before our eyes, the people-as-father and Spain-as-mother—a strange avatar of that Reproductive Couple that provokes the ironic and iconoclastic wrath of

Juan, *sin Tierra* (the Landless), Goytisolo—make love, and as they fart around with "fecund breath" and "fruitful soul" they engender Dolores. She is thus the daughter of the virile people and gentle, feminine Spain. But at the same time, as all those cantos, odes, and elegies never tire of repeating, she is also our mother who is in heaven. The mother and the matriarch of the proletarian combatant, that is to say. Or rather, Dolores is at once the daughter and the mother of the people. The daughter and mother of herself, in the final analysis. The family romance of the neurotic poets of the era of the personality cult, among whom I must necessarily count myself, has, as can be seen, a rather transparent plot line. If Oedipus were to happen by, he would see through it immediately.

But I am not going to analyze here all the poems that were published in that issue of *Cuadernos de Cultura.* There was naturally one by Juan Rejano, a specialist in obsequious odes. But it is not possible to forget that the precursor of all of us, the unsurpassable master, was Miguel Hernández. His poem dedicated to La Pasionaria in his *Viento del pueblo (Wind of the People)* is a sort of prototype. And it is a very interesting poem to study, for it dates from 1937, the moment when the personality cult was making great strides in the Soviet Union, following the elimination of all Stalin's possible opponents in the great political trials. It is also interesting because in Miguel Hernández, whose origins were Catholic and peasant, there are forcefully—and effectively—expressed all the religious clichés of the leaders cult characteristic of a Catholic and peasant culture that has come to fuse with Marxist culture and hence pervert it.

Some day, doubtless, some university researcher with a grant from Harvard, let us say, will write a solid, semiological study of Hispanic Communist language that will bring to light its subject matter, its toponymy, its topology, its system of codification and censorship, its stereotypes and its polysemantic terms; that will investigate its evolution; that will describe its esoteric, quasi-religious functioning. I may even take on this study myself, so as to keep it from falling into the hands of one of our latter-day young pedants: one of those vulgar village idiots dipped in the herb-tea of the pseudo-Freudian baptismal font, one of those academic asses who weary us with their semioseminarial braying.

In any event, my *Canto to Dolores Ibárruri,* written in the late forties, was the result of a totally personal, gratuitous, ritual act. Not only was this poem never published: La Pasionaria never learned that I had written it. When I had the occasion to speak with her, it never occurred to me to mention this interminable unfinished poem that I had dedicated to her in my fervent youth. In short, in my case the poetic personality cult was a sort of solitary vice of my long-ago youth.

Well, almost solitary. If I am not mistaken, two persons came to be acquainted, at least partially, with these and other political poems of mine dating from this period in my life. Benigno Rodríguez, first of all. Benigno liked these dreadful—I can say it now—verses of mine. He kept urging me to finish them, to publish them. Today,when I think of it, this does not particularly surprise me. Benigno was a terrific, almost incredible, person, a self-taught man with a very vast and solid culture and extremely acute political and human intuition, but he had a Stalinist superego that never let up and constantly repressed his innermost impulses. Because of the admiration I felt for him in these years from 1946 to 1952, Benigno is doubtless the person principally responsible for my own ideological Stalinization.

In my case, as in that of all Communist intellectuals of bourgeois background, the complex of social origins functioned as the prime motivation of this process of ideological glaciation. But this could not have been the reason for Benigno's own Stalinization, for he was from a working-class family. In Benigno the complex of origins functioned differently; it was more subtly mediatized and obeyed different mechanisms: he had been an anarcho-syndicalist militant before joining the party. What Benigno constantly repressed in order that others would forgive him for it was this libertarian background of his.

Pepe Bergamín was the second person who read or heard me read some of my poems of those days. I remember one afternoon in Paris at Jesús Ussía's, for example. Bergamín's criticism was merciless. He tore the clichés, the rhetoric, the religious allusions of all these poems apart in a masterful way. No doubt this critcism of Bergamín's struck me as excessive at the time. I thought to myself that what he had had to say could not possibly be right on every score. But because of this and all the rest, I abandoned the interminable unfinished *Canto to Dolores Ibárruri.*

So, as I was saying, this accursed folder full of poems came to light again recently. I had forgotten these verses. I hadn't forgotten writing them, generally speaking: I had simply forgotten their precise content. Like the return of the repressed to conscious awareness, or to the penumbra of memory, this sheaf of yellowed sheets of paper, some handwritten and some typed, conjures up the specter of what I was in those years. In the mirror of the political poetry that I wrote in my long-ago youth there appears the face of a person of whom I can now speak with equanimity.

I shall speak of myself with equanimity. Tano doesn't need to subject me to self-criticism. I shall do so myself.

The two brief extracts that I have quoted are sufficient proof of the entire mental and ideological structure of my poetry of that period, and by extension, of my Communist religiosity. My reader will note, first of all, the philosophical flirting with Hegelian terminology: "in the depths of buds flowers were preparing their graceful negation. . . . " As I was a fairly well-read intellectual, I knew this passage from Hegel's *Phenomenology of Mind* by heart. And since I was multilingual as well as being fairly well-read, I knew it in German: *Die Knospe verschwindet in dem Hervorbrechen der Blüte.* . . . I had read quite a bit of old Hegel in my brief but profitable years as a student. Then in Buchenwald I reread him. Not all of him—one never finishes reading all of Hegel—but I did get through *Logic* and *Phenomenology.* I have no idea why the works of Hegel were in the library of the concentration camp at Buchenwald, but the fact is that they were. There were dozens of copies of *Mein Kampf,* and other books by the theoreticians of national socialism. But there was also Hegel. When it was my turn to work at night in the *Arbeitsstatistic* office—every three weeks or so—I read Hegel.

Among Marxists at universities it is no longer fashionable to read Hegel. That is not to say that Hegel was very widely read in the past. His works are not easy going. But in any event it was not a bad thing once upon a time to show signs of a certain knowledge of Hegel. But since Louis Althusser has imposed his paranoiac aversion to Hegel on the ideological apparatus of the bourgeois university—which is where Marxism is taught of course: where, if not there?—it is no longer fashionable to read him. What is fashionable is to proclaim, stupidly, that Marx broke with Hegel on epistemological grounds, thanks to a sort of theoretical razor that in one stroke separated the young Marx from the mature one and the same young man from his fetal, ideological prehistory. The problems begin when one must establish the exact date of such a fortunate Adamic or Edenic birth of Marxism. It is a truism that chronologies of genesis are always complicated. (Sometimes this is so because they are oversimplified, as in the Bible and in Althusser.) Marx's genesis and epistemological razor stroke was first said to have taken place in the year 1845. But this did not prove very convincing: it made it look more like a castration than a razor cut. And the later works, that is to say those of Marx's maturity or at least his maturation, continued to be haunted by the ghost of old Hegel. This was true of the *Grundrisse* [*Notebooks*], for example, which date from 1857. Well then, out with the *Grundrisse!* —they are not important, they are mere stammerings, Althusser decreed. In the end the epistemological razor cut, which was something very clean and beautiful, very dialectical, was reduced to an evolutionary process—the worst thing that can happen to a dialectical phenomenon.

But I am not going to speak here about Althusser or about his typically French positivist lack of understanding of the extremely complex relationship between Hegel and Marx. I will merely say, to finish with the subject for now, that Althusser misconstrues Marx. It must be said that he is in fact a specialist in misinterpretation: he falls into the same error with Stalinism. Because the problem lies not in knowing *when* Marx ceased to contend with Hegelian dialectic but in knowing why he *never* stopped contending with it. Or in other words, why Marxism has never managed to establish its own philosophical lineage. (Perhaps it is simply because Marxism is not a philosophy. Perhaps because it does not have a father.)

Anyway, I was merely saying that the obvious flirting with Hegelian terminology that can be noted in those lines from my *Canto to Dolores Ibárruri* could easily allow the reader to deduce that I belong to the generation that still arrived at Marxism through reading Hegel, and, more concretely, through George Lukacs's reading of Hegel in his *History and Class Consciousness,* a key book in my life when I was eighteen.

Another aspect that leaps to the eye in the extracts from my poetry of long ago is precisely that having to do with what I have called "the complex of origins": the feeling of guilt aroused in the bourgeois intellectual because of the fact that he was born in the bosom of an exploiting class. It is a guilt that is of course merely another version of the original sin of Christian mythography; the desire, at once an expiation and a realization of oneself, to join the working class, not only (nor even primarily) because it has been given the historic mission of transforming society, but also (and most importantly) because it is a humiliated, exploited, suffering class; the eucharistic vision of a future of justice, which on the one hand is inevitable since it is prefigured in the very course of history, but which on the other hand requires effort and purifying sacrifices. All of these profoundly popular, religious themes are commingled in the political poetry of my young days. These themes clearly reflect a state of ideological alienation. Perhaps it is the poem that I shall now cite, one from this same period, that is most revealing in this respect.

> I am the son of a vanquished class,
> of a world in ruins.
> And in the sound and fury of the struggle that is life,
> of what prospers or dies, from me there has spurted
> the blood of this wound,
>
> of this uncertain, moribund existence.
> And I tasted the bitterness,
> night after night. Its dripping from deep within

destroying roots of beauty,
ravaging the world.

I knew blind searching,
fumbling in the dark
along the path of youthful anguish,
and shedding sadly, one by one,
sad visions of the future.

I want to tell you now how it was
to be born to happiness,
to the horizon and the heartbeat
of the future, to the new day
agleam with the light of my Party.

To be born, to be born to the rhythm of a class
moving upward, attacking,
spring-like, as though an April star
had risen, that I hail with joy.
Being born again: new. A new class.

The "dripping from deep within" of bitterness in this poem of mine has its remote but obvious origin in Rubén Darío. "Do you not hear the drops of my melancholy falling?" the Nicaraguan poet had asked. And as it happens Rubén Darío was one of the poets my father was fondest of, along with Gustavo Adolfo Bécquer. For years and years I heard my father recite entire poems of the two of them, in any number of circumstances, including those that did not seem to lend themselves to such an activity. Something of Rubén's sonority will always linger in my memory, in the infra-language of my innermost monologue.

But this is not what is most important. The most important thing is that the poem is a perfect reflection of the movement that impels a bourgeois intellectual to trace his anguish to his class origins and project an illusory solution to this anguish in the form of a militant incorporation within the working class, whose eucharistic representative is the party. The Party, that is, with a capital letter. The difficulty, both for the intellectual and for the working class, is that one does not meet the latter: one meets Manuel Delicado, Antonio Mije, or Jesús Izcaray, let us say (and there are even worse, of course), who are not the working class, naturally, but merely its dismal, bureaucratic specter; and its overlords, or its petty chieftains.

But I do not have time now to go more deeply into this subject. La Pasionaria has asked for the floor and I am not)

you are not in a novel. You are on the outskirts of Prague, in an ancient castle of the kings of Bohemia, where a plenary session of the Executive Committee of the Spanish Communist Party has been meeting for several days. Through the great windows of the room there enters the grayish, damp light of a bleak month of March—in fact it is April already: these are the first days of April, though it doesn't seem like it, days of pouring rain and hail. Outside is a dreary, deserted park with bare, leafless trees.

The park might also remind you of other parks. That of La Granja, doubtless, that afternoon with Nieves and Ricardo, and Berta when she was very small. Other parks. The one surrounding the palace of the Empress Zita, in Lekeitio. And you know very well why it would be pleasant to remember that park in Lekeitio.

Well, you aren't in a novel and you aren't going to start morosely calling to mind here all the parks that would be strangely reminiscent of the one today, the one in this month of March, or April, 1964, when you were forty years old, the park surrounding an ancient castle of the kings of Bohemia. You are not going to be able to show off by coming out with a few literary frills, by playing with the possibilities offered by traveling back and forth in your memory.

The fact is that La Pasionaria has asked for the floor and you know that this is a decisive moment.

Not that it will change anything, of course. Everything has already been said, decided, nailed down, firmly nailed down. And it is obvious that neither you nor Fernando Claudín will persuade the others and that the others will not persuade you and Fernando. On the other hand, it is also obvious that you are not going to capitulate. Or, rather, you are not going to agree to their making a self-criticism of you. Everything is clear therefore. There is no solution, at least within the narrow framework of democratic centralism. The time has come to end things. And in a certain sense that is what everyone is hoping that Dolores is going to do: end things. Or, rather, give the two of you the *coup de grâce.* After she has spoken all of you will probably ask for the floor again, ritually. But what Dolores says now, and how she says it, is going to be decisive, for the simple reason that she is who she is.

From the summit of the sacrificial pyramid of democratic centralism, forty years of party history look down upon you in irritation and amazement.

So you raise your eyes from your papers and look at La Pasionaria, who has asked for the floor. You look at your comrades on the Executive

Committee, who have appointed themselves a tribunal of the Holy Office. You look at them one by one at this decisive moment. But it so happens that two people are missing. Romero Marín is missing; he couldn't be bothered to come. His presence in Madrid was indispensable, he said: at any minute crucial events were about to take place, a powerful mass movement he said. The same old thing, in short, the same damned story that never ends. We are still waiting for this famous steamrolling movement that will sweep away everything in its path. What really happened was that Romero Marín was enough of an old hand at things to know how the whole farce was going to turn out. In a word, he couldn't be bothered. Simón Sánchez Montero is also missing, but for other reasons. Simón is in Dueso Penitentiary, and has been ever since they arrested him on that night in June, 1959.

And then, at the thought of Simón, and that night in June, you remember number 5 Concepción Bahamonde.

2 NUMBER 5 CONCEPCIÓN BAHAMONDE

It has always seemed amusing to you that you lived on Concepción Bahamonde: Ventas Prison is just around the corner.

But then you also thought it amusing, a few years before, to live in the Travesía del Reloj. You sometimes went down to the barbershop, and the barber would be shaving the army recruits on guard at the Special Tribunal of Colonel Eymar, on the Calle del Reloj. If they had managed to catch you in those days, a bare thirty yards separated your tiny garret —with a terrace and a panoramic view on all the north of Madrid, but seen in Velazquian reverse, or rather the reverse of the profile that Velázquez once painted—thirty yards separated this clandestine hideout of yours from the tribunal that would sit in judgment of you. Then on Concepción Bahamonde, at the end of the fifties, it was Ventas Prison that was just down the street.

It is true that it is a women's prison and thus you would not have ended up in it. You would have gone to the Carabanchel House of Detention, to begin with. You sometimes contemplated the cupola of Carabanchel from a garret on Cinco Rosas, when you met there with Ignacio Romero and the comrades of the university committee. You would contemplate the cupola of the prison building, and there were always comrades inside. In your imagination, identifying with one or another of those who were inside at that moment, you had already been in Carabanchel.

You were in the garret on Cinco Rosas, and you knew, in a vague sort of way, that the name Cinco Rosas had something to do with some episode in the history of the Falange. Five roses of blood, if you remembered rightly. So the name of the street where you sometimes lost yourself in contemplation of the cupola of Carabanchel was a vague reference to a horizon of tragic rhetoric, of words soaked in the blood of years past that were still powerful because of their sheer dead weight. In a certain sense, spontaneously, thanks to the peculiar resonance of language, "Cinco Rosas" and "Carabanchel" transported you, crushed you against that gray and bloody wall of the past that was still present, a wall of spongy, cottony material, with the smells of a field hospital, through which you were obliged to pass, to make a narrow, stifling path for yourself, endlessly, beneath the dead light of the past.

Ignacio came over to you.

Ignacio: "You looking at something?"

You: "That's right. I'm looking at something."

Ignacio: "Carabanchel?"

You: "That's right, Carabanchel."

Ignacio: "Do you know it from inside?"

You: "No, not from inside."

Ignacio: "Some other one then?"

You: "What's that?"

Ignacio: "I mean: some other prison?"

And you: "Several."

Ignacio didn't question you any further that time, perhaps because he thought there was no reason to know any more. And you didn't say anything more either. You limited yourself to that bare statement that you for your part were acquainted with several other prisons.

It is true that, however much you might have forced yourself, supposing that you had wanted to force yourself in this way, you would not have managed to present this memory of yours of other prisons as something especially moving. In your memory prison was a succession of brief experiences in your youth and for that reason, doubtless, not marked with the stamp of sadness, desperation, helplessness.

The autumn light, very early in the morning, in Auxerre, when they let you out into the courtyard of the prison, and the pure, cold water of the fountain in the courtyard. You had flooded your eyes, your face, your back with the living water of the fountain, pure and cold, and were beginning to dry your hands, your back, your face, with one of your shirt-tails. A woman suddenly began to sing. You raised your eyes. There in the street on the other side of the prison wall, within reach of your hand but invisible, a woman, singing. Sewing and singing perhaps, what a miracle. Everything was in its rightful place. The houses, the women, sewing, songs. This wall, this courtyard, these tiers, these cells, your loneliness were all only a part of reality. Outside, things were in their rightful place. The women, absorbed in their morning tasks, went on singing. You stood there motionless, alert, and it was a moment of happiness: a little shard of happiness entering your soul, your heart, your blood, the silent flow of your life. Houses, women, trees, seasons of the year, dreams, tasks to be undertaken, songs, comrades still existed. Tomorrow, that very afternoon, they might shoot you, but all that would continue to exist. A tiny happiness suddenly overcame you.

And then the German soldier, a tired old man immured in his bawling prison-guard routine, shouted: "*Los, los!*" Your total immobility surprised him, displeased him: it was not normal. You returned to the prison, to the cell, to the four walls you were locked up in. But not alone: anchored to the world again, anchored in it. Reassured.

You could thus enumerate tiny instants of irrational and serene happiness, all of them from your years in prison or in a concentration camp.

But on that June night in 1959, as you passed by the garage of the Navy Motor Pool, on Marqués de Mondéjar, as you were about to turn into Concepción Bahamonde, you had neither the time nor the inclination to summon up, with obvious narcissistic pleasure, your personal prison memories. Something much more important had happened: Simón Sánchez Montero had disappeared a few hours before.

It had all begun at 9:30 p.m., on the corner of Martínez Campos and Castellana, near the newspaper stand.

At 9:30 p.m. on the dot, on June 17, 1959, Aurelio arrives at the appointed place. It would be more exact to say that he is suddenly there, suddenly visible, like an apparition. Because Aurelio doesn't simply arrive at a rendezvous, he just suddenly materializes without ever giving the impression that he has been on his way there, moving through space in your direction. He is simply there all of a sudden

(all right then; it is years and years later—today, August 1976—as I begin to write this book, that I am revealing that Aurelio is Francisco Romero Marín: it doesn't matter anymore: it is no longer a secret: Aurelio was the name Romero Marín went by among us: on the Executive Committee: among the comrades of the central apparatus: in Madrid Aurelio had many other names—Gonzalo, Paco, "the Tank," and who knows what others: but it doesn't matter now: Aurelio/Romero Marín has just gotten out of Carabanchel: good news, hooray, happiness, things are looking up: every prisoner that gets out of Carabanchel or any other prison will be a victory: and as long as there is a single prisoner left this victory will not be complete, I say: Romero Marín was not at the plenary session of the Executive Committee in March–April '64: he didn't want to be: I resented it: not only because the reasons he gave seemed grotesque to me —a clumsy pretext—but also because I was disillusioned: in my naiveté I had imagined that the presence of Romero Marín would prevent certain things from happening—even though he was in agreement with the majority of the Executive Committee—the presence of Romero Marín who had shared life underground with me in Madrid since 1956:

yes, I remember it very well: in 1956, at the end of that spring: a historic one, as they say: a very heated discussion in the Spanish Politburo: and simultaneously the Twentieth Congress of the Russian party: student demonstrations in February: a government crisis: the workers' strikes: it was at this point that Federico Sánchez came into public existence: the ninth of February: when the entire press of the movement reprinted an article by Federico Sánchez: mine: published in *Mundo Obrero* the previous autumn: on the work of the Communists in the university: the article was entitled "Sin dogmatismos preconcibidas" ("Without Preconceived Dogmatisms"), and the Falangist press regarded it as proof of a plot: the hand of Moscow: the fact is that the Fascists have—like Stalinists, I add today—a metaphysical and policeman like conception of history: but I will speak later on in this book of that year 1956: a decisive one: I will speak of the comrades of that era: Carlos Semprún—my brother, an underground militant, a party official, nowadays he signs himself Semprún Maura, as he has a perfect right to do, but it's doubtless because he doesn't want my name and his confused, as though that were possible—well anyway, Carlos Semprún; Enrique Múgica—on the Executive Committee of the Spanish Socialist Workers' Party (PSOE) now, a friendly hug to you, Enrique, it's lucky they can't take the past we had together away from us; Julián Marcos—I haven't seen him for years, that's how life goes, or rather doesn't go; Jesús López Pacheco—he called me the other day: the telephone rings in my house in Paris: it's Jesús López Pacheco calling: we have dinner together at the home of Juan Goytisolo and Monique Lange: in the warmth of Monique's and Juan's friendship: Jesús has just arrived from Canada with Marisol and the children: we reminisce about the old days: like excombatants, but with tenderness: and even a certain pride: why not?: we remember that April 1 of 1955 when the first nucleus of Communist students was formed in a vacant lot of the Ciudad Universitaria: with Jesús: and with Julián and Enrique: and the others too of course: Julio Diamante: I know nothing about you now, Julio: I remember you: I hope I haven't left you with a bad memory of me: whatever happens:

Diamante introduced me to Javier Pradera one night on the Gran Vía; early in the summer of 1955: we were getting ready for the Congress of Young Writers: that legal cover that allowed us to organize mass actions: Javier: our nightly talks together that summer: Javier was studying for some competitive exam, I don't remember which one: we would meet at night: discussions: the divine and the human: then he would go off to work till dawn: I remember that summer, Javier: I'm on the far side of life today as I draw up the balance-sheet of those years, and I still have friends left from that time: I mean real friends: Javier Pradera for certain: another one died: Domingo González Lucas: Dominguito: the telephone rang; Javier Pradera calling me from Madrid: Dominguito has committed suicide: far away in the fabulous Americas: how can that be possible: Domingo was the life-force itself: the stubborn happiness of living: the dream of living: how can life kill itself?: it's not possible, Javier: shit: how terrible: our youth is over, Javier: how stupid: till victory: till defeat: till death: till forever, Javier: and then the others: the comrades of that extraordinary year 1956: Ramón Tamames: known as *zoon politikon,* the very opposite of the utopian animal that man is said to be: an animal who believed in the possible: one who would never try to get an elm tree to bear pears: let us be reasonable: please: but a hard worker with personal charisma: an excellent leader of today's Communist Party, whose aim is not to transform reality but to administer it more rationally: where are you heading, Ramón?: toward power: a peerless partner for Carrillo in the days to come: leadership with two faces: Carrillo the incarnation of the mythological tradition: the heroic, sterile bloodshed of this tradition: the bloody, miserable secrets and the ruses of historical reason: pragmatism as the red thread leading from yesterday to tomorrow: Ramón the incarnation of the new forces of culture: the smiling but authoritarian technobureaucracy of the future State: a Christian ought to be placed alongside the two of them at the head of the party so as to produce the sacrosanct trinitarian formula: someone leaning to the Left and if possible a prophet: that's more impressive: and there is no lack of candidates: but anyway: to return to the subject at hand and to sum up briefly: the comrades of that era: Carlos Semprún, Enrique Múgica, Jesús López Pacheco, Julián Marcos, Julio Diamante, Javier Pradera, Ramón Tamames, and a few more: Fernando Sánchez Drago, Jaime Maestro: an excellent team in every respect: they can't take that away from us: but I was speaking of Romero Marín: at the end of the spring of 1956 he appeared in Madrid: I had a rendezvous with someone sent by the party leadership, and Romero Marín turned up in his place: Aurelio: smiling: like a fish in water: he brought me the first news of how the heated discussion in the Politburo had ended: he informed Simón and me of the beginnings of the policy of national reconciliation: he announced to us that a plenary session of the Central Committee was to be held in the summer of 1956 to ratify the new orientation and modify the makeup of the groups leading the party: he worked in Madrid regularly beginning in February, 1957: Romero Marín, Simón Sánchez Montero, and I directed party activities: and then Julián Grimau joined us after Simón was arrested: all of that under my responsibility: I was the one in charge of coordinating the efforts of the clandestine center: a good underground companion, Aurelio: calm and courageous: not like others whose names I prefer to forget: "the Tank": but these memories of Madrid are nonetheless not going to make me lose my critical spirit: Aurelio is a man without political imagination: a bureaucrat: there are also "heroic bureaucrats," as Alfonso Sastre reminds us in his "Ballad of Carabanchel": an iron-fisted bureaucrat: with great gifts for playing the role of political boss: a feudal overlord exercising his seigneurial rights all around him, in his work and in his life: but I was saying that Romero Marín did not come to the plenary session of the Executive Committee that resolved our case: that of Claudín and Sánchez: and I felt his absence and inwardly regretted it, thinking in my naiveté that his presence would have prevented certain things: some of the slanderous attacks on me by Eduardo García for instance: vicious Eduardito, elevated to the secretariat of the organization by the grace and favor of Carrillo: Carrillo's guard dog that he set on us: a police dog: a spy of the Russian Special Services in the Executive Committee: a KGB dog: as has since become evident: he was soon to bite Carrillo's paternal hand: but I'm not going to shed tears over it: he who sows dogs reaps sons of bitches: the bastard sons of bitches of the KGB: but as I was saying: Romero Marín was not at the meetings in the Kafkaesque castle of the kings of Bohemia: but his presence would have changed nothing: obviously: the last time I saw him was in September of 1964: on the third, to be exact: in Paris: at a meeting I had with a delegation from the Executive Committee: the last one before I read in the papers that I had been expelled from the party: the only one after the plenary sessions in March–April: and Romero Marín *was* present at *this* meeting: with poor Delicado: a stupid ass: a petty prince from Andalusia: because there are petty princes in all classes including the humblest: and with Ignacio Gallego: an Andalusian too, but not a petty prince: and not stupid either: not at all: a Stalinist, however, down to his very bones, it would appear: marked forever by his training during the Civil War and the exile in Russia: Gregorio López Raimundo was also present: one of the leaders of the party closest and most loyal to Carrillo: the latter's instrument in the United Socialist Party of Catalonia (The Communist PSUC) during the Comorera era: one of those who knows the dirty and bloody secrets of the party best: from the dawn death walks of '36 to the summary executions of the era of the guerrillas in '45–'48, passing by way of the liquidation of the POUM: one of our great pragmatic sharks with a very short memory: and in this meeting Romero Marín did not distinguish himself by his moderation: nor by his ability to listen patiently: as violent and as deaf as all the rest: I say this because it is true, but it leaves me cold: it leaves me completely cold that those who were wrong in '64 and have continued to be wrong every since are still leading the party: those who have never seen a single prognostication or prediction that they have made come true: those whose one merit is the fact that they have survived all their errors: pushed onward by the flux of a history that they neither understand nor dominate: those who nonetheless go on believing that they are the demiurges of reality and will persuade themselves that Franco's death was the result of their strategy: and now Romero Marín is out of prison: fine, I say again: amnesty, amnesty: and I go back to my memory of that night in June of 1959 when Simón Sánchez Montero disappeared: I go back to the life, to the memory of Federico Sánchez)

and Aurelio suddenly appears with that look of his that he has at bad moments. The tense mouth, the dead, expressionless face of the bad moments.

Aurelio says: "Simón wasn't at the rendezvous." Like that, coming straight to the point.

And you: "What's that you say?"

You have heard Aurelio's words perfectly; they are perfectly comprehensible and raise no problem of interpretation. "Simón wasn't at the rendezvous." A sentence, an assemblage of words that are totally transparent, devoid of all ambiguity. If you ask: "What's that you say?", it is only to gain time, so that the shocking impact of these words may be deadened by this bit of time you give yourself, this bit of time you gain, as if it were possible to interpose this brief lapse of time between the explosive meaning of these words and their actual explosion in your consciousness.

Aurelio says again, insistently: "Simón wasn't at the rendezvous."

And you: "You were to meet at nine o'clock, right?"

And Aurelio: "That's right, nine o'clock."

And you: "What other rendezvous did Simón have late in the day?"

The two of you had started down one of the walkways paralleling the wide avenue, between the trees, after having turned to the left as you came onto the avenue.

Aurelio: "I know he had a rendezvous at seven, with the comrades from the building trades, and one after that, but I don't know who with."

You: "I saw him at noon."

Aurelio: "And I saw him at five, as we'd arranged."

It is not a usual practice, of course, for the three of you to meet so many times in a row on the same day. It is not a good practice, of course, for the three members of the Executive Committee (or rather the Politburo: in 1959 this was still the name of the group of top leaders) in Madrid to meet so many times at such short intervals. And on the street moreover. You usually meet once a week, in some absolutely safe house whose existence is known only to the three of you. But it is June 1959, the seventeenth of June, and tomorrow is the day that a Peaceful National Strike, the HNP, has been called. For this reason you have been meeting more often lately than you ordinarily do: in one of the safe houses sometimes, the one on Concepción Bahamonde or on López de Hoyos, for example. These were meetings for discussion and analysis of the situation, of the progress being made in organizing the strike, of the difficulties that had arisen; "pencil and paper sessions," as Dominguito classes this sort of get-together. At other times you see each other two by two, in rapid contacts on the street, to exchange information or settle some small problem. And so today, the seventeenth of June, on the eve of the planned strike action, you have seen Simón at noon, Aurelio has seen him at five, and has had to see him again at nine, and tomorrow at ten the three of you are to get together on López de Hoyos to analyze the first results of the Peaceful National Strike in Madrid. But between five and nine something has happened to Simón.

As though you were resisting accepting this idea, you speak again as you walk in the shadow of the trees along the wide avenue. People are sitting on the terraces of the little bars, in the night shadows of the trees. Families, sweethearts, the usual people. Snatches of conversation, laughter, hands clapping to call the waiter can be heard. A night in June like any other, calm and peaceful. You speak again.

You: "Maybe he's just late."

Aurelio: "Maybe." But he shakes his head dubiously.

You persist: "Or there's been a mixup. Couldn't he have made a mistake about the meeting place?"

Aurelio, emphatically: "No, it wasn't that—absolutely not. The arrangement was quite clear. There's no use even discussing that possibility."

All right, it was clear; there couldn't have been a mixup. But you cling desperately to the idea nonetheless.

"He might have turned up late for the rendezvous with you and gone back to his place."

Aurelio says nothing in reply.

You have come out from under the shadow of the trees, crossed the wide avenue, and are now walking in the direction of the Plaza de la República Argentina in silence.

The burning, cruel truth lies hidden in the silence. A few indisputable facts mark off the progressive coming into being of this brutal truth. You have seen Simón at noon. Aurelio at five p.m. Simon had failed to turn up at nine. Between five and nine Simón had other rendezvous. Something might have happened at any one of them. If you think about it, something might happen at any rendezvous. Between five and nine something doubtless happened.

The two of you have turned down Vitruvio, and on reaching Serrano, Aurelio speaks again.

"Well," he says.

And the moment has come to make decisions, to break this silence, to move, to look for Simón, to try to find out where the betrayal has come from, if there has been one.

You decide that Aurelio will look for Pascual, one of the comrades responsible for the building-trades sector, with whom Simón had a rendezvous at seven. You must find out whether Pascual saw Simón at that hour. If Pascual has also disappeared, this will mean that the betrayal has come from someone in the building-trades sector. Meanwhile, you are going to go to the apartment where Simón has been sleeping these last few weeks. That's easy. It was you who found this apartment when it was decided that Simón should leave his so as not to be discovered in some routine police raid. You have found Simón a temporary refuge at Gabriel Celaya's and Amparo Gastón's, in the Calle de Nieremberg. You are going to go there.

You finally decide to meet again at eleven o'clock on the esplanade of the Paseo de Ronda, between General Oráa and Juan Bravo, to pool your information.

You have arrived at the square and you say goodbye to each other. Aurelio crosses over to the corner of Commodore, where it's usually possible to get a cab.

You will remember this moment.

You lighted a cigarette. Aurelio had just left you. You had suddenly noticed a stone bench, on the sidewalk of Serrano, on the right-hand side as you go toward the square. You had a vague memory of something. The sight of this stone bench reminded you of something, in a vague sort of way. Then the memory became clearer.

Sitting here on that bench, you had a rendezvous with Francisco Bustelo in late March of 1956. You had sat down on the stone bench three minutes before the appointed time and Bustelo arrived on the dot. You saw him coming toward you and you knew it was Bustelo because Javier Pradera had given you a detailed description of him. What is more, Bustelo had to ask you a certain question, agreed upon beforehand, and you were to give him a certain answer, also agreed on beforehand. Bustelo arrived, on the dot. You saw him coming, saw him come over to the stone bench, heard him ask you: "Has it been long since the last trolley went by?" And you, rising to your feet and picking up the package that you had laid down beside you on the bench, answered: "There aren't any more trolleys." And the two of you began walking toward the square together and then down Joaquín Costa. A little farther on, at the first street cutting back toward Serrano, Bustelo took the package and walked off, saying "good luck." And you said the same thing to him: "good luck." And that was all there was to it; Bustelo had already disappeared down that street, taking with him the package containing several hundred copies of the appeal of the First of April, which the University Socialist Associaton (the ASU) had approved and was also going to distribute.

(today—twenty years after, as in a novel by Alexandre Dumas— I get up from the table at which I'm writing: I go over to the shelf on which I keep my records of these years: I look for a copy of this appeal of April 1, 1956: I find it immediately because I am not as disorganized as some people claim: it begins this way: "On this day, the anniversary of a military victory that has resolved none of the great problems standing in the way of the material and cultural development of our country, we students of the University of Madrid again address our comrades all over Spain, and public opinion. And we—the sons of the victors and of the vanquished—do so on this day because it is the constitutive date of a regime that has not been capable of anchoring us to an authentic tradition, of carrying us into a common future, of reconciling us with Spain and with ourselves. . . ." : that's enough, for heaven's sake, I say to myself twenty years afterward: what a flood of rhetoric: what fuzzy concepts: and I am the one in the best position to say this: no one needs to make a self-criticism of me: I can make it all by myself: because I was the one who wrote the final draft of this appeal: after consulting the university comrades: the little handful of those days: Javier Pradera and Francisco Bustelo in particular: this latter acting in the name of the University Socialist Association: I know very well the reasons behind this rhetoric: behind these fuzzy concepts: the appeal claimed to be speaking in the name of the majority of university students in Madrid still mobilized after the great struggles of February: it was not a party appeal: nor even one by the leftist opposition: hence I doubtless copied, parrot-fashion, a language that was not my own: the cliché-ridden, typical language of the day: "constitutive" and "authentic tradition," for instance, or the "common future" that so closely resembles the expression "common destiny": the Ortegan origins of this language seem apparent to me: as a minor historical fact I offer the information that this is the first clandestine document in which the idea of reconciliation appears: an idea that got badly trampled on later: the same idea that is formulated, also with a certain overblown rhetoric and a certain vagueness, in the seventh point of the Affirmation of Principles of the ASU: a document of this same period that states: "Socialist youth repudiate the bloody hatreds of the past so as to enter an era of fruitful work in which all Spaniards may peacefully resolve their differences": well anyway: I am not going to hold myself responsible for this rhetoric: every mast must bear up beneath its own sail: end of parenthesis).

And so as Aurelio crossed over to the corner of Commodore in search of a taxi, you remembered this first meeting with Francisco Bustelo.

There had been many others later on. Bustelo had a little car; he would pick you up on the Plaza de España and take you to the Casa de Campo. You would get out of the car and walk then. You would take a turn around the lake, perhaps, deep in discussion, or stroll under the trees amid the verdant sound of spring. This year and other years, this spring and other springs.

When you were with Aurelio—you thought as he crossed over to Commodore—the Casa de Campo was peopled with sounds of war. The luxuriant leafing of the trees turned into a continuous thunder of explosions. Companies, battalions, brigades moved about like cohorts of phantoms. The hummocks and rises turned into steep hillsides, and in the background, like the sound of a riptide, like a horizon lashed by a hurricane, the artillery of Mount Garabitas hammered away at the buildings of Madrid. Aurelio seemed to come alive again with the memory of those Civil War days in the winter of 1936.

But nothing like that could happen with Bustelo. The fragrant slopes of the Casa de Campo stretched out before you in all innocence, beneath a sky of ever-changing blue: deep indigo or Velazquian azure, depending on the season. With Bustelo, the Casa de Campo was spring, autumn, oaks, evergreen oaks: a landscape without Moors and without Christians.

You lighted a cigarette, walked away from the stone bench, looked over toward the corner of Commodore: you saw Aurelio getting into a taxi. You were alone.

Centuries ago, or so it seems to you, the streetcar line ended here and this was almost open country.

The very first houses of the Colonia del Viso were going up in the vacant lots. The streetcar conductors would get out and the ticket-collector would grab hold of the trolley cable so as to turn it around in the other direction, as the conductor moved through the car, carrying with him the steering handle that he was about to place in the black metal motor box at the other end. When you stepped in alongside the conductor you could read the name of the city where these apparatuses had been manufactured, and it was the name of a foreign city: CHARLEROI. Then the conductor and the ticket-taker would roll a cigarette, waiting for it to be time to head back to downtown Madrid.

You were walking away from the stone bench, Aurelio was going off in a taxi, and this place was open country. The wind from the Sierra was raising little clouds of dust and dead leaves. From time to time, perhaps, flocks of sheep from the hinterlands passed by, as in the time of La Mesta, about to cross Madrid following the path laid out for sheep along the royal way.

But you walked away from this stone bench and this far-off landscape of your childhood. You were alone and you began walking toward Amparo's and Gabriel's place, on Nieremberg. You passed by the NO-DO building, all lit up, crossed the street, and found yourself near the Béisbol Cafeteria.

You had sometimes met Simón here. During a certain period in the course of these last years, you used to meet him here in the mornings.

As eras of natural history become legible in geological strata, so certain eras in your long years of meetings with Simón crystallized in your memory around certain places: a cafeteria, a stretch of sidewalk, a garden gate, a façade suddenly whitewashed by the sun of three o'clock in the afternoon. Later, in front of one of Tàpies's canvases, you had seen how there was awakened in you the same sensation of direct, almost physical, perhaps painful, contact with some material element of the universe: a rough, dense surface, smooth or marked by the imprint of time, or work, or mere wear and tear, as though in this limited material landscape, in itself inexpressive, human feelings, human undertakings had gradually encrusted themselves, as though a memory had come to reconstruct itself around those sandy surfaces, as though this inert material had been humanized by a possible memory. In the same way, the peeling wall with damp spots and grayish stains there in the Béisbol Cafeteria is like a screen in your memory onto which there is projected the recollection of your meetings with Simón, the recollection of all the events, the images, the experiences of those days.

But you had now left the Béisbol Cafeteria behind, you were now at the traffic roundabout, you were starting down López de Hoyos, intending to make a phone call from the post office halfway on the way to Amparo's and Gabriel's.

The clerk put a token for the phone down on the counter and took your money without even looking at you.

"A token, please," you had said.

She had been talking on the phone herself. She had fished a token out of the little metal box on her table and gone on talking.

"The doctor at the clinic says it's nothing, but my dear, he's not well at all."

You picked up the token and walked away.

"Listen, he can't even stand up on his own two feet, physically, I mean, and the doctor says it's nothing, nothing at all, that he should rest and it'll go away. That's easy to say, isn't it?"

You walk over toward the phone booths, continuing to hear the clerk's voice at your back.

You can see the row of booths occupying all the rear of the post office. In the last booth on the right is a young girl leaning on the little wooden counter under the telephone, speaking into the phone in a whisper. You go to the other end of the row of booths, put your token in the slot and dial the number, but it's busy.

At this moment the young girl who's speaking on the telephone turns around and looks at you. It seems to you that this dark-haired young girl, there in the last booth, that she is winking at you, or making some sort of sign, as though she knew you. You don't remember her. You dial the number again, but it's still busy. If it's Amparito on the phone, you have a wait ahead of you.

The dark-haired girl has turned all the way around toward you and put her left hand over the mouthpiece of the phone.

"Hi there. How goes it?"

"Okay," you say, still not able to place this dark-haired chick.

She sees that you don't know who she is.

"You don't recognize me, right?"

You make an evasive gesture.

"We met each other this winter, at Carlos Saura's."

It's possible, but you still can't place her.

"Of course, excuse me, my mind was somewhere else."

She laughs, still covering the mouthpiece of the phone with her left hand.

"I'm talking to my fiancé," she says.

And she laughs again.

"He can babble on for hours."

And she laughs again.

"I just say 'yes darling,' 'of course darling,' every once in a while— it makes him so happy."

She takes her left hand away from the mouthpiece and says:

"Yes darling, of course darling."

She puts her hand back over the mouthpiece and laughs.

"I don't have to tell you the time I while away doing this. It's great having a fiancé like mine!"

But you've dialed the number again and Amparo has hung up on her last caller and comes on the line immediately.

"Amparichu?" you say, lowering your voice almost without realizing it.

Yes, she says, and asks who it is and you say Rafael and she says good evening, Rafa.

"How are all of you there at the house?" you ask.

And Amparo says they're all fine and you ask if Ángel is there, because that's the name that she and Gabriel know Simón by, and Amparo says they're waiting for him to come home for dinner, and you ask if you can come over, and Amparo says sure, whenever you want to, Rafa.

You are out on the street now.

Across the street the lights of a cafeteria cast a harsh gleam on a stretch of sidewalk and part of a wall that disappears in shadow higher up.

Sharply outlined in the fluorescent light, like exotic fish in an aquarium, the silhouettes of several men move along the counter of the cafeteria across the way. From one sidewalk to the other, the street is a tunnel of spongy heat. You need only cross this dense, stifling, night space in order to enter the air-conditioned establishment, sit down at the counter, and order a beer. Your throat is suddenly burning with thirst coupled with a strange anxiety. As though your throat, your stomach, the whole interior of your body had turned into a slatelike substance, as though it had crumbled to a gray gravel creaking in the sun. As though living were no more than a long walk in the outskirts of the city, amid refuse, bright greenish shards of broken bottles, whirlwinds of dust, and eroded hillocks of dry earth. As though living were this anxiety that has overcome you, whose origin you know, but whose brutal immensity nonetheless never fails to surprise you.

You begin walking down the street again, toward Nieremberg, along the dense, dark tunnel of night and you are suddenly assailed with the terrible suspicion—the certainty, rather—that tomorrow's strike is going to be a disaster. A certain inexplicable causal relation absurdly establishes itself between this feeling of alienation that came over you as you left the phone booth and the presentiment—the conviction—that tomorrow will see the failure of the Peaceful National Strike.

Three hours later, at one in the morning, you were starting down Marqués de Mondéjar and walking past the garage of the Navy Motor Pool.

The entrance to Concepción Bahamonde awaited you, deserted, on your right, in the hot silence of June

(now, many years later, again at night, but in another place, I find it strange that that silence, on that June night, struck me as hot; that is to say, that this surprising, quite inappropriate adjective came to me all by itself, merely through the inertia of language articulating itself, writing itself: why *silence* and *hot* together, intermingled, superimposed? A silence can be described only as silent, if one uses language with the maximum rigor possible, if one eliminates from language all subjective coloration, which in a certain sense is indecent, if one extirpates from language all psychological accretions: devoured by the rigorous purity of a possible, conceivable language: limpid, restored to its original substantiality: now, many years later, on reading the words that have been written to the rhythm of my typewriter, a rhythm at times hesitant and fumbling, at times inexorable, triumphant, I think that an entrance to a street cannot await anyone, that that is sheer anthropomorphism, a mere superimposition on reality that in itself means nothing, sentiments of the narrator, or of the character, or of the Narrator turned into a Character, and hadn't it been decided to do away with the Narrator and the Character once and for all, giving language back its precise function of revealing things in the world round about?)

but the entrance to Concepción Bahamonde was awaiting you, there on your right, in the hot silence of June, an almost sticky, sweaty, oozing silence, like the sweating of night, of stones and iron, brick and cement, concrete and glass, of all the material elements of night, and of the very nocturnal essence of night, its nightness: a hot, oozing silence, sticking to your very skin, injected into your body, decanted into you from out of the night.

As always, almost without your realizing it, your way of approaching the door of the building in which you lived obeyed rules that one day, months ago, you had imposed on yourself. Your movements were mechanical, conditioned reflexes. It was simply a matter of avoiding the night watchman. You had a key to the outside door and in any case if you had given the watchman a peseta he would merely have said good evening to you, commented on the weather, and perhaps on some more solemn occasion ventured a few remarks about soccer or the bullfights. Nonetheless, ever since the day you first came to live here you decided that the watchman should not be able to recognize you, should never be able to describe your physical appearance. And thus far that was how things were.

In a certain way it was like a child's game, like the ones you played long ago in the Retiro—especially in its densest, leafiest parts—secret, sometimes cruel games, when a prisoner had to be rescued or a make-believe stagecoach attacked, as in Zane Grey's novels and American westerns.

The whole trick was to wait for the watchman to go take a rest in some distant doorway or enter one of the neighborhood bars still open at that time of night to have a little chat, or, simpler still, to wait for the handclap of some neighborhood resident to summon him out of the Calle de Concepción Bahamonde so that you could then cover the distance that separated you from the door of number 5 in great long strides. Thus far you had always managed to get in unseen and your one relation with the watchman was auditory: the only thing you knew of him was the very characteristic sound of his traditional stick striking the sidewalk, there in the distance, in the tiny immensity of the night.

Tonight however, in the short stretch that separates the garage of the Navy Motor Pool, on Marqués de Mondéjar, from the entrance to Concepción Bahamonde, the memory of childhood games doesn't enter your mind, nor does that other sonorous memory associated with them: the croaking of frogs in the pond of the Retiro. Your attention tonight is on the world round about you, your eyes are focused on the doorways, your ears are attuned to the sonorous silence, bearing witness to a tension that tears you away from yourself, away from your own memory.

Because Simón has disappeared.

On the dot of eleven you had met Aurelio again, on the esplanade of the Paseo de Ronda. You had come out on it from General Oráa, and he from Juan Bravo.

Aurelio had spoken with Pascual, the comrade from the building trades. Pascual had seen Simón at seven, as planned. They had spoken about the action tomorrow, the damned HNP. Entering a bar with Pascual, Simón had gone to make a phone call and returned saying he had to go to an urgent rendezvous. "Who with?" you ask. "Did Simón say?" Aurelio nods his head. "Simón said he had an urgent rendezvous with a comrade from printing," Aurelio says. "Printing?" you say. "Well, that must be So-and-So!"

So-and-So is an old Communist whom Simón knows from his prison days, a party contact in the printers' sector. Simon has been seeing him more often lately, in connection with the organization of the HNP. You and Aurelio know this.

What you don't know yet is that So-and-So has turned Simón in to the police. What you suppose at that moment, as you walk along the main esplanade of the Paseo de Ronda toward Manuel Becerra, on this hot night of June 17, 1959, is that perhaps So-and-So has been followed by the police, who recently, as you know, have been tailing certain old militants who have been let out of prison and are relatively easy to keep track of. You presume that So-and-So has unwittingly led the police to Simón, and hence Simón has fallen into the trap by chance. You do not yet know that So-and-So, under pressure from the police, has deliberately betrayed Simon, that he set up a supposedly urgent meeting with him in order to hand him over to them.

On the following day, June 18, in the afternoon, while you were with Manolo Suárez, an employee at Aguilar who also knew So-and-So, you telephoned the printer's where the latter worked. It was necessary to find out if So-and-So had disappeared too. No, he hadn't: he was at the printer's. He came to the phone and Manolo Suárez spoke with him. He asked So-and-So in a roundabout way, without mentioning names, whether he had seen Simón the night before, whether anything out of the way had happened. So-and-So's reaction had been violent. He shouted that he didn't know a thing, that he hadn't seen anybody, that he wanted to be left alone. And then he hung up.

That was how you began to suspect So-and-So, from the printing sector.

But that was the next day.

That night, the night of June 17, talking with Aurelio on the esplanade of the Paseo de Ronda, only one thing was clear. And that was that at 7:30 p.m. that day, in a bar with Pascual, Simón had telephoned a comrade from the printing sector (at that moment at any rate you could still believe he was a comrade). When Simón came back from making the call, he had said that he had to leave right away. The two of them had gone out of the bar and Simón had climbed into a taxi. Then at nine he had failed to turn up for the rendezvous with Aurelio. Between 7:30 and 9, therefore, Simón had begun to disappear, so to speak. And perhaps this disappearance had something to do with the urgent and somewhat unexpected rendezvous with someone from printing.

That was the only thing that seemed clear to the two of you.

You walked toward Manuel Becerra, as though you were out for an evening stroll, amid people who really were just out for a walk, on a warm night in June, and a long silence fell between the two of you.

Then you tell Aurelio that Simón hasn't come back to Nieremberg, to Gabriel's and Amparo's. And it was already plain that Simón wouldn't be coming back to the Celaya apartment, on Nieremberg. But you tell Aurelio anyway, so that there won't be any doubt about it.

(I remember it very well.

I had been waiting for Ángel for a while, at the place on Nieremberg. Ángel was one of Simón's pseudonyms. Gabriel and Amparo knew him as Ángel. The three of us were having a few glasses of red wine. Waiting for Ángel. Talking about this and that. Time went by and Ángel still hadn't come. I would have to meet Aurelio again in a little while. I had to tell Gabriel and Amparo that maybe Simón wouldn't be coming back, that maybe he'd been arrested. Ángel, that is. That probably they'd arrested Ángel. We had another glass of red wine, standing up, the three of us right next to each other, thinking of Ángel doubtless, feeling closer to each other than before, certainly. As though Ángel's possible disappearance had brought us even closer together.

Amparo looked at me and asked me what to do. What to do? The thought came to me that if they'd really arrested Simón they'd surely be interrogating him by now. I looked at Amparo and told them that if they would rather sleep somewhere else than there in the apartment they should do so. Sleeping somewhere else was logical, the best thing to do. Just in case. But I quickly added that Simón wouldn't talk. Ángel, I mean. That Ángel wouldn't talk. I had no intention of leaving my place, I added. And Ángel knows where I live, I said.

We emptied our glasses. We embraced. I left.

I had met Gabriel Celaya in 1953. In June of 1953. At the end of my first clandestine trip to Spain. I began it in Barcelona and ended it in San Sebastián.

In Barcelona, after arriving at the Francia train station, I first found myself a cheap hotel. Then I began walking, looking for the Ramblas and the Plaza de Cataluña. I had never been in Barcelona before the war. Everything I knew about the topography of the city I learned in Malraux's *Man's Hope*. I found the Plaza de Cataluña and walked up the Paseo de Gracia, ready to drink my first beer in the Navarra bar.

NAVARRA,

NAVARRA

NAVARRA!

you suddenly see the name of this bar, on the corner: NAVARRA: a sudden visceral warmth comes over you: you remember: it was here: you are here once again: you have regained all the time lost: all the time that has gone by: twenty-four years later you are back in the place where it all began: you were sitting on the terrace of the NAVARRA and you ordered a beer and drank it: twenty-four years ago: beneath a June sun in Barcelona: and today you raise your eyes and see this same terrace and you are mingling with the crowd parading down the Paseo de Gracia: it is the Day of Catalonia, September 11, 1977: the entire population is in the streets: and you are one with the entire Catalan people: anonymous: and the flags of Catalonia are being raised: and you have just heard Raimon's voice over the loud speakers: singing: *quatre rius de sang—terra polsosa i vella:* and it is years, dusty centuries perhaps, since you have felt your eyes bathed in a sea of happy tears: but happy tears fill your eyes because nothing has been in vain, though nothing has been as foreseen or dreamed of either: no, you did in fact dream of this: this great dream of flags and *vivas:* this surging tide of Catalonia on the march toward the statue of Rafael de Casanova: and your old hands and very old heart tremble: the hands that once took up the outmoded arms of the Maquis: that turned the handle of the copy machines in difficult times: the very old heart that wore itself out on the hard stones in the path: but here you are: one with this serene and resolute collective happiness: shouts of "*volem l'Estatut!*" ("We want the Statute [of autonomy]!") from little boys and girls who were born after you had made that first journey to the depths of your people: we want the status of men and of a people: the stature of Catalonia standing on its feet: the statue of the dead on Montjuich: and you think that perhaps nothing has been in vain even though everything has been different from the way you all dreamed of it: and you are with Oriol and Georgina and Sergio, who is thirteen and raises his fist as so many thousands of solitary dead did in the face of the rifles; and you are with Berta Muñoz, who had just been born on Joaquín María López, a street in Madrid, when you began to make your trips back to the scene of the struggle and of your childhood: she is now a militant in the United Socialist Party of Catalonia (PSUC), and listens to you telling your old stories: smiling: and now she is singing "Els Segadors" (the Catalan national anthem): you don't know how to sing "Els Segadors": you only know how to murmur, amid this surging tide of flags, that perhaps nothing has been in vain: that perhaps something is germinating here this day that you and the militants of the difficult times sowed: so few of them that you could count them on the fingers of one hand: perhaps two clasped hands: and it is the glorious Day of Catalonia and you can hear Raimon's voice and your very old heart beats as it hasn't beaten for centuries: with the beat of that blood that has perhaps not been shed altogether in vain: perhaps: perhaps:

The program of that first clandestine trip had been prepared by Víctor Velasco, one of Carrillo's aides on the Commission of the Interior. The Secretariat had approved of this program. In all truth, it was a rather unrealistic plan, if not downright insane. In the space of three weeks, according to this plan, I would have to visit Barcelona, Valencia, Seville, the Canary Islands, Madrid, Salamanca, and San Sebastián. Furthermore, in none of these places was it simply a question of making contact with already-established groups by way of already-established passwords. It was a question, rather, of exploring the possibilities of establishing, for the first time, some sort of relationship with groups, or isolated intellectuals, with whom no organic relation existed. That is to say, it was a question of a task requiring more time than the routine inspection trips that used to serve as the basis of party emissaries' usual reports back to the Commission of the Interior predicting imminent party triumphs. And as if this were not enough, as if the lack of time to accomplish all the objectives outlined in minute detail by Velasco and the Secretariat were not enough, the money supplied me for expenses was quite plainly insufficient. It was, in short, a program that could not possibly have been carried out. But we Bolsheviks, as is well known, are men of a different stripe from common mortals. Nothing can resist us, or at least so it says in books, in poems, and in reports to the plenary sessions of the Communist Party. Not even the enemy, not even reality can stand in our way. But to tell the truth, reality had the last word as usual and I was obliged to make changes in the program from the very outset. Thus, beginning with my very first experience, I was able to see how great a distance separates the illusions of the party and the demands of reality, even as regards so simple a thing as a trip of this sort.

Another strange thing was that the party apparatus failed to provide me with a false passport, or rather a falsified one, for this first clandestine trip. I was asked to procure one myself, at my own expense, to hunt up some French comrade or other whom I trusted and ask to borrow his passport. And that is what I did. I asked an intimate friend, Jacques Grador, to lend me his. He agreed and the party changed the photos. When I think about it, this is absurd. More than absurd, irresponsible: contrary to all security regulations. Grador was a fantastic comrade, but he had no experience underground. He might very well have talked too freely in circles that we both frequented in Paris, with all the possible consequences of such an involuntary indiscretion. Why was this the procedure in my case? It was so exceptional that I never came across another instance of it in all my years in the party. Was it in order to put me to the test? Or bureaucratic indifference to the safety of a comrade who was a neophyte at this sort of dangerous mission and not one of the circle of initiates? I have never explained it to myself to my own satisfaction, and to tell the truth, I never asked for an explanation, despite the fact that it seemed absurd to me. I was so eager to make this trip, to return to Spain, that I would even have agreed to cross the border without any passport at all, get myself smuggled across, go on my knees, crawl, swim, anything.

So I made the trip under the name Jacques Grador. My mission, as I have said, was to carry out an initial exploration of intellectual circles, since the death of Benítez in a railway accident had cut off the very few contacts that the party had with these circles in those days.

In certain places and with certain persons, after feeling out the situation, I was able to reveal that I was an emissary from the party. That was what I did in Madrid, at the home of José Antonio and Colette Hernández, at number 94 Ramón de la Cruz. I had a letter of introduction to them from Emilio García Montón, whom I had met in Paris, at the Spanish College at the Cité Universitaire. In Madrid, José Antonio and Colette opened the doors of their house to me, the doors of friendship. There were not many open doors, faithful friends, sheltering houses in 1953. They could be counted on the fingers of one hand. José Antonio and Colette Hernández's house on Ramón de la Cruz was one of the fingers of this hand. I shall never forget that.

On other occasions I introduced myself as a French Hispanist interested in Spanish cultural problems. That was how I happened to find myself, in that month of June, 1953, in the house of Vicente Aleixandre, on Wellingtonia. I don't remember who it was that gave me a letter of introduction to Vicente Aleixandre. I don't recall whether it was Herrera Petere or someone in Valencia. In any case, I telephoned Vicente Aleixandre when I arrived in Madrid and spent a few hours with him, talking of the human and the divine, of poetry and politics, with complete freedom; on his part, I mean. I remained on my guard, and contented myself with asking questions. After all, I had come to listen, not to make speeches. What was hardest for me was to speak with just the trace of a French accent during the entire interview, as suited my role of a foreign Hispanist. At the end of my visit, Aleixandre congratulated me on my fluent Spanish and presented me with a copy of his speech that he had delivered on the day he was received into the Royal Spanish Academy. I still have it: "The Life of the Poet: Love and Poetry." That was the title of the speech he gave at the public ceremony that day. Aleixandre's handwritten dedication reads: "To Jacques Grador, in memory of our first friendly chat, his friend Vicente Aleixandre." There was no second chat, but I remember that first one very well, there in the house on Wellingtonia. I hope that Aleixandre will forgive me for having played this little trick on him.

In Madrid I also talked with Jorge Campos, and again I did not reveal that I was Spanish. At the end of our conversation Campos invited me to go with him to a café—the Gijón, naturally—where he was to meet a friend. As we walked down the street to this meeting, he happened to mention that it was Fernando Baeza who was waiting for him at the Gijón. My heart skipped a beat, as the saying goes. Baeza had met me in Paris a few years before and knew me by my real name, as was quite natural. We had had dinner together several times, with his father, Ricardo Baeza, and Pepe Bergamín, if my memory is correct, at Jesús Ussía's. I had to make up some sort of excuse to leave Campos and take off before we got to the Gijón. It would have been terribly funny to come into the café with Jorge Campos and be received by Fernando Baeza with a resounding, surprised: "Well, if it isn't Semprún! What in the world are you doing here?" There's never a dull moment when you're working underground.

San Sebastián was the last stop on this first trip.

I had read Gabriel Celaya's books, and I had a letter of introduction to him. So I presented myself at the little apartment he had on Juan de Dios, in the old quarter. The office of Norte, a publishing house that he had set up, was in the apartment. So was Amparo. We got along famously from the very start. After a few hours' conversation and a few drinks, I let them in on the secret that I was Spanish, and a member of the party as well. Things went better still after that.

One afternoon, on the second day of my stay in San Sebastián, as I was talking with Gabriel in the apartment on Juan de Dios, a very young boy turned up, terribly nervous and talking a blue streak, pronouncing his r's gutturally, as a Frenchman does. He began to rant and rave against the Falange and the regime, I don't remember on what grounds exactly. It was Enrique Múgica. Active, imaginative, full of plans. That was where we first met and that was how our friendship began. In those first years, Enrique Múgica's contribution to party activities in university circles was decisive. Without him neither the "Poetry and the University" series of meetings, nor the Congress of Young Writers, nor the University Manifesto of February, 1956, would have been what they in fact were. Things as they really are—*Las Cosas Como Son*—as the title of one of Gabriel's books of poems went.

On the last day of my stay in San Sebastián, the newspapers were full of headlines about the workers' insurrection in East Berlin. Stalin had been dead only a few months, and the border territories of his bureaucratic empire were already beginning to fall apart. But the real significance of this event did not become clear to me until later, years later. Up until 1956, up until the publication of Khrushchev's secret report at the Twentieth Congress of the Communist Party of the Soviet Union, the veil of ideological illusion had not yet been completely torn away. I will come back to this subject, naturally.)

But it is the night of June 17, 1959, and you are heading down Marqués de Mondéjar toward Concepción Bahamonde.

Suddenly, as you approach the door of number 5 Concepción Bahamonde, you realize why you have decided to come sleep here, despite the fact that Simón knows this clandestine address.

You had talked it over with Aurelio an hour before.

"Do you have some other place you can sleep?" Aurelio had asked.

"I have several," you had replied.

"Well, go to one of them," Aurelio had said.

"Simón won't talk," you had replied.

Aurelio shook his head.

"Of course not," Aurelio had said. And he had continued to shake his head. "Of course Simón won't talk," Aurelio had said.

Then the two of you had fallen silent for a moment.

"Even so, it's a question of taking the proper precautions."

And he was right: it was a question of taking the proper precautions.

Hadn't you decided to take every conceivable step so that if Simón were arrested it would have the fewest possible repercussions? Hadn't you asked certain comrades to leave their houses so as to keep them from falling into a police dragnet, no matter what happened?

Of course it was a question of taking the proper precautions.

When someone gets caught by the police, the first thing to do is to try to keep that person from being traced back to the organization. When someone gets caught, you adopt the most pessimistic hypothesis as your working assumption. And that is what you had been doing from the moment it had become plain that Simón had disappeared.

In the chain of measures logically deducible from this working hypothesis, not sleeping at the place on Concepción Bahamonde was the last link, the ultimate logical consequence.

"And what are *you* going to do?" you asked Aurelio.

Aurelio looked at you with that fleeting smile that sometimes transformed his face, which was usually grave and even somber.

"I'm staying," Aurelio had said.

And the smile had disappeared.

"I'm staying at my place," Aurelio repeated.

Naturally Simón also knew where Aurelio lived.

And that was all. You said no more about the subject that night.

But now, as you step into the doorway of number 5 Concepción Bahamonde, you understand why you have come here to sleep, to this place that Simón knows about, that is to say an address that the police can also hypothetically come to know. You haven't come just to feel that you are in a safe place, a feeling based on the absolute certainty that the police won't get a word out of Simón, not a single word. You've also come for the opposite reason, to be in a place that may hypothetically be in danger. As though braving this hypothetical danger were the only way to help Simón, as though placing yourself in danger were the one possibility of sharing Simón's suffering with him, of participating in a certain sense in this suffering, of relieving Simón of some part, however small, of his suffering.

You had imagined yourself in the headquarters of the Security Police. It didn't require any special effort of imagination. A great many comrades had described the place to you. Moreover, you had known that you might find yourself in the same situation at any moment. Every morning during those years as you began your usual daily round of contacts and meetings, you had thought that that might be the day that you would get caught. You had never tried to repress this idea. You had never tried to hide this truth from yourself. You had contemplated it, you had tried to foresee what moment of the day you might be arrested so as to prepare yourself inwardly. As a matter of fact, you sometimes had to go to a rendezvous that was set up with some comrade or other weeks before. And it was not always possible to verify that nothing had happened to that comrade during those weeks. Perhaps he had been arrested. Perhaps he had been interrogated, tortured, and had told the police that he had a rendezvous, on such and such a day, at such and such a time and place, with a party leader. The comrade knows very little about you. He doesn't even know that you are Federico Sánchez. He knows you by some name or other, that's all. "Rafael," let's say. But he knows that you're one of the party leaders. Well then, the comrade has given in under pressure and squealed about the rendezvous. The rendezvous is still a week away. It's autumn; the weather is nice and warm, as soft as silk. You are happy in the mornings as you drink a cup of good strong coffee in a bar on Manuel Becerra. You believe you are free. After so many years underground, you have even come to halfway believe you're immortal. Or untouchable anyway. You smile to yourself as you slowly sip the strong coffee, and you don't know that the machinery leading to your arrest has already been set in motion. As a matter of fact you've already been arrested. The Social Brigade has already set in motion the operation that will trap you. Your arrest is already woven into the warp and woof of the days to come. You have been at Buchholz's looking at books, but your freedom is simply an illusion. You've already been arrested. You've been with the comrades from Getafe and the first party committee for this area has been set up. Tonight you are going to have dinner with Domingo and Javier, on the Calle Ferraz. They are going to talk to you as though you still existed, as though you were not already only the shadow of yourself. You have just a few hours of freedom left, but you don't know it. The day of the rendezvous will arrive. It's on the Calle Gaztambide, on the corner of Cea Bermúdez. The thought will cross your mind that this is one of the moments of your day when you might be arrested. Well, what of it? Half an hour before the rendezvous you enter the Café Inglés, on the San Bernardo traffic circle. You never go directly to a rendezvous of this sort, leaving only minutes to spare. You walk to it slowly, detouring first in one direction then in another, sniffing the atmosphere of the neighborhood, observing the meeting place from a distance. You leave the Café Inglés and head for the appointed meeting place, following a roundabout path. Nobody is tailing you, of that you can be certain, after abruptly changing direction two or three times. You arrive by way of Cea Bermúdez, five minutes before the appointed time. There is a newsstand on the sidewalk across the street, the even-numbered side. You stop and look at the headlines of the afternoon papers so as to use up the remaining time. You buy an afternoon paper, you walk slowly away, just a few steps, scrutinizing the meeting place on the opposite side of Cea Bermúdez. You notice nothing suspicious. No unusual car, no movement out of the ordinary, no passerby loitering about the meeting place in a suspect sort of way. You appear to be absorbed in reading the sports pages of the afternoon paper, but you are really inspecting everything around you. You are yourself and your circumstances, you think with a slight smile, quoting Ortega to yourself. Right this moment, it's quite true. The appointed time for the rendezvous has arrived. There's not a sign of the comrade. The minutes go by, they're endless, and the comrade you had the rendezvous with, on Cea Bermúdez, on the corner of Gaztambide, on the odd-numbered side of the street, hasn't shown up. You've finished the sports pages. The comrade isn't going to turn up.

The fact is that he's been arrested. You will find that out the next day. You will also find out the next day that he hasn't said a word about this rendezvous with you in the course of the interrogations that he's been subjected to. You are free again. You steel yourself to face another one of these moments of danger that are always possible. You ponder once again what freedom is. Your freedom in these concrete circumstances at any rate. Your freedom is the silence of comrades who have been arrested. They are the ones who ensure your freedom. Their silence at the headquarters of the Security Police makes it possible. Your freedom depends on others. Others are your freedom, as you know very well. You will never forget it.

Then suddenly you are overcome with the mad desire to be arrested sometime yourself, finally, so that the freedom of others, of the comrades who work with you, will depend on your holding out: on your will to be free, on your will not to give in under torture. You are overcome with the mad, proud, perhaps narcissistic desire to be in a position to give other comrades the gift of their freedom, to ensure it and confirm it by your silence at the headquarters of the Security Police in the Puerta del Sol.

For years, in order to prepare yourself for it inwardly, you have imagined the torture to which you might be subjected. It is not difficult for you to imagine. You have had a certain experience of torture. You have been in the hands of police who were at least as skillful and expert at this sort of thing as Spanish ones. You have been in the hands of the Gestapo. Fifteen long days of interrogations by the Gestapo gave you, years ago, a relative experience of torture, a relative knowledge of what it means to resist it without revealing a single name, a single fact about the underground organization. That was in autumn too, in Auxerre, in 1943. There were autumn roses in the garden of the villa occupied by the Gestapo in Auxerre. Today, however, when you think of possible torture you do not remember the roses in the Gestapo garden, or the gold-capped teeth of Haas, the Gestapo chief. When you think of torture, you do not think of the past, but of the future. And the future has a name. Its name is Conesa. The image of Conesa looms up before you. It is a generic image: you don't know Conesa. Simón Sánchez Montero has told you about Conesa. Lobato has told you about Conesa. Antonio Pérez has told you about Conesa, and has described him to you in great detail. He has told you that he was sickly pale. During the first interrogation, back there in the very hard years that followed Franco's victory, as Gilabert was beating him, Antonio saw how Conesa idly stirred bicarbonate of soda into a glass of water with a spoon, his mind seemingly elsewhere. Antonio stared into Conesa's empty eyes, gray ones or dark brown ones, which accentuated the weary look on his face. In fact all the comrades who have passed through the basement of the Puerta del Sol since 1939 have told you about Conesa. Pilar Claudín has also told you about Conesa. Students nowadays are beginning to talk about other guys in the Brigade: Campanero; or "the one with the purple birthmark." Other guys, other names, other nicknames. But Conesa continues to be the name, the generic image, of a violent and bloody past. And this past may well be your future. If they arrest you, it is probable that Conesa will personally take the trouble to deal with a member of the Executive Committee of the Spanish Communist Party.

As a generic, protean image, the personification of the Social Brigade, Conesa on the prowl haunts the geography of Madrid. In such and such a street there is a harness-maker's shop, a little place where a party family works. It's best not to drop by there, because Conesa sometimes comes sneaking round to sniff the atmosphere, to try to find out if anything's up. So Madrid, some parts of Madrid, are dotted with neuralgic spots, infected ganglia, danger signals that light up in the night like a hallucination: they must be avoided. You can't walk around in certain neighborhoods, on certain streets with Simón, for example. These streets and neighborhoods must be skirted, left off your itinerary. Like the areas shown on old maps as still unexplored—*hic sunt leones*—certain corners of Madrid are mentally colored with gray or sepia: dangerous deserts. Deserts that are avoided so as not to suddenly meet the dangers that come from the cold of the past, the knots that the past has woven into the fabric of the years as they go by. And Conesa, as a protean, generic image of the Social Brigade, is the cunning, pitiless little god of this mental geography that covers the houses and the neighborhoods, the avenues and the squares of Madrid like a fine transparent latticework.

And that is why when you imagined Conesa, on this night when Simón Sánchez Montero had disappeared, you had thought that if it were you yourself who were at the headquarters of the Security Police, your resistance, your ability to keep silent would have been all the greater if you had been sure that there were comrades counting on your silence, certain of your silence.

So you had returned to the place at number 5 Concepción Bahamonde, so as not to leave Simón by himself, so as not to abandon him. So that between Simón and you there would continue to be this link, this tie, this relation, like a shared secret.

It's true that Simón knows where you are. He knows this room, with its iron bedstead, its wardrobe, its night table. He knows the next room, in which you work: a table, a chair, the typewriter, a few books. He knows these two tiny, bare rooms. He has lived in this place on Concepción Bahamonde before you did. And when you cease to live in this place, Julian Grimau will live in it.

Simón has lived here in these two rooms. That is to say that at this very moment, Simón, if he so desires, can imagine you in one of these two rooms. He can presume that you are here, still awake, spending a sleepless night, listening to the hot sounds of June, trying to guess, or deduce, what is going to happen tomorrow. Or rather today. It is already tomorrow, it is already today: June 18, 1959.

Simón can imagine you in one or the other of these two rooms, he can presume that you are still awake, that carried along by a flood of mental images you are thinking vague thoughts about what is going to happen tomorrow—today, it's dawn now—or about what is perhaps not going to happen. Simón can also imagine Aurelio there at his place, which he also knows. On this June night he can imagine, one by one, all the comrades.

Simón, in the police headquarters on the Plaza de Pontejos, with a cruel light shining in his eyes, deafened perhaps by the incoherent shouts of the guys from the Brigade, perhaps about to faint; Simón, coming to perhaps; Simón, shut up in his silence, enveloped in his victorious silence, can project onto the geography of Madrid the faint, flickering lights of a few rooms, a few lamps lighted: signals, signs, messages, sentinels, on this June night.

That is why you have come here to sleep, to the Calle de Concepción Bahamonde. So that in Simón's memory, as he is interrogated, tortured, there may be lighted this lamp of yours, this fraternal lamp among others. So that Simón will not be alone. So that you will not be alone either. So that you will be with Simón this night.

So that you will be together on this June night.

3 THE AITCH EN PEE

Ten years later, you saw Simón Sánchez Montero again. It was in the summer of 1969, in Madrid. Many things had happened since that long-ago night in June. You were no longer Federico Sánchez. That ghost had vanished. You were yourself again: you were now me.

Ten years later, I saw Simón Sánchez Montero again.

When I was expelled from the party in 1965, I applied for a passport at the Spanish Consulate in Paris. The months went by and every time I inquired again, they told me the same thing: that the minister of the interior was opposed to their giving me a passport, even though the functionaries at the consulate unofficially admitted that I had a perfect right to one. Finally, after all else had failed, I asked Luis Miguel Dominguín to intervene on my behalf.

I had met Luis Miguel some time before, at Domingo's at number 12 Calle Ferraz. Domingo had introduced me to his brother by my official name of those days, that is to say, the name that was on one of my false identity papers: Agustín Larrea

(and here, in this story or memoir in which it is my intention to reveal all, I am going to hide the name, to purposely fail to identify the comrade who provided us with papers: that comrade to whom so many of us owe our freedom, and some of us our lives, because the papers he made for us or doctored for us so amazingly resembled authentic ones that nobody would ever have found them at all suspicious: I happened to see him at work on occasion, handling the inks, the glues, the plastic coverings, the stamps, the bunsen burners almost lovingly, in a workshop where false papers became works of art, fraternal safe-conduct passes for weathering the possible storms of life underground: I am not going to reveal his name, but as I keep it secret I nonetheless recall this nameless name and do it honor in my memory, because—who knows?—perhaps we may still need this comrade's diabolical, or angelic, skills, his genius as a counterfeiter, some day: In any event one of the false identity papers he had made for me bore the name Agustín Larrea, and this was the name that Luis Miguel Dominguín knew me by).

I'm fairly certain that Luis Miguel soon guessed that preparing for competitive exams for a professorship in sociology was not my principal activity at the time. He accepted this fiction Domingo put before him, but his behavior toward me in the public places where we sometimes chanced to meet was always extremely circumspect, as though he had tumbled to the truth, as though he had made the connection in his mind between my recent appearance in his brother's company and Domingo's no less recent political activity—not knowing the concrete details, doubtless, but still having a general idea of what Domingo was up to.

This was how matters stood between us until the month of October 1961, until the celebration of Pablo Picasso's eightieth birthday in the south of France. For the occasion, as everyone remembers, kites were flown and bonfires lit, there was lots of feasting and carousing, and there was even a bullfight at Vallauris, fought by Domingo Ortega ("the real philosopher—lots more interesting than the other Ortega," Domingo Dominguín said), Luis Miguel, and a third bullfighter whose name I don't remember. Anyway, at these festivities in honor of Picasso, which went on for two or three days, I happened to be representing the Spanish Communist Party, and this naturally officially confirmed Luis Miguel's intuition that I was a Communist leader.

We spoke of this again later in Cannes, at a dinner at which Colette (my wife), Lucia Bose (for whom this dinner had been the occasion of a reunion with Antonello Trombadori and other Italian comrades of her youth), and Domingo were also present. During this dinner Luis Miguel, with the keen instinct so characteristic of him and the cynicism he so often displays, doubtless as a defense and to reassure himself, predicted to Domingo and me that if the party eventually triumphed in Spain, we would soon be disillusioned. "You don't like power," he declared, "but power is the only thing that matters. You are men of the opposition, to the very bone—men who fight viscerally against power, not for power. You're against Franco today, and tomorrow you'll be against Carrillo, if he's the one who represents power. It's the opposite with me: I side with power every time. But don't worry: just as I'd intervene in your favor with my friend Camilo Alonso Vega today, I'll intervene on your behalf when Carrillo's my friend and you're being persecuted."

Be that as it may, at the beginning of the year 1967, after two years of getting nowhere at the Spanish consulate in Paris, I sought Luis Miguel's help. Without hesitating a minute, he wrote a letter on March 6 to General Camilo Alonso Vega, then minister of the interior.

On March 16, 1967, Camilo Alonso Vega sent Luis Miguel the following letter in reply, which I quote word for word:

The Minister of the Interior
Sr. Don Luis Miguel Gonzalez Lucas
Segre, no. 8
Madrid

My dear friend:

I have received your letter of the sixth of this month which expresses such interest in the case of Don Jorge Semprún Maura, at present residing in Paris, who wishes to return to Spain and has asked our Consulate in that capital to normalize his situation as a Spanish citizen.

I regret very much not being able to give you good news in this regard, since his conduct during the last twenty-five years and, in particular, his activities abroad may well give rise to his being prosecuted by the Judicial Authority.

With a fraternal embrace from your good friend,

(Signed)
CAMILO ALONSO VEGA

Attached to this letter was a report or resume drafted by the Security Police of my political activites. I cite this document in its entirety, word for word. I think it deserves to be quoted.

JORGE SEMPRÚN MAURA

Born in Madrid December 10, 1923, son of José María and Susana; at present residing in Paris.
POLITICAL EXILE.

He is the son of José María SEMPRÚN GURREA, former civil governor of Toledo, Chargé d'Affaires of the Republican government at The Hague, ambassador to Rome and minister without portfolio in the Republican government. Represented the government in exile in the Italian capital.

He arrived in France in 1939 with his parents, as an exile.

Because of his participation in the French Resistance during the German occupation, JORGE SEMPRÚN MAURA was arrested as a member of the Emigré Workers' Movement and deported by the Germans to the concentration camp at Buchenwald.

In the year 1963 he received the "Formentor Prize" in literature for his work entitled *The Long Voyage.*

He has a master's degree in Letters and works or worked for UNESCO as a translator. He wrote the Spanish version of the work *The Vicar.*

He was married to the French actress Lola BELLON, who belonged to the board of directors of the France–USSR Association; he was divorced on a date that has not been determined.

He has two brothers, Carlos and Francisco, the first of whom was a pupil at the Film Institute of Paris and is well known as a distributor of Communist literature.

On May 3, 1965, the Italian newspaper *La Stampa* stated that JORGE SEMPRÚN was active in the clandestine Communist organization in Spain, and went so far as to call him "the successor of Julián Grimau."

He has been pointed out as an assiduous participant or at least one present at numerous public protests against the regime that have been held outside the country. Among these there might be mentioned his lecture at the "House of Culture" in Genoa on October 10, 1963.

On this occasion, SEMPRÚN MAURA, after having predicted the imminent fall of the Spanish regime, said that the recent manifesto by the intellectuals of our country had for the first time exposed the rest of the world to the problems of censorship, torture, and the fight for freedom and democracy in Spain. He added that the anti-Franco forces inside the country could now count on the aid of Catholic and ex-Falangist circles. He ended his remarks by asking for the aid of all Italian intellectuals, regardless of their political creed, in the fight against Franco.

When the so-called "European Conference for the Amnesty of Political Prisoners and Democratic Freedoms" was held in Venezuela in 1965, the subject of this report sent an expression of his support.

In the October 15, 1964 issue of *Le Monde,* SEMPRÚN MAURA published an article, entitled "Burgos," on Spanish political prisoners.

He also contributed to the white paper published by the Italian Communist Party on "Political Prisoners," in a chapter entitled "Spain in Prison."

It should also be pointed out that this individual is considered to be the author of the screenplay for the film *La guerre est finie,* directed by ALAIN RESNAIS, on our differences with our adversaries.

According to reports, the screenplay mentions an exile who feels himself obliged to return to Spain, not to see his aged mother, but to fight at the head of a group of guerrillas, of which he is the leader and which sees itself in danger of being liquidated by the "Fascist police."

Under the pseudonym of FEDERICO SÁNCHEZ, Jorge SEMPRÚN MAURA was elected a member of the Central Committee of the Spanish Communist Party at the Fifth Congress held in Prague in November 1954.

A collaborator of Fernando Claudín Ponte's, the two of them were excluded from the Central Committee and from the Spanish Communist Party in January 1965.

The fact that certain Communist leaders were supporters of Stalin's policy has been attributed to the influence of CLAUDÍN and SEMPRÚN. This current of opinion was termed "regressionism" by the orthodox leaders.

December 12, 1966

This incredible document, a string of harmless well-known facts that the most inept journalist could have turned up, and of egregious errors and gaps, bears the official seal of the *General Technical Secretariat— General Headquarters for Social Investigation* of the *Security Police Authority.*

It goes without saying that this text amply explains, *a posteriori,* how it was possible to work underground in Madrid for ten years—to have permanent relations with several dozen party cadres and a similar number of personalities of the democratic opposition—without ever having fallen into a trap set by the police. The fact is that Franco's police, Conesa's police, were not worth shit, to put it frankly. The only thing they were good at was keeping all the old militants with police records under surveillance once they had been released from prison. They were only relatively effective, until the end of the sixties at least, at keeping workers' sectors under special surveillance. But in this latter case it was not only the Social Brigade that kept an eye out for possible militants, but the entire institutional apparatus of capitalism. The built-in despotism of capitalist power greatly facilitated police surveillance in factories. The very mechanism of exploitation, of the production of surplus value, greatly helped to neutralize the activities and the propaganda of militant workers in industrial plants, and to ferret them out. But the moment one was outside of this closed capitalist universe steeped in a diffuse terrorism, the moment one was—as was true of me—not only a Communist without a prison record but also a leader who even old party cadres could not identify, then, given that Conesa's Social Brigade had to rely on informers and beatings, one could move about Madrid like a fish in water. And that is what I did. I could laugh as hard and as often as I pleased at Superagent Conesa.

In any event, the accumulation of errors in this report is surprising. After the description of my family background and public activity, which, I repeat, anyone could easily have found out about, the report begins by saying that Semprún Maura "works or worked for UNESCO." This was dated December 1966, and I quit as a translator in this venerable, useless, and bureaucratic institution in 1952, the year in which I became a party official. The report then adds that I wrote the Spanish version of *The Vicar,* when it is obvious that what I wrote was the French version of Rolf Hochhuth's play. Anyone who reads the newspapers would have known this.

In the next line, the General Headquarters for Social Investigation of the General Technical Secretariat of the Security Police Authority— such sound and fury over nothing—proclaims that I have "two brothers, named Carlos and Francisco, the first of which was a pupil at the Film Institute in Paris and is well known as a distributor of Communist literature." The truth is that I have not two but four brothers; and two sisters, just to keep the record straight. There are seven children in the family: proof enough, if any is needed, of my traditional Catholic background.

As for the information concerning Carlos, the best that can be said for it is that it was not current. To describe Carlos merely as a "distributor of Communist literature" is almost an insult to his hundred percent activism, which led him, after leaving the Spanish Communist Party in 1957, to militate in the Popular Liberation Front (FLP), and then, down through the years, in purer and purer, more and more chimerical splinter groups of the FLP, all alike in their eagerness to proclaim themselves the only authentic vanguard of the class struggle in Spain, and finally ending up—after a 180-degree ideological turn that made him forget, at last, his Leninist fetishism as regards organization—playing the role of an arcadian and archaic armchair prophet preaching an opposition to all authority that no doubt conceals a very real and profound, and perhaps even unbearable, despair at the historical failure of the revolution.

But to return to what I was saying: the report by the Security Police totally ignores Carlos Semprún's activity as a clandestine official of the party in Madrid from 1955 to 1957 or thereabouts, thus shedding significant light on that agency's lack of information about the organization that Carlos and I were setting up in those years with young militants and with the help, primarily, of Ricardo Muñoz Suay, Juan Antonio Bardem, Javier Pradera, and Enrique Múgica, an organization that had its ups and downs but somehow managed to survive all the raids, repressions, and run-ins mounted by the police.

I am nonetheless not going to emphasize here all the errors in the report that Camilo Alonso Vega (may he rest in peace), army general and minister of the interior, passed on confidentially to Luis Miguel Dominguín in March of 1967.

But I do want to have my fun, and allow myself to burst into peals of merriment and whoops of laughter, even though it is solitary laughter, on rereading the last paragraphs of this confounded report.

It says there that "it should also be pointed out that this individual" (and the individual is you, and you accept that label with pleasure, despite its obvious pejorative connotation: now that poor Althusser is trying to demonstrate to you that man is only an ideological illusion of the bourgeoisie, that not even man—in the final analysis what the bourgeois call a man—is the subject of his own history, now that this history is a process without a subject and without a purpose, which is tantamount to saying that it is not a process in the last analysis but an immovable spiral structure, a sort of self-movement of a second-hand Absolute Spirit: now that poor Althusser is proclaiming that man is a joint invention of the bourgeoisie and Stalinism, that man is only a mask and a myth concealing real entities from us, whose one definition is that they are no longer bearers of eternal values, as in the simplistic or simpleminded mythology of José Antonio (Primo de Rivera, founder of the Falange), but rather bearers of relations of production; now that man, as fashionable philosophers proclaim, is merely an incidental feature in the historical landscape, an ambiguous and ineffective hole in the texture of massified relations of production; now that being a man, generically, is so looked down upon by the latter-day philosophers of university Marxism, with their white gloves and spongy brains, you are now pleased to accept the label of individual and, even worse, of "this individual," which further accentuates, if need be, the contemptuous nature of the expression: and you accept it because, when all is said and done, the individual is what is not divisible; what is irreducible to social and political mediations; what the mechanisms of state power cannot replace; what rises from the bottom of the holes in the relations of production, every time that it is necessary to rise up against injustice, against the impossibility of life, against slow death from alienation: the individual, therefore, is what ideologies, beliefs, norms, powers cannot replace; that is why the fact that the Security Police called you "this individual" neither disturbs you nor displeases you), and "this individual," then, it says in the report, "is considered to be the author of the screenplay for the film *La guerre est finie.*" In view of the fact that I am, indeed, the author of the screenplay, it seems logical to me that I should be so considered. But the Security Police are probably not film fans. Not only are they uncertain whether I really am the author of the screenplay of *La guerre est finie,* but they've also confused the screenplay of this film with an American film by Fred Zinnemann, in which Gregory Peck plays the part of an exile who returns to his country to see his dying mother and falls into an ambush by the Civil Guard, whose local head, if I remember correctly, is Anthony Quinn. A very weak film, in the bargain, so I am irritated to see it compared to mine; or rather, to Alain Resnais's.

And to top it all off, a pearl I won't even bother to elaborate since it speaks for itself and demonstrates once again the supine stupidity and the encyclopedic ignorance of the specialists in the General Headquarters of Social Investigation, the grotesque statement that makes Fernando Claudín and me "supporters of Stalin's policy." The informer, doubtless someone from the party ranks, must have been someone who had swallowed the Carrillists' lies hook, line, and sinker. An argument of this sort was in fact widely used against us in the internal campaign to facilitate the militants' acceptance of our exclusion without batting an eye.

When Luis Miguel Domínguín sent me the photocopies of Camilo Alonso Vega's letter and the Security Police report on April 28, 1967, following his return from a long trip to America, I had just been summoned by the Spanish vice-consul in Paris, whose name, by one of those ironies of fate, was Sánchez. The vice-consul told me that he had just received permission to issue me a passport, but that he was obliged to inform me officially that if I used this passport to go to Spain, I would be doing so "at my own risk." The vice-consul was obviously worried about such a risk. I wasn't. The most superficial analysis of the situation indicated that the risk was minimal, if not nonexistent, at least so long as I didn't intend to reside permanently in Spain. So I accepted the passport—and the risk.

And as was predictable, nothing happened.

I made my first legal trip to Spain in July of 1967, by way of Havana, where I had been invited by Carlos Franqui, along with a large group of European artists and writers. Faithful to our long friendship and worried about what might happen, Luis Miguel and Domingo were waiting for me on my arrival in Barajas. They had also brought with them, just in case, a cousin of mine, a certain Gamazo who was working at the time, if I remember correctly, in the president's office and was later briefly a minister of Franco's. But his intervention was not necessary. The one thing the border police wanted to know when they saw my entry card was what hotel I was intending to put up at and how long I was going to stay.

And that was the end.

The end of the excitement of clandestine trips across the border, of yesterday's joy every time I crossed the old Behobia bridge to go back into my country without anyone's permission. The sun shining on the waters of the Bidassoa, or maybe the gray waters of the border river flowing slowly along beneath an overcast, perhaps rainy sky. And making it. Crossing that invisible, radical line once again. Once again returning to the scenes of my childhood, to the solid, stubborn happiness of clandestine political work, to the fraternity of Madrid, with Nieves and Ricardo, with Javier and Gabriela, with Domingo and Carmela, with all the comrades. Once more returning to the imaginary territory of plans never carried through but always feasible, of dreams that were never realized but that made my soul navigable, as Rafael Alberti would have said in the days when he was a real poet, centuries ago.

So then, that was the end. I was just one more tourist now, one more traveler, a Spaniard residing abroad who was returning to breathe his native air, a sort of old colonial hand returning from the Americas.

Someone of really very little importance, someone who didn't really amount to much. Just a French writer of Spanish origin.

A real tear-jerker, wouldn't you say?

Ten years, as I was saying, after that night in June when Simón Sánchez Montero was arrested in Madrid, I met him again. It was in the last days of summer. He sent me a message via Domingo Dominguín. He told me he would be pleased to see me again. I'd be pleased to see him too, of course. So we saw each other. We spent a whole long afternoon together.

We met in Pozuelo de Alarcón, in a very luxurious house done in the most vulgar taste which Elias Querejeta had rented for a French actor who was a friend of mine, Jean-Louis Trintignant, and who was acting in a film directed by Antón Eceiza, *les Secrètes Intentions (Secret Intentions)*. It was partially my fault that Trintignant had agreed to make a film with Eceiza and Querejeta—I say fault because Anton's film turned out to be very mediocre, despite a great screenplay. I had introduced them to each other in Paris early that summer.

Anyway, Simón and I spent a whole afternoon together talking in the garden of that so untastefully done house, on the edge of a swimming pool that was trying to look Hollywood without quite making it. But then this wasn't Beverly Hills, it was Pozuelo de Alarcón. But never mind, the decor didn't matter at all. What mattered was that Simón and I were talking. Simón was the first leader of the Spanish Communist Party who had been willing to speak to me since I had been expelled. Which shouldn't have surprised anyone.

At least it didn't surprise me.

The first thing Simón Sánchez Montero asked me on that afternoon at the end of summer in 1969 was what I had done on that long-ago June night. Had I gone back to my place on Concepción Bahamonde to sleep?

We were in the garden, sitting on chaises longues set out on the technicolor lawn. You could hear the murmur of water flowing into the pool. I looked at Simón and he looked at me. For the space of an instant a ray of sunlight glinted on the thick lenses of his glasses.

That glint of light vaguely reminded me of something.

Yes, of course. Many years before, in 1956, in February. On Doctor Esquerdo, on the esplanade, in front of the hospital. I had a rendezvous with Simón. I saw him arriving in the distance, laughing. A burst of laughter like an explosion of joy. And the sunlight glinting on Simón's glasses in the distance. In his hand was a copy of *Arriba* with an article by Federico Sánchez, published in *Mundo Obrero* some weeks before, on political activity of Communists at the university. It was in the days of the student demonstrations. The struggle of the masses, open battle, was beginning at last. I remember Simón's happiness over this success of ours, one of the first we had been able to chalk up to our credit in Madrid in a long time.

I looked at Simón.

The glint of sunlight on his thick glasses recalled to my mind many years of meetings, discussions, illusions, of weaving and unweaving the fabric of days and dreams. For a second that was like an eternity, I was totally absorbed in this memory. Then I answered his question.

Yes, I had gone back to Concepción Bahamonde to sleep that night in June 1959. I explained to him why I had gone back there. Simon looked at me and shook his head. "That's what I thought you'd do," he told me. "I hoped you'd go back to your place. It gave me strength thinking you were at your place."

There was a silence. The sun was no longer glinting on his glasses, but on the postcard-blue water of the swimming pool.

"The next morning I went out into the streets very early," I said to Simon. "The HNP was a complete fiasco!"

The Peaceful National Strike! The HNP, or *Aitch En Pee,* three charismatic initials that for so many long years—from 1959 to the death of Francisco Franco—had made the Communists live in the phantasmagorical world of dreams. At other times it was *Aitch Gee Pee,* the *Gee* standing for General and the *Pee* this time standing for Political, while the *Aitch* kept its permanent meaning: HUELGA—STRIKE—as though the word HUELGA, down through the years and down through its multiple metamorphoses—its last reincarnation being the ADN, the National Democratic Action, which Santiago Carrillo announced as imminent in September 1975, just a few weeks before Franco's death— as though the HUELGA had continued to be the possible, the dreamed- of explosion of everything that existed, giving us access to a new reality, one perhaps engendered by the sheer magic virtue of this word, of this fantastic, mythological action postponed from month to month, from year to year, but always imminent, always just about to explode.

And doubtless the Holy Church needed learned doctors to explain to the militant faithful the extremely subtle dialectical mediations between the HGP, the HNP, and the ADN, to explain their constant objective maturation, which somehow never managed to objectify itself, except subjectively, in the dichotomized, schizophrenic consciousness of the activists.

Hence, through the years, eaten away by the cancerous proliferation of ideological illusion, the General Strike ceased to be a strategic objective, capable, at least partially, of transforming reality, having gradually taken on an almost religious significance, continually oscillating between extremist triumphalism and the most inconsistent opportunism. It was as though, through yet another irony of historical reason, the *Aitch En Pee* had turned itself into the final incarnation of the Hegelian Absolute Spirit, the autonomous Conscience of the Party—and, more exactly, of Carrillo, who is the latter's personification—from the In-Itself to the For-Itself, the creator of its own positivity, of its own ideal objectivity, in the illusory world of representation. It was as though it were enough to modify the universe of representations, to modify the opaque and resistant universe of reality.

The general strike!

As I look back on it, my entire life as a militant Communist has unfolded beneath this sign

(your entire life, ever since you reached the so-called age of reason, has unfolded beneath this sign, as you look back on it: what has happened is that this sign has changed sign through the years, or, to express it in current language, this signifier has changed signification: in fact, the general strike begins in your mind as something vaguely disquieting, apocalyptic: the general strike in your first memories of it has the sound of sniping and bursts of rifle fire: but even without this background noise it is disquieting: in Santander, for example, in the summer of 1931, at the time when your father was civil governor of the province after the Republic had been proclaimed, the CNT declared a general strike: there was no sniping, there were no bursts of rifle fire: but you heard your father and your father's friends discussing matters, on the veranda of that house in El Sardinero: they said that the CNT was committing a criminal error, that the workers had to defend and consolidate the Republic, before all else, that the solution of social demands, just ones moreover, completely justified ones of course, would come later: thus on the veranda of that house in El Sardinero, where for years you had spent the summer, a house you have described in some book or other and that you will continue to describe, doubtless because it is one of the secret corners or hiding places of the tiny earthly paradise of your memory, on the veranda of that house in El Sardinero where you lived in 1931, because your father had not wanted to occupy the official residence of the civil governor, on that veranda you discovered, at the age of eight, without knowing that you had just discovered it, the contradictions of the bourgeois Republic and thus the inner rents in the liberal conscience: and three years later, remember, in Madrid, hearing Alfredo

Mendizábal telling your father about the days he lived through in Oviedo during the proletarian insurrection of October 1934, you again had the same sensation of   vaque malaise: and the fact is that,   listening silently to your elders, to Alfredo Mendizábal and your father, you seemed somehow to understand that the cause defended by the Asturian workers was just, but that the means that they were using to defend it were not: worse still, that they were counterproductive, because the legitimacy of the Republic could be preserved only through legal means: but)

my entire life as a militant Communist has unfolded beneath the sign of the general strike, which continued, doubtless, to be something apocalyptic, though no longer disquieting, but rather quite the contrary: the immediate and festive explosion of a new social reality. *In hoc signo vinces. . . .* But profane history never has as beautiful an ending as sacred history: beneath the sign of the general strike we did not conquer.

In 1947, at any rate, when my party cell met in the building of the Learned Societies on the Rue Danton, the mythology of the general strike found concrete nourishment in an attempted workers' strike in Vizcaya.

On May 1, 1947, in fact, there had taken place in Bilbao a rather large-scale work-stoppage, which went on for several days afterward. But the analyses by the party failed to place this action in its proper setting, seeing it instead as a decisive turning point, the beginning of the final step leading to the liquidation of Francoism. Despite different shadings due to particular times and places, this type of analysis never ceased during the decades that followed. Despite the changes in the groups exercising leadership, despite tactical shifts, despite the global change of strategic organizations, which led from the creation of clandestine labor unions to the exploitation of the legal possibilities inherent in the vertical labor unions, and from guerrilla fighting to peaceful mass action, ideological subjectivism continued to be the leading thread of the activity of the Spanish Communist Party during the entire period of Franco's dictatorship. It can even be said, I believe, that subjectivism has been a specific malady of Spanish Communism.

In the spring and summer of 1947, Vicente Arroyo was the joyful, optimistic spokesman of this subjectivism. With the enthusiasm of an old fighter buoyed up by illusions, he would tell us in the meetings how the strike in Bilbao had gone, what its consequences would be. Arroyo published an article on this strike in *Nuestra Bandera,* the party's theoretical review, if I remember correctly (you get up, you go to your library: you look on the shelf for the copies of *Nuestra Bandera* of this period: your memory is correct: in the June 8, 1947 issue is an article by Vicente Arroyo, "Antecedents and Experiences of the Euzkadi Strikes": in this same issue are two other articles on the subject: one by Vicente Uribe, "The General Strike in Vizcaya and the Euzkadi Communist Party," and another by Cristóbal Errandonea, "The Vizcaya Strike Has Been a Great Lesson in Unity": you remember Cristóbal: Errandonea was a member of the Politburo when you met him: he was that up until around August 1956: in 1951, after the arrest of Gregorio López Raimundo and the other comrades of the PSUC, a commission was created to organize a campaign to free them: Cristóbal was the head of this commission: Serrán, Ramón Ormazábal, and you were members of it: there were others too, perhaps, but you don't remember: perhaps: your work was quite effective: the campaign attracted international attention: you were an employee at UNESCO then: your participation on that committee for prisoners, for amnesty, was the first somewhat responsible work you ever did in the party: since besides being a translator at UNESCO and an unpaid activist you also continued to be an unknown but prolix poet, the Barcelona strikes inspired you to write another interminable poem that you also never finished, *Spring Begins in Barcelona:* you have just found it again in the dusty packets of your Stalinist verses: an extract from this new canto was published in *Cuadernos de Cultura,* no. 7: "We publish below a poem by the Communist poet Jorge Semprún from his recent work, *La primavera comienza en Barcelona.* In forthcoming numbers we will publish other poems from this work, which represents a precious contribution to the development of a Spanish poetry linked to the struggles of our people," the introduction stated: fortunately no more extracts were published: this one was entitled "The Yankee Invaders": but you have gotten up from your work table to see if you can find Vicente Arroyo's article: you have found it: you go back to your work table with the three copies of *Neustra Bandera* corresponding to the spring and the beginning of summer 1947: the review was put out in Toulouse: in a 14 x 20 cm. format: price was 20 francs: on the cover of the publication, under the name and alongside a five-pointed star, were the words, "Monthly review of political, economic, and cultural orientation, published by the Spanish Communist Party": too much orientation doubtless for a single review: but that was the way the subtitle read: on the inside of the cover was a frieze with the marmoreal profiles of your masters: four of them, like the musketeers and the Evangelists: beneath it a caption read, "Beneath the banners of Marx, Engels, Lenin, and Stalin": you leaf through these three copies of *Nuestra Bandera,* that is to say the banner of Marx, Engels, Lenin, and Stalin: above all the last: there is no doubt of it: you find nothing by Santiago Carrillo: there appear the signatures of Vicente Uribe, Antonio Mije, Manuel Azcárate, Fernando Claudín, Tomás García, Juan Modesto, Antonio Cordón, among others: you plunge into the reading of these old copies of *Nuestra Bandera,* beginning with the article by Vicente Arroyo, "Antecedents and Experiences of the Euzkadi Strikes": and)

during that spring Arroyo reminded us at all the cell meetings, or after the meetings, on the sunny terraces of the cafés in the Latin Quarter, of a sentence that La Pasionaria had uttered at a recent plenum of the party: "One must have a passionate faith in the cause that is being defended; one must will to triumph over heaven and hell and heaven stand in the way of our path." And we did not lack faith, of course, but hell and heaven came to stand in the way of our path. Or rather, objective conditions came to stand in the way of the path of our triumphalist subjectivism.

A few weeks before the Bilbao strike a plenum of the Spanish Communist Party had taken place, from the 19th of March to the 22nd, in Montreuil. (It was in precisely these days of the plenum, though I don't remember whether it was before or after, that my first meeting with La Pasionaria had taken place, on Kléber.)

But I am not writing the history of the Communist Party in exile (an exciting history, moreover, which it will be imperative to write, to the scandalized outrage of certain people). I am therefore not going to analyze the content of the plenum in Montreuil in detail. All I am interested in is emphasizing the subjectivism that dominated all the speeches that were given, the certainty of imminent triumph that runs through all of them like a red thread. Reading the reports presented at the plenum, as well as the editorial comments on it in subsequent issues of *Nuestra Bandera,* one gathers the impression that the Franco regime was tottering, that its death-throes had already begun.

Thus the main report by Dolores Ibárruri begins with a categorical statement: "We are holding this Plenary Conference in the final days of the Franco regime." This was in the year 1947, let us not forget. And then La Pasionaria develops the various points in her argument:

Francoism, wounded to the death, is collapsing, and democratic Spain is rising from its prostration.

Workers' organizations, which Franco brutally dissolved, are being clandestinely reconstructed; strikes and demonstrations against hunger are taking place; dozens of illegal periodicals are being published; the peasants are resisting Francosim.

In Catalonia, Euzkadi, and Galicia national sentiment, repressed by force, is arising once more, stronger and more active than ever.

Anti-Franco military personnel and intellectuals are organizing: the parties on the right that formed the Francoist bloc are embarking upon independent political activity, and monarchists and unaffiliated are now beginning to appear as more or less coherent political formations.

Capitalist and financial groups are questioning the authority and the efficacy of the Fascist methods imposed by Franco. . . .

A part of the Church, whose instinct for self-preservation alerts it to the danger to its future of going along with Franco to the end, is beginning to show public signs of its lack of agreement with the regime.

Franco's authority is waning even in the army. Certain military leaders who supported him in rebellion are inwardly returning to their old dynastic sentiments and seeking other new paths that will put an end to the Fascist histrionics of the Caudillo. . . .

Spain is falling apart in Franco's hands. Spain is sinking into poverty, into ruin, into the degradation of Fascist corruption and the inability to govern. . . .

Doesn't it give rise to a strange sensation to read these words of March 1947? Was it not precisely this sort of analysis, with some variation, that persisted until a few weeks before Francisco Franco's death?

At the plenum in Montreuil, thirty years ago, La Pasionaria concluded the first chapter of her report—the title of which was unequivocal: "The Situation in Spain: Francoism is Crumbling"—with an analysis of the mass struggles ending with the following paragraph: *"And it is this popular national resistance that is growing day by day, morally stimulated by international democracy's condemnation of Francoism and by the irremediable economic catastrophe into which Spain is sinking, thus obliging monarchists and conservatives in general to think of a change of regime before the violent explosion of popular wrath brings down the temple and all its Philistines."*

Dolores Ibárruri's biblical metaphor is a perfect reflection of the tone and the general cast of all the speeches delivered at the Montreuil plenum. In the spring of 1947 the Spanish Communists' view of the situation was that the fall of Francoism was imminent.

Unfortunately, reality, perhaps through the fault of heaven, or hell, or both, was quite different. In the spring of 1947 "popular national resistance" was not growing day by day. The triumphalist enumeration of strikes of all sorts that Santiago Carrillo drew up in his speech on March 21 at the Montreuil Plenum is totally false. Likewise the conclusions drawn by Carrillo from these struggles are false, thus pitifully misleading those militants present.

It is false to say that "strikes, demonstrations, protests of all sorts have agitated the whole of Spain." It is false to say that "what is new in this movement is that, going beyond previous situations in which the struggle was carried on by small groups of Communists and other vanguard anti-Francoists, today the participation of the great popular masses is a fact." It is misleading to tell militants that "workers' unions are again being formed clandestinely. The General Workers' Union is being reconstituted in factories and workshops, as meanwhile the vertical labor unions, the instruments of oppression on the part of Falangists and owners, are totally losing their influence, their strength in the factories." It is childish to proclaim that "the repercussion of all these strikes and mass actions on the political situation, despite their apparently economic character, has been tremendous. The regime has felt itself shaken to its foundations." It is to stray from the truth, finally, to conclude that "it is necessary to show the working class that in its hand, within its reach, is a weapon that, if it can be combined with the action and the struggle of all anti-Franco forces inside the country, with international democratic pressure from the outside, can put an end to the Franco regime: this weapon is the general political strike that Spanish workers gallantly brandished in 1917, 1930, 1934, 1936. . . . "

As can be seen, the general political strike, or *Aitch Gee Pee,* is a long-standing obsession of Santiago Carrillo's. From the Montreuil Plenum, in March of 1947, to the Second National Conference of the Spanish Communist Party, held in September 1975, a few weeks before the long death-agony of Francisco Franco, Carrillo had kept rousing this ghost to life. As the years went by, naturally, as we kept approaching this "inevitable" and never realized action, the formulations that defined it were gradually modified, in keeping with Carrillo's fantasy and without taking the slightest account of Spanish social reality. Thus in 1975 the *Aitch Gee Pee,* or *Aitch En Pee,* came to be called the ADN, Democratic National Action, a formulation doubtless more in accord with the language of the civilized Left that had grouped around Carrillo in the form of the meteoric and ill-fated Junta Democrática, and that included everyone from José Luis de Vilallonga to Rafael Calvo Serer, plus a very amusing Princess de Borbón-Parma and a not at all amusing Garcia Trevijano.

There is one fact that demonstrates, in my opinion, how deeply entrenched the conception of the HGP, HNP, or ADN was in Santiago Carrillo's mind. At the end of 1976, in fact, when history had demonstrated that the transition from Franco's despotic dictatorship to the bourgeois democracy of the Franquistas had been produced without the intervention of that mythological popular uprising, when the *Aitch En Pee* had been put back in some storeroom of the national theater by the stagehands of the political class, Santiago Carrillo nonetheless kept mentioning it as something that might have been possible, something that had been on the point of taking place; as though it were something that only happenstance had prevented from taking place. In his pamphlet entitled "What is a Democratic Break?" Carrillo states: *"If chance had brought it about that Franco's life had been prolonged a few years more, we would have seen how popular pressure, probably accompanied by a 'palace coup,' would have removed Franco, more or less politely."* I do not believe it is easy to find in the writings of political leaders who proclaim themselves to be Marxists any more unreal or surreal text than this one, or one so inflated with unfulfillable desires or frustrated dreams. The question must be asked whether Carrillo's early political vocation did not cut off a possible career as a writer of science fiction or cheap fantastic novels.

In any event, a summary analysis of Carrillo's initial statement of 1947 with regard to the general strike will be sufficient witness to all the contradictions, all the confused thinking that surrounded the strike order at that time, and which continued to surround it up until the biological withering away of the dictatorship.

Let us begin with the historical examples used as references by Carrillo. Carrillo stated that Spanish workers gallantly brandished in 1917, 1930, 1934, and 1936 the weapon of a general strike. I shall pass over the vulgar adverb. Gallantly? One wonders what the class struggle has to do with aristocratic gallantry. But let us go straight to the heart of the matter. And the heart of the matter is that Carrillo lumps heterogeneous and incomparable historical events together.

The general strike in 1917, in fact, took place within the historical context of a Europe-wide crisis, and whose epicenter—unfortunately for the future of the revolution—was Russia. It was an openly revolutionary mass action, which inaugurated in Spain what some have called the "Bolshevik triennium."

The general strike of December 1930 was something quite different. It was an action against the Monarchy of Alfonso XIII, unleashed in support of the uprising in Jaca of Galán and García Hernández, which was very soon put down. Strictly speaking, it was not a class action, as in 1917. It unfolded beneath the political hegemony of the Republican-Socialist coalition that had signed the Pact of San Sebastián. This frontal action that attempted to combine a military coup and a general strike was a failure in both respects. And it was not until months later that the Republic was established, on the occasion of certain municipal elections, and as a result of the internal decomposition of the monarchical institution and the narrowness of its social base, which had been undermined by popular actions and protests.

The situation in October 1934 likewise had nothing to do with either the one in 1930 or the one in 1917. What took place then was an attempt of an insurrectional nature headed—without sufficient unity or perspective—by workers' parties in opposition to the rightist overthrow of the democratic-bourgeois Republic through parliamentary means—which Hitler had just successfully used in Germany, let us not forget—that was threatened by the relative victory of rightist parties in the latest legislative elections. The general strike in 1934 was also a failure, except in Asturias, where the struggle took on the form of armed insurrection on the part of the miners, bloodily repressed by the army.

In 1936, finally, we again find ourselves confronted with an unprecedented situation. The general strike was the popular, working-class answer to the military uprising. This was only the first step toward the armed uprising of the people, toward the replacement by a new popular power, crushed soon, of the apparatus of the bourgeois state, which had been incapable of opposing the military conspiracy.

Hence it is not possible to sum up in a single all-purpose, superficial phrase the mass actions of 1917, 1930, 1934, and 1936 as Carrillo does. If the soul of Marxism is the concrete analysis of a concrete situation (though this phrase of Lenin's is far from being totally satisfactory, since it may well lead to Realpolitik pragmatism if it is taken literally), Carrillo's statement is anything but Marxist. In the ideological darkness of its formulation, all concrete situations become unreal.

Yet all these historically heterogeneous actions have a number of common traits: the very ones that Carrillo neglects to analyze.

The first trait that they have in common is the fact that the mass actions were directed by parties and labor unions that were acting within the law, that had at their disposal all the means of propaganda, organization, and mobilization permitted by a democratic system. In 1947, on the other hand, when Carrillo proclaimed that the working class had, "in its hands, within its reach," the weapon of a general political strike, parties and labor unions were completely illegal, a situation aggravated by the fact that this illegality followed upon a historical rout of popular forces, in which all their leadership groups were exterminated or scattered throughout the world. When Carrillo addressed Spanish workers in March 1947 and urged them to "gallantly" brandish the weapon of a general strike, he did so from Paris, from exile. Carrillo was speaking not only from outside the situation, but also from a long way away, and the workers whom he was addressing not only could not hear him, but would not understand him even if they could hear his appeal.

The second common feature of all these actions, which Santiago Carrillo also fails to mention, is that they were offensive actions, produced at high points in the movement of the masses. Even that of October 1934, which at first glance has other features, is a counter-offensive action, a dynamic reply of the masses to reaction on the rise. It was not the working masses who had lost the legislative elections of December 1933: it was the reformist and bourgeois coalition of the first two years of the Republic. The electoral defeat had been proof of the lack of resolution, of perspective, of strategic firmness on the part of the Republican–Socialist coalition. But the working class, agricultural day laborers, peasants, and the urban petty bourgeoisie that constituted the radical and revolutionary wing of the bourgeois Republic were not demoralized by the defeat at the polls, which, moreover, was relative. Their forces remained intact. Even the bloody rout in Asturias in October did not check the rising tide of the movement. In other words, all the general strikes that Carrillo mentioned as a historical precedent for his appeal had taken place in moments of flux (yes, Tano, yes!) of the democratic workers' movement. In 1947, on the other hand, when Carrillo again began to raise the specter of the General Political Strike, this movement was in a phase of profound depression, as a consequence of the crushing defeat suffered after three years of civil war.

Furthermore, any sort of reasonably rigorous analysis of the content itself of Carrillo's statement in 1947 would demonstrate that the general political strike he called for was impossible. Or better put: once all the conditions that would make it possible were hypothetically at hand, the *Aitch Gee Pee* would no longer be necessary.

What did Santiago Carrillo in fact say? He said that the general strike could put an end to the Franco regime if it could be combined *"with the action and the struggle of all anti-Franco forces inside the country, with international democratic pressure from the outside."* Of course, but this was to combine a lot of things. Naturally a general political strike brought off under these conditions would have put an end to the regime. Perhaps it would have been enough merely to announce such a strike, merely to prepare it politically, to attain such an objective. In fact, it would have been a genuine political revolution. But—and herein lies the entire problem—was it possible to think in March 1947 of the combination or conjunction of all these factors? Wasn't this merely an academic hypothesis, or a chimerical theme for heated discussions among exiles in the back rooms of cafés?

In reality, a serious analysis, as opposed to a doctrinaire and self-justifying one, of the Bilbao strike, which was set in motion a few weeks after the Montreuil Plenum, would have afforded genuine understanding of the real meaning of the workers' struggles in Euzkadi.

The fact is that the strike of May 1, contrary to the illusions of the Spanish Communist Party, was not the culmination of a period of partial struggles and the beginning of a stage of qualitatively different activities. Quite the contrary. It was the last gleam of the past, the moving light, still glowing brightly, of a dead star. It was the last dying twitches of the struggle linked to memories of Republican unity, which was falling to pieces at precisely this time. It was also linked with the orientation of the democratic powers of the anti-Hitler coalition for a change of regime. But this orientation was disappearing forever. A few days after the beginning of the strike in Bilbao, before order had been totally restored in Euzkadi by Franco's forces, on May 5, 1947, the Communist ministers were unceremoniously expelled from the French government. It was the beginning of that turning point that later came to be called "the cold war." The United States was to launch the Marshall Plan, thus giving new impetus to the expansion of the capitalist mode of production. In September of this same crucial year—which De Gaulle called "the terrible year"—Stalin was to organize the Cominform, in order to unify the action of the European Communist parties and make it entirely dependent upon the foreign policy of the Russian state.

It was necessary to wait four years, until the spring of 1951, before any notable movements of popular struggle again came about. Four years during which party organizations were dismantled, swept from the scene of Spanish reality by the police brigades of the Conesas and the Creixes, who, though they successfully used torture and infiltrated informers into Communist organizations, in point of fact achieved their aims because the unrealistic appeals for action and the excessive offensive tactics of the party exposed the organizations at work by isolating them from the masses: the fish of the Spanish Communist Party found themselves out of water.

Terrible years, no doubt. Years of obscure and heroic effort by obscure and heroic militants. Nonetheless, in view of the meager results obtained, in view of all the blood spilled uselessly, blood that brought forth nothing but flowers of rhetoric at meetings, one has the right to wonder whether it would not have been more useful for the party, for the future of the fight against Fascism, to have had a little less heroism and blind faith and a little more Marxist analysis of Spanish society and of the correlation of forces on the international scale. Hadn't we agreed that Marxism is an instrument for procuring objective knowledge of reality, with a view to transforming that reality? Well, that was the moment to prove it.

I say all this today, *a posteriori.* It is easy to say it, and not much merit in so doing. History has already settled the question. I say this after having reread the minutes of the Montreuil Plenum and the issues of

Nuestra Bandera of those months. I had also read that material in 1947, doubtless. But it did not surprise me then. It aroused no critical zeal on my part. I was only a rank-and-file militant, after all. I wasn't invited to the party plenum in March, nor did I attend the big meeting in Toulouse in July that Benigno Rodríguez told me about, in the course of which La Pasionaria had delivered an incendiary speech. But the strike in Bilbao filled me with enthusiasm and I was completely persuaded that it would help bring Franco down.

During the months that followed, in the white-hot heat of this enthusiasm, I wrote a play. A play in three acts called *Soledad (Solitude)* that I wrote in French, despite what the title might suggest.

(You have the manuscript of *Soledad* here on your work table, next to the typewriter. The yellowed, typewritten sheets are in a faded blue folder. SOLEDAD, Play in Three Acts, it says in the center of the first page. And below, in the left-hand corner of the rectangular sheet of somewhat faded paper, is your name and address of those days, 42 Rue Fontaine. You read your address of those days and begin to laugh to yourself. That apartment in which you lived for a few fleeting days (or days when you were fleeing?), at 42 Rue Fontaine, had belonged to André Breton. He turned the lease over to you when he moved to another, larger apartment in the same building. It was a studio apartment for a painter, with the big window of the studio facing the north light, which was the light of Montmartre, of course. You arrived one day with the 250,000 francs— mere centimes in today's money—that was the price of the lease. André Breton opened the door looking exactly like the poet André Breton, the way he looked in the photos of illustrated surrealism histories. Almost all the poets you've known have in fact looked like poets. As a child, you saw Rafael Alberti in the Lyon d'Or combing his hair and inspecting his profile in the mirror, and he certainly looked like a poet. Pablo Neruda too had that same unmistakable look, many years later. In fact, you knew Neruda was a poet even before you knew a poet existed whose name was Pablo Neruda. Explain yourself. The fact is that in 1937, at the chancellery of the Legation of the Spanish Republic in The Hague, when your father was Chargé d'Affaires during the Civil War, there was a Dutch creole woman from Java or Sumatra who worked there and who had been married to Pablo Neruda. Only a poet could have had a wife like that, so outsized, so like a gentle, sleepy giraffe. Then ten years later, when you met Pablo Neruda personally you weren't surprised to see how much he looked like a poet. Only a poet could have married a somnolent giraffe-woman from Sumatra or Java. And Blas de Otero had also looked like a poet when Manuel Azcárate introduced him to you, around 1952. Blas had left Spain with the intention of going into exile and publishing an explosive book of poems. The party gave you and Benigno Rodríguez orders to look after Blas de Otero while he prepared this book that was to be published by Pierre Seghers. It was no easy task, clearly no sinecure. Looking after a poet like Blas, solving literally all the problems of daily life for him one by one, was something like having to look after a runaway horse, a horizon full of thunder and lightning, a star dancing on a tightrope. But you are not going to tell here about the surprising peripeteias of living with Blas de Otero and his difficulties in living. You will merely say that the book never reached print, although the majority of the poems included in it were used by Blas, at times with slight revisions, in other volumes of his published later. In a trunk somewhere you still have a folder of poems by Blas in his own hand that date from this period. And the book did not reach print because as the publication date came closer and closer, with the text already in galleys, Blas was plunged into a state of desperate, frantic anxiety. The best specialists were called in and, marshaling all their knowledge, came up with contradictory cures. But there was only one solution, of course: give Blas back his freedom, or in other words give him the possibility of turning back, of not publishing the book, of forgetting that most unfortunate expedition abroad and returning to Bilbao. That is what you recommended to the party comrades—Manuel Azcárate, Víctor Velasco—and that is what was done. You accompanied Blas to the Gare d'Austerlitz one night. Standing on the step of the railway car, throwing his head back with the unmistakable gesture of the poet, Blas de Otero said in a solemn voice that you remember very well: "Don Quixote's first sally into the world!" You were no longer around to supervise the second sally of Blas-Quixote. You continue to search your memory, recalling the poets that you have known. Ángel González, it is true, didn't look like a poet back there in the sixties in Madrid. But he was already a marvelous poet nonetheless and a marvelous underground companion as well. Ángel's house served you as a hideout more than once in those years. But Ángel assumed the look of a poet later. You have just seen some photos of him in a copy of *Viejo Topo,* and nowadays he does look like a poet, with his flowing beard and his kindly, direct gaze. But you were telling about how you arrived that day at André Breton's. He opened the door for you, and there was no doubt about it: he looked like a poet. The leonine look of a nineteenth-century poet à la Victor Hugo: the look of a seer seeing, in a word. Breton showed you into the apartment that he was about to lease to you and took you through it. On one side was the studio, looking out over the Boulevard de Clichy and the Butte de Montmartre. You stood there dumbfounded contemplating the vast accumulation of art works piled up in that small space. Naturally André Breton wasn't going to lease you the canvases by Picasso, or the masks from Indonesia or Black Africa: only the bare walls and the floor were included in the terms of the contract, as was only to be expected. You contemplated the paintings by Picasso, Juan Gris, Braque, Soutine, lost in thought, but André Breton called to you. He led you over to the window that looked out on the Boulevard de Clichy, doubtless so that you could enjoy the view. Down below, on the Boulevard de Clichy, on the sidewalk across the street, you saw the façade of a cabaret, painted a gloomy black. Le Néant. The name of the cabaret was LE NEANT (NOTHINGNESS). André Breton noticed your gaze riveted on the name of this cabaret. He smiled. "At night," he said, "the neon letters blink on and off. It's an intermittent nothingness." He put a hand on your shoulder and laughed. "It's rather amusing," he added. Despite his air of a lion-poet, his stature and his bearing, Breton turned out to be most approachable, surprisingly open and unassuming. You laughed in concert, commenting on the metaphorical meaning of that intermittent nothingness. "In short," you said to Breton, "it's Being and Nothing." But naturally you did not tell him that some time before, under the *nom de plume* of Falcó, you had written a very harsh criticism—doubtless inspired, you think now, by the Marxistoid rigorism that characterized you in those days—of his latest book, *Arcane 17.* You had published this critical piece in *Action.* But you didn't tell Breton this. You continued your inspection tour of the apartment with him. In the bathroom you noted with amused surprise that the bathtub was unusable for its customary purpose. It was full of paintings, piled one against the other. If these were works by Picasso, Juan Gris, Braque, something you did not dare verify, this was of course the most luxurious bathtub imaginable, despite its humble, almost dilapidated outward appearance.

But anyway, this memory comes back to you only because on the first page of the yellowed copy of *Soledad* that you still have in your possession is written your ephemeral address of those days, 42 Rue Fontaine. On the second page, as is customary, is a list of the characters, the *dramatis personae.*

THE MOTHER, 55 years old, blind, a little touched in the head
SOLEDAD, her daughter, 18 years old
JUAN, her son, 22 years old
SANTIAGO, 26 years old, an opponent of the Franco regime
RAFAEL, 45 years old, a worker from Bilbao
LUIS, 35 years old, another worker
THREE WOMEN'S VOICES

Below this is the following information:

"A single stage setting for the three acts."

"The action takes place in the first days of the month of May 1947, during the general strike of the workers of the Basque city of Bilbao against the Franco regime."

As can be seen, you had conceived a work that would not be complicated to stage. A single set, a small cast: any theatrical director would congratulate you, and as a matter of fact)

one did congratulate me. He liked the play, but explained to me that it was too political, too *engagée* to be able to be put on at that time, given the general situation in the theater.

I had also submitted *Soledad* to the critical judgment of the party; or rather, to the judgment of Antonio Mije. In those years, at the end of the forties, Antonio Mije was the party leader with whom I was in most frequent contact. Mije was acting at the time as press and propaganda secretary. As I was one of the collaborators on *Independencia,* and then later on *Cultura y Democracia,* and also wrote notes and little unsigned articles in *Mundo Obrero,* which was still being published legally in France, I had to attend meetings with Mije or have personal interviews with him from time to time. It was not much trouble of course to go talk with Mije: all I had to do was cross the Avenue Kléber, passing from the odd-numbered side to the even-numbered, to get from my office at UNESCO to the party offices.

The fact that Antonio Mije is dead now (may he rest in peace at the right hand of God in all his Andalusian glory!) will not prevent me from saying that he was the exact opposite of what one imagines a Communist party leader to be when at the age of twenty one joins the party out of profound historical and moral motivations, out of a desire for intellectual clearsightedness, out of the undeniable attraction of a global vision of the world. Antonio Mije was superficial, bombastic, coarse-tongued, an improviser, an opportunist, of Bolshevik iron with subordinates and of softest velvet with his superiors in the hierarchy, petty-bourgeois in his tastes and conception of life, compliant, and possessed of a mental vulgarity that was well-nigh incredible. May he rest in peace, or rather may he continue to rest in peace, because during his lifetime Mije was never noted for any real inclination toward work. He talked a great deal, he bustled about a great deal, he was extremely demonstrative, but sowed absolutely nothing.

Despite the fact that Mije never inspired in me the slightest intellectual respect, I took my first literary work to him. It was an illogical attitude, but one typical of a Stalinized intellectual, prepared to humbly accept

Mije's or Zhdanov's judgments on, let us say for instance, music and philosophy, as though either of the two, aside from their scant personal worth, could possibly have been authentic interpreters of party opinion, which would in turn be the opinion of the working class, as though the working class had the possibility of any sort of definite opinions on literature, music, or philosophy!

A few weeks after my submitting my dramatic creation, Mije revealed to me what he thought of it. *Soledad,* he told me, was not a positive work. In the first place, the role of the masses and the party in the Euzkadi strike was not correctly emphasized. This considerably reduced its interest. In the second place, the principal characters did not appear to have a clear perspective, did not appear to be sufficiently convinced of the inevitable and imminent triumph of the struggle of the masses in Spain. I heeded Mije's advice and abandoned Soledad to the corrosive criticism of time.

Some years later, when Colette Audry published and staged a work with the same title, which also dealt with an episode in the fight against Fascism in a Spanish-speaking country, the coincidence attracted my attention. But I quickly forgot about *Soledad* again.

Rummaging about in my papers recently, I again came across the manuscript of that forgotten dramatic work. I read it again. Aside from any literary value that it may have—which is not a great deal, even though for reasons diametrically opposed to those put forward by Mije, the characters do not manage to free themselves completely of the abstract, false ideological exigencies of the moment—it is an extraordinarily enlightening text. All my obsessive personal themes already figure there and in a form that is so authentic and profound that they consistently go beyond the limits of my own self-awareness. Clandestine life, not only as an adventure, that is, the pleasure or satisfaction at being outside any and every norm, but also as a path toward the conquest of a genuine identity. Politics as individual destiny, and thus not dependent on the question of victory and the conquest of power, which is always secondary or derivative, bur rather related to a risking of oneself and a realizing of oneself, perhaps through death freely contemplated. Freedom, in fact, as a decisive factor in any political and existential commitment. In *Soledad* all these themes also had a utopian dimension, by which I mean that they were centered on an imaginary future. No doubt my concrete experience of the French Resistance, of the concentration camp, had lent substance to this imaginary projection into the future. But the central character of the work, Santiago, was in certain respects the first imaginary incarnation of Federico Sánchez. He was a fictional being who prepared my access to the reality of Federico Sánchez, a reality that doubtless bore the imprint of fictional characteristics as well. That is to say, Federico Sánchez, as is luminously demonstrated in that old forgotten work of mine, was not a pure happenstance in my existence, an avatar due entirely to circumstances, but rather the expression of a very profound homing instinct. That is why I have to deal with him, with this phantom and its dense, compact reality. In the final analysis, Santiago, the character who represents me—and whose name, I should perhaps make clear, is in no way a reflection of the personality cult paid to another Santiago . . . when I wrote *Soledad,* the only charismatic figure in my ideological universe was La Pasionaria; I did not yet know Santiago Carrillo at that time; I knew almost nothing about him; I had seen him only once, from a distance at Kléber, around 1947, it must have been; I was at Kléber, in the antechamber, waiting for Antonio Mije to receive me; anyway, there in the waiting room of those offices on Kléber Enrique Líster and another personage whom I had no difficulty recognizing and who was Santiago Carrillo suddenly appeared; what most attracted my attention was that both men had felt hats on; Líster's was gray and Carrillo's a Tyrolian green; the two met, exchanged a few words, and started to enter one of the offices; at the door, each of them went through the pantomime of insisting that the other go in first; they began to speak, ironically, in French: "Après vous, mon général," Carrillo said; and Lister replied: "Après vous, monsieur le ministre"; finally they disappeared through the door; this is the first image of Carrillo preserved in my memory; that of a short, squatty man with glasses and a green felt hat going through an exaggerated routine in front of a door in the party offices on Kléber; I had occasion to meet with Líster several times in those months; in those days, in fact, Benigno Rodríguez used to invite me to go with him to the home of Antonio Cordón, a professional soldier in the Artillery Corps who joined the Communist party during the Civil War and was promoted to general by Juan Negrín a few days before the Republican rout; the house was on the Boulevard de Sébastopol; I sometimes met Enrique Líster there; some days we would sit around an Asturian *fabada,* a Gallegan *potaje,* a *paella valenciana,* or a *cocido a la madrileña* (as is well known, we exiles adore the typical regional dishes of our lost homeland that we so sorely miss: eating them in the company of a few friends is like communing with national essences: it is as eucharistic as though we had ingested a windmill: but this type of relation with the mythified homeland is given the crowning touch in a phrase turned by Santiago Carrillo, a phrase of dumbfounding vulgar pretentiousness: people say that in one of those television interviews, all pomp and circumstance, in a studio with central heating and wool wall-to-wall carpeting, which he used to give during his brief but flashy underground period at the time of the "negotiated rupture," which in fact was more one authorized by royal decree, people say, then, that he declared: *"I am impressed by this blue sky of Madrid: I do not understand why I have been forbidden to look upon it for so long a time, I do not understand it . . . . "*: a phrase that is not only vulgarly pretentious but enlightening: we finally learn the real and deep-seated motivation behind "bunker anti-Communism": preventing Carrillo from seeing the blue sky of Madrid: how could we have failed to realize sooner that Carrillo's contemplation of the sky of Madrid was the hidden objective of the class struggle, what was at stake in this struggle?: now that we know this, we can breathe freely: we now understand why Carrillo's mind seems so often to be in the clouds), but I was saying that on certain days, in Paris, around 1947, Benigno and I would get together with Antonio Cordón, Juan Modesto, Enrique Líster and their wives over typical national dishes; the fact is that exiles, above all military personnel, have most decorously upheld the sacrosanct institution of the traditional family, which along with *fabada* and political fables has been the vital props of life in exile; it was also at Cordon's house that I saw for the first time Romero Marín, who was to work with me much later, ten years later, in the underground in Madrid; I remember very well what Romero Marín said to me that day we first met: "Do you know Gustavito Durán?" he asked me rather abruptly; I did not in fact know Gustavito Durán, or even who he was; "Well, he works at UNESCO, the same as you," Romero Marín spat out at me; I began to feel oddly guilty, without knowing why; "He's a renegade, an agent of the Americans," he said to me; I didn't know what to say and the conversation ended there; but the fact that Gustavito Durán, "a renegade" and "an agent of the Americans," worked at UNESCO seemed to place me personally under a cloud, as though, objectively, I were in some obscure way guilty simply because I worked in the same organization as Gustavo Durán, who was the real-life model for Manuel in Malraux's *Man's Hope,* and who, naturally, was not an "agent" of the Americans, although he was no longer a Communist; in any event, those occasional lunches on the Boulevard de Sébastopol were attended by a large part of the staff-level Communist officers of the Republican Army; all of them heroes; all colonels or generals; and all of them graduates of the Frunze Academy in Moscow where they had continued their studies following their heroic defeat in Spain; and there at Cordón's house, amid the French beans and the sausages, amid the chickpeas and the choice bits of meat, listening to Líster winning *a posteriori* the battle of Brunete, let us say, or presenting the crossing of the Ebro by the Fifth Army Corps as the most brilliant military operation of the twentieth century, I gradually became certain of something I have never since had occasion to doubt, that the Spanish Civil War was something too serious to be abandoned to the ex-combatants of either side; I know, in fact, many "sons of the victors" who had, in the opposite camp and confronted with a different mythology of the Civil War, that of the Crusade, an analogous critical reaction; who very soon felt the same need to historicize the problems of the Civil War, which does not mean locking them in the dungeons of the past but approaching them and dealing with them critically, so that they may give shape and substance to a strategy; it was there, at Cordón's, hearing Líster tell of his military exploits against the confederated forces of the Council of Aragón, let us say, that I began to understand that the Civil War would be merely a mythology so long as it was their appanage, something that belonged to those who made it and who unmade us by making it so badly; that it would be history, in the end, a body of practical knowledge, that would permit us to live with it, assuming it critically rather than spending our lives aimlessly wandering in its deceptive labyrinths; only when it was our appanage, something that belonged to those of us who had not made it, to those of us who were crushed by the ideological weight of such a great legend marked by such contradictory signs. . . .

But I was saying that Santiago, the central character of *Soledad,* a clandestine militant of the Spanish Communist Party during the Bilbao general strike, opens before me, by way of imagination, the path leading to Federico Sánchez. Twenty years later, Diego Mora, the character in *La guerre est finie,* a person who is beyond question fictional, fulfills an identical function, though in reverse. He makes possible—though in a hesitant, stumbling way—the concrete, vital, not at all easy passage from the ghostly but effective—relatively effective—reality of Federico Sánchez to the flesh-and-blood, but hypothetical, reality of Jorge Semprún: both inventions of a writer who's gotten mixed up in politics, no doubt.

Be that as it may, Antonio Mije's devastating criticism of my *Soledad* did not prevent me around 1947 from continuing to immerse myself in the arcana of lyrico-Stalinian poetry. I continued to work on the interminable unfinished *Canto to Dolores Ibárruri* that I had begun in the heat of my first meeting with La Pasionaria.

> The door opened. You came in. We rose
> from our chairs. You shook each of our hands,
> smiling.
>   And at that moment the waters of spring burst forth.
> I thought to myself: it seems as if the years
> were asleep at the loom of time,

that there is no escaping anguish, pain.
The day's toil seems endless. Will we see one day
the dawn of love,
                            of justice?
It seems that all that replies is the echo
suffering in a barren desert of saltpeter and sulphur.
But this is not true. There flows
from each fiber of the night a drop of dawn
from each ice-sheet of winter there spurt forth
the waters of spring, from each man enraptured by
the heat of life is now born not the cold
wasteland of panic but the valorous
creative word, the passionate password
that tempers souls borne on
toward what is to come.
    Death at each step is becoming life once more.

I thought to myself that this is happening
in our homeland too. Hundreds and hundreds
of revolts in factories and workshops, thousands
of protests, partial strikes with limited ends,
propaganda and guerrilla actions,
peasants defeating wheatfield and hearth, and sometimes
open struggle, the entire populace in the street, women
at the head.
    And in the middle of the line of fire from the enemy
in the vanguard of the masses, the Party. Its clandestine
voice multiplies and guides actions,
however small; its organizations
are the flesh of the bare flesh of the people,
the blood of its blood drained to the last drop; its men
are seeds; its passwords polar stars.

Our Party, creator of horizons,
virile juice of popular fruits.
There is no doubt, comrades, the day will come:
spring is growing and swelling:
                            it will burst forth.

I suppose that's enough of that.
    This is sufficient to give some idea of my personal contribution to the
alienated subjectivism of the period. Every mast must bear up beneath

its sail. It would be too easy to forget what mass I sang at, and what responsory.

Despite such lyricism, such "passionate faith in the cause that is being defended," so great a "will to triumph over heaven and hell," the general strike that the working class had "in its hand, within its reach," as Santiago Carrillo put it, did not take place in 1947; nor in the decades that followed, as history has demonstrated.

In fact, a year after the Bilbao strike, despite so much trumpeting of imminent victory, the Spanish Communist Party was obliged to modify its methods of struggle radically.

In 1947, the tactics of the party revolved around two principal axes: on the one hand, the stimulus of the guerrilla movement, and, on the other, the creation of clandestine class labor unions. But by 1951, when the mass movement again resurfaced, though still timid and confused, both methods of struggle had been abandoned. The guerrilla movement had been liquidated, and, in the process of exploiting legal possibilities, however minimal these might be, clandestine labor unions had been replaced by the vertical labor unions of the National Confederation of Syndicates (CNS). There is no need to underline the fact that this was a decisive change in party tactics, and essentially a correct one.

How did the leaders of the Spanish Communist Party determine that such a fundamental change of party tactics was necessary? The answer to this historical problem is very revealing.

In his last book, *Eurocommunismo y Estado (Eurocommunism and the State* [Westport, Conn.: Lawrence Hill & Co., 1978]), Santiago Carrillo makes a surprising and totally false statement, as will be seen. He says that " . . . for some parties—and naturally for the Spanish Communist Party—the dissolution of the Communist International had considerably altered relations with the Communist Party of the Soviet Union. *I remember no change of party line, no important political decision concerning which our Party held prior consultations with the Soviet party after this dissolution; if perchance on certain occasions—or rather quite fortuitously, because it coincided with travels for other reasons, we had a large emigration there in the USSR—we informed them, we did so after the fact.*" (my italics)

Let us note these words carefully.

From 1943 on—the year of the dissolution of the Communist International by Stalin, the significance of which can be gathered by consulting Fernando Claudín's exhaustive essay, *La crisis del movimiento comunista (The Crisis of the Communist Movement)*—Carrillo thus remembers no consultation with the Russian party or its leaders. The Spanish Communist Party decided all the changes of orientation in its strategy independently, Carrillo states, on its own account and at its own risk, perhaps limiting itself to informing the leaders in Moscow after the fact. This is what Carrilllo claims in *Eurocommunism and the State,* Chapter 5, "The Historical Roots of Eurocommunism," dedicated primarily to arguing—if cynical lapses of memory and deliberate falsehood can be called arguments—in favor of the autonomy of the Spanish Communist Party.

Carrillo had already said something similar to an Italian journalist, Bernardo Valli. In Valli's book, *Gli Eurocommunisti (The Eurocommunists),* published in September 1976, are interviews with the Frenchman Jean Elleinstein, the Italian Paolo Spriano, and Carrillo. Bernardo Valli asks this latter how to explain "the fact that a Communist party such as the Spanish one, which has been clandestine for thirty-seven years and thus ripe for the development of conspiratorial sectarianism, managed to create an autonomous line and establish such close ties with Spanish reality." And Carrillo answers that the evolution was permitted by "the very difficulties in which we found ourselves, not only because we were a clandestine party, but also because of the cold war, which held us fast as in a pair of tongs and prevented us from choosing our autonomous path. Obliged as we were to beat our heads against a wall, we said to ourselves: we must search, we must use our imaginations. These are the fundamental reasons that forced our party to move ahead."

As can be seen in these two texts—which are from the same period—Carrillo stresses the autonomy of the Spanish Communist Party's strategy decisions at moments of decisive change. But the truth is quite different. The truth is that in 1948—*that is to say, five years after the dissolution of the Communist International*—obliged to "beat our heads against a wall," and finding no solution to its problems, the leadership of the Spanish Communist Party (represented by Dolores Ibárruri, Francisco Antón, and Santiago Carrillo) went to consult with Stalin and ask his advice. The truth is that it was the trenchant and categorical directives of Stalin that were responsible for the Spanish Party's change of strategy. If that is what Carrillo calls autonomy, heaven help us all!

The time has come, thus, to refresh Santiago Carrillo's memory. What is more, it will be easy to prod the brain and the memory of our forgetful Great Helmsman—one must only remind Carrillo of his own statements. The fact is that Carrillo appears to have no scruples about saying the most contradictory things based on identical facts, as suits his immediate objectives any any instance.

As regards the tactical change of party line in 1948—a decisive one, I repeat, and essentially correct, even though it is owed to Stalin, the god of Theory and the Gulag—Santiago Carrillo has already given us another version that is closer to the historical truth.

But before examining what Carrillo stated in this regard in his book

Dialogue on Spain, it behooves us to recall that the first Communist leader to publicly allude to the role played by Stalin on this occasion was Enrique Líster. In his pamphlet, *!Basta! (Enough!)*, Líster states at the end of the second chapter, *"And so we limped along until October 1948, at which date, following Stalin's advice, we introduced into our policy the changes that I shall come back to later on. But we did this, once more, without any real analysis of the stage that we had just gone through, without any study of the errors that we had committed. And so we presented to the party the idea that we had introduced changes, not because we were carrying on a mistaken policy, but because there was a change in the situation."* At the beginning of Chapter 6, Líster states, *" . . . the weightiest argument, and practically the only one that was employed to bring about approval of this decision was the argument that this was what Stalin had advised.*

"A month before, in September 1948, a delegation from the Party had had a meeting with Stalin. On their return they informed the Politburo that Stalin had advised a change in Party tactics: dissolving the clandestine labor organizations, joining the official unions that all workers were obliged to affiliate themselves with, and dissolving the guerrillas."

The only thing that interests me at this moment is the concrete historical fact of the meeting with Stalin in 1948, which gives the lie to Carrillo's stupid boast in *Eurocommunism and the State* about the autonomy of the Spanish Communist Party. I therefore leave aside all Líster's interpretations and personal comments.

Líster's pamphlet must be read in fact with an extremely acute critical eye. It must be placed within its historical and moral context. There are some truths in it, of course. I say this because I can personally verify them, or because I heard them directly from comrades whose honesty I cannot question. There are also a fair number of lies and evasions based on partial truths and, above all, statements that may well be true but are nonetheless unverifiable so long as historians do not have access to party archives (if they ever do, and if these archives do not somehow conveniently disappear).

However, in reading Líster's pamphlet with its strong bias against Carrillo, the most important thing to keep in mind is that Líster is not speaking in his own name, that he is merely the voice of his masters; the voice, that is to say, of Brezhnev, Suslov, and Ponomariov; of those Russian leaders who manipulated this vain old general as a result of the bitterness he harbored against the secretary-general of the Spanish Communist Party for his condemnation of the Russian military intervention in Czechoslovakia in August 1968.

The fact that Líster bowed to the political and ideological interests of the Russian leaders radically limits the value that some of his criticism against Santiago Carrillo might otherwise have. Thus, for example, attacking Carrillo "from the Left," in the name of Leninist orthodoxy and claiming, as Líster does, that this theoretical orthodoxy continues to be incarnated, to be materialized in the national and international policy of the Russian leaders, is either comical or repugnant, depending on the humor one is in at a given moment. For even though Carrillo's policy in recent days doubtless contains a good number of revisions of Leninism and Marxism—revisions that should be analyzed globally to disentangle their positive and negative aspects, for there is a little bit of everything in them—this policy nonetheless is situated to the left of Brezhnev. By situating himself in the terrain of the democratic way to socialism—even though he does so expediently, making corrections of past errors without analyzing them and without consulting the militants; even though he occupies this democratic terrain without imagination and without a strategy; despite the fact that his realism is in fact a Realpolitik, that is to say a capitulation to reality rather than a transformation of reality— Carrillo's policy, despite all its limits and confusions, by the very fact that it is concretely, practically situated in the terrain of democratic pluralism, is a policy of the Left in comparison to Brezhnev's neo-imperialism in the sphere of international relations and his bureaucratic neo-Stalinism in the internal sphere of Russian civil society.

Precisely because of the influence of the Russian leaders on Líster, it is impossible for him to attain a dialectical vision of Carrillo's policy that could embrace its contradictions. Hence, even when he rightly criticizes some of Carrillo's past errors—which were also, of course, shared by the entire Spanish Communist Party leadership, including Líster himself— he is incapable of any sort of profound analysis of their causes.

I shall give a single example.

In his pamphlet *!Basta!,* Líster states: *"I accuse Carrillo of having formed a tribunal to interrogate and investigate the case of all comrades who returned from the Nazi concentration camps in Germany. The fact that they had not died made each of them a suspect and an accused traitor. Carrillo maintained that if anyone got out alive it was because he had been a 'Kapo,' an executioner of his comrades."*

In and of itself, this is certain fact. The party cadres who survived the Nazi camps (though not "all comrades," as Lister says: I for one was an anonymous rank-and-file militant, and no one called on me to account for my attitude and my work at Buchenwald) were, in fact, subjected to a sort of police-style investigation and prohibited from having any sort of important political responsibility. Thus, for example, and I shall speak only of those whom I know personally, the principal leaders of the clandestine party organization in the concentration camp at Buchenwald, comrades Nieto, Lucas, Lacalle, and Celada, all of them Communists with ties to the Resistance in France and with a long history of high-level participation in the party struggle, were subjected to such an investigation and censured. And it is also true that the person most directly responsible for these investigations and punitive measures was Santiago Carrillo.

In a public speech by Carrillo, reprinted in *Nuestra Bandera,* no. 2, published in Toulouse in June 1945, in a paragraph entitled, very significantly, "We must fight implacably against the Fascist agents of the POUM," the political "justification" of these repressive measures is formulated. After stating that "we must bar the path of the Trotskyites, we must combat and attack them wherever they are, not because they are enemies of the Communists but because they are an agency of Fascism and their mission is to sow discord and confusion in the anti-Fascist camp." In the next line of this typically Stalinist proclamation, Carrillo goes on to say:

> As regards provocation, I also wish to warn comrades about something that we are living through in these days. Comrades liberated from concentration camps are returning from Germany, those who have not succumbed are returning, for from a single camp of 10,000 Spaniards only 1,800 are returning. We must welcome these comrades with open arms. We must help them get back on their feet, we must inform them of the situation, adapt them to our work, allow them to participate in it, reinforce our activity with their participation. But it must not be forgotten that the Gestapo may take advantage of the confusion and send us a certain number of infiltrated Falangist agents among these comrades. There were many Spanish Falangists who went to Germany to work as volunteers. There was the Blue Division (40,000 Spanish volunteers who fought for Nazi Germany on the Russian front). Do you believe the Gestapo won't send us some of them among those who are returning? It is even possible that a number of anti-Fascists of yesterday have capitulated in the face of Nazi terror in the concentration camps. We have seen that here in France. We are seeing it in Spain. We must be very attentive, very vigilant, so as to prevent Franco agents who will be coming back in this way from infiltrating the ranks of our Party and the ranks of the anti-Fascist movement. Without mistrusting our comrades, we must know what it is that they have done, how they have behaved, we must keep a close watch on those whose situation is somewhat suspect, all this with the aid of the comrades coming back from Germany, since they themselves are the first who will permit us to exercise this control.

This was how far Santiago Carrillo went in a speech in May 1945. It does not seem necessary to comment on it at length, for it speaks for itself. It is a text typical of that metaphysical-policemanlike conception of history that is basic to Stalinist ideology. Under the pretext of revolutionary vigilance—which indeed is always necessary, providing that the masses and militants are involved, as opposed to its being a weapon of the dominant bureaucracy to use as it pleases, thus creating a Manichean mentality—systematic suspicion and the spirit of denunciation and submission are introduced into the party. In the atmosphere of a "witch hunt," in fact, militants will have a tendency to shut themselves up within a prudent silence, in an atomized subjectivity that leads to the diametrical opposite of Communist morality. They will not dare defend accused comrades, since the accusations heaped upon them—Trotskyism, Titoism, Comoreraism, Monzonism, or any other damaging epithet of the moment—are based on secret data known only to higher-ups, to whom in the end one can do nothing but capitulate or else leave the party. And it is never easy for a militant to abandon the party. It is easier to capitulate and keep entirely to oneself the doubts and questions that in the end gnaw at the conscience of the militant, that sooner or later demoralize him.

This said, how is it possible that Carrillo can state with such certainty that the Gestapo is in a position to infiltrate its agents within the ranks of the Spanish Communist Party? Let us not forget that this is May 1945. Hitler has killed himself in the bunker of the chancellery. The German armies have been wiped out or scattered. It is every man for himself. Where would the Gestapo find the forces and the prospects sufficient to organize the infiltration of a party as insignificant on the international scene as the Spanish one? The explanation is simple. And chilling. The fact is that Carrillo is not speaking to us about the real, historically localizable Gestapo, but rather of the mythological Gestapo of Stalinist delirium. If the Gestapo were capable, according to the official version, of converting Trotsky, one of the most clearsighted organizers of the October victory, as well as the most seasoned leaders of the Leninist old guard into Gestapo agents, why would it not in fact have been capable of taking in a few middle-level cadres of the poor Spanish Communist Party? Such a thesis requires no proof: it is a revealed truth of Stalinist theology.

And it is not by sheer happenstance that Carrillo's speech concludes, in the passage immediately following what I have just quoted, with a vulgar, highflown peroration dedicated to the personality cult of La Pasionaria, who is characterized as *"the person who represents the spirit of our nation,"* no less. All this is of a piece and begets an ideological monster that is absolutely typical and absolutely stereotypical.

In reality, Carrillo's handling of the returning Communist cadres from

Nazi concentration camps was an exact replica of what the Russian Special Services were then doing with regard to all the Soviet deportees and prisoners of war, the majority of whom were sent directly from the German camps to the camps of the Stalinist Gulag. It is impressive to note the synchronism of these two procedures. It is impressive to note, despite Carrillo's statements referred to above, how nonexistent the autonomy of the Spanish Communist Party was in this period, two years after the dissolution of the Comintern: how closely its rules of internal security followed the criteria of Stalin's political police. The one difference—a considerable one for the individuals involved—was that Carrillo was not in power, or, in other words, that the existence of a bourgeois democracy saved the lives and the freedom of those who had been proscribed.

But this is, naturally, what Enrique Líster was unable to say. This decisive root of the monstrous errors of the Spanish Communist Party on this occasion—i.e., the blind submission to Stalin's police criteria— was what Líster could not analyze, because he himself was still living in that universe of abject, blind, deaf submission.

But let us return to the change in party line in 1948.

In Chapter 5 of his essay, *Eurocommunism and the State,* Santiago Carrillo stated the following, which I repeat here: "I remember no change of party line, no important political decision concerning which our Party held prior consultations with the Soviet party after this dissolution [of the Communist International]." But in his earlier book *Mañana, España (Dialogue on Spain),* which is the Spanish edition of interviews with Max Gallo and Régis Debray, published in France several years previously under the title *Demain l'Espagne.* Carrillo himself gave the lie to his own later words:

> In 1948, Stalin invited a delegation of our Party, made up of Dolores Ibárruri, Francisco Antón, and myself. A meeting with Stalin ... I had already seen him, from a distance, in 1940, but this was the only interview I ever had with him. For a Communist in those days, going to have a talk with Stalin was a capital event. Dolores had already talked with him once: I never had. We were very moved. On the day after our arrival, they told us late that afternoon, "Comrade Stalin is waiting for you." We went to the Kremlin, to the area where his office was. Molotov and Suslov were with Stalin. You know what his physical presence was like, and there is no need for me to describe it. He was a man of more or less my height, dressed in a very simple military blouse and wearing army boots; in short, resembling his photographs. He received us very cordially and impressed us by asking for news of each one

of our comrades, mentioning them by name. He said something very odd to us: 'It would appear that Líster doesn't feel much affection for the Soviet Union." I didn't know what he was referring to. But Dolores did, and she said: "He's becoming more prudent." We immediately sat down at the conference table. He asked us: "You wage guerrilla campaigns, but why don't you work in legal mass organizations? Your work with the masses in these organizations is very weak. Bolshevik experience proves that this sort of work should be done. It is necessary to be patient (and he repeated the word *tierpienietz*—patience—in Russian). Then when you're strong, strike." The essential question for him was the necessity for us to work in the Fascist labor unions and in mass organizations. He did not propose abandoning guerrilla activities, except indirectly.

And a little farther on, Carrillo adds:

We had a very animated discussion with Stalin about work in legal mass organizations. How were we going to work in Fascist labor unions, which were so discredited among workers? The truth was that we had a sectarian and leftist position on the subject. He insisted, saying *niet* and repeating: "Our experience is this," and so on. After an hour and a half of discussion, we left without being very convinced. He had allowed us to glimpse the possibility of receiving arms, but at the same time advising us to use the guerrillas more as a support for the political leadership, to guarantee its security, to support clandestine contacts in the cities. The idea wasn't a bad one, though perhaps a little late, but basically his entire position was correct.

Just one point remains obscure on this page of *Dialogue on Spain* that I have quoted: the reference to Líster. What does the sibylline phrase that Carrillo has Stalin say really mean? "It would appear that Líster doesn't feel much affection for the Soviet Union." Carrillo says that he didn't know what Stalin was referring to but that Dolores Ibárruri did and that she hastened to reassure Stalin by saying, "He's becoming more prudent." What Carrillo doesn't tell is whether Francisco Antón, who at this time was all-powerful in the Spanish Communist Party, knew what all this was about. In any case, we are left in the dark. Nothing is explained to us. What was happening with Líster in the autumn of 1948? It must have been something serious for Stalin to have bothered mentioning it. What differences of opinion could Líster have had at that particular juncture with Stalin's policy? It must be remembered that a few months before this interview in the Kremlin the offensive mounted by Stalin and the Cominform against Tito and the group of Yugoslav Communist leaders had begun. Could Enrique Líster have expressed certain doubts on this score? It should also be remembered that the offensive against Titoism went hand in hand with the beginning of a general discrimination against, soon to become a systematic persecution of, the Central European Communist party cadres that had fought in Spain in the ranks of the International Brigades. Could Enrique Líster have somehow been taken aback by this aspect of the Soviet Union's policy? *Dialogue on Spain* sheds no light on this particular point.

All this having been said, we may conclude that the allusion to Líster Carrillo has Stalin make is simply an obscure settling of accounts between leaders who are or were in on the secrets of gods. We mere mortals are not in on the secrets of gods. We must confine ourselves to inferring that something was happening to Líster at the time, and that Carrillo maliciously remembered it, many years later. But if Enrique Líster, in 1948, "did not feel much affection for the Soviet Union," according to the phrase attributed to Stalin; if Líster had doubts about some aspect or other of Stalin's policy, this would be something of a point in his favor. The fact that Stalin was not exactly happy with Líster in 1948 is a bit of evidence that redounds to the latter's credit. It is very odd, therefore, but also very significant that in 1974 Santiago Carrillo mentions this mysterious remark in *Dialogue on Spain* as though Stalin were still the god of theory, the coryphaeus of science, the indisputable patriarch, as though his words were still the criterion of truth and falsehood. We can see that Carrillo's memory has played him another bad trick. He has forgotten that Stalin is dead and that his corpse has been thrown in the dustbin of history. He has forgotten that Stalin's little sally against Líster no longer has the same weight when measured on the scales of history today. Carrillo's memory, and his lapses of memory, are unquestionably worthy of detailed analysis.

But in any event the long passage cited from Carrillo sheds definite light on the problem of the shift in tactics of the Spanish Communist Party in 1948. It makes it clear that in 1977, in his essay on *Eurocommunism and the State,* Santiago Carrillo was guilty of a barefaced lie when he affirmed, with his habitual braggadocio, with his peculiar party chauvinism, that following the dissolution of the Communist International the leaders of the Spanish Communist Party at no time held prior consultations with the Russian party regarding any important political decision. In his eagerness to demonstrate the Eurocommunist autonomy of the Spanish Communist Party, to seek out roots and historical antecedents, Carrillo has had a memory block that would merit psychoanalysis. He has forgotten Stalin. Which is no minor lapse of memory, of course.

As if that were not enough, Carrillo has also forgotten the attitude of the Spanish Communist Party leadership to the Tito case. A few months before the aforementioned interview in the Kremlin, in fact, the first resolution of the Cominform against the Yugoslav Communists had been published, in June 1948. How did the Spanish Communist Party leadership react in this concrete instance? Was there in its attitude the slightest trace of the autonomy that Santiago Carrillo claims for it today?

I am not going to refer here to the general historical context of the Cominform's offensive against Tito and Yugoslavia under Communist leadership. Nor shall I refer to the political content of the questions debated. There is already an abundant bibliography on the subject. Without looking any further, the reader may consult—or reconsult—Fernando Claudín's essay *La crisis del movimiento comunista* (*The Crisis of the Communist Movement*). In Chapter 3, Part II, entitled "La Brecha Yugoslava" ("The Yugoslavian Breach"), this question is examined with the minute scrutiny that characterizes Claudín's work. My intention is merely to underline, within this context, certain characteristics of the Spanish Communist Party's behavior in the face of the Cominform's condemnation of Tito.

The Cominform passed a first resolution against the Yugoslavs on June 28, 1948. Three weeks later, on July 17, a meeting of the Spanish Communist Party cadres was held in Paris, at which two reports were read. In the first one, for which Vicente Uribe was responsible, the general problems raised by the Cominform were taken up.

Need it be said that in the name of the Spanish Communist Party Vicente Uribe approved, without any reservations whatsoever, all of the points presented by the Cominform? A number of Uribe's turns of phrase were already a clear indication of what sort of criticism would be offered. "The documents that have been published," Uribe states, "make it evident that certain of its [the Yugoslav Communist Party's] leaders, headed by Tito, are maintaining an attitude and pursuing conduct that I permit myself to call indecent, scandalous, and traitorous to the international Communist front, the democratic camp, the Soviet Union, and, in the final analysis, to the people, to the working class, and to the Yugoslav Party." And a little farther on: "In their insolence, these men, Tito and Company, have lost all sense of reality." And finally: "Each one of the things being denounced is a grave fault. Taken as a whole, they constitute a monstrosity that tells us very clearly how far these Yugoslav leaders have descended on the downward path of political degeneration." (Vicente Uribe, "La penetración imperialista norteamericana pone en grave peligro la independencia nacional de España" ["The American imperialist penetration places the national independence of Spain in grave danger"], *Nuestra Bandera,* August 29, 1948.)

As regards this aspect of the question, that is to say, its unconditional approval of Tito's condemnation by Stalin's Cominform, the Spanish

Communist Party leadership has already engaged in acts of general self-criticism. The most recent of these can be found in *Eurocommunism and the State,* where the following can be read: "In 1948 many Communist parties, following the tradition of unconditional allegiance to the USSR, upheld in this case by the important group of parties constituting the Cominform, went along like sheep with the condemnation of Comrade Tito and the other Yugoslav leaders, and we went so far along the path of unconditional allegiance that when Khrushchev had the courage to publicly tear the maneuver to pieces we felt so cruelly deceived and humiliatingly manipulated that this finally destroyed everything mythical and almost religious that remained in our attitude toward the Communist Party of the Soviet Union."

I will not discuss here this formulation, which leaves aside what is most essential, that is, the ideological mechanisms of unconditional allegiance. But even if we recognize it as a good thing, this self-criticism is nonetheless only partial. For the leadership of the Spanish Communist Party did not confine itself to following the condemnation of Comrade Tito like sheep; it also instigated an anti-Tito campaign in the very midst of the Spanish party, a witch hunt that culminated in the expulsion and condemnation of Joan Comorera, the secretary of the PSUC. And in so doing the leadership of the Spanish Communist Party did indeed demonstrate "autonomy" and "ideological creativity"! But about this Santiago Carrillo says nothing at all. And perhaps he says nothing because it was he, very directly and personally, who was above all responsible for the anti-Tito campaign in the ranks of the Spanish Communist Party and the PSUC, whose limited national autonomy represented a danger for Carrillo's autonomous but unconditional Stalinism.

In the meeting of the Spanish Communist Party cadres held on July 17, 1948, two reports were given, as I have already mentioned. I have alluded briefly to the one presented by Vicente Uribe. The second report was the work of Santiago Carrillo. And apparently the Spanish Communist Party leadership considered it important, for it was published even before Uribe's, a month before, in *Nuestra Bandera,* no. 28, under the heading, "In the Light of the Bucharest Communiqué: The Liquidationist Tendencies in our Party during the Period of the National Union in France."

In this report Carrillo adopts that peculiar Stalinist dialectic that consists of reinterpreting the past in the light of the ideological necessities of the present. In this case the reinterpretation involves "errors" committed by the party leaders in France and Spain during the Second World War, "errors," moreover, which must be regarded as purely hypothetical, so long as all the historical facts of the situation have not been established and the positions of Jesús Monzón and his comrades of this period have not been studied. It was the period in which the party launched the policy of National Union, which was a specific reflection of the strategic interests of the USSR at the time of the alliance with the anti-Hitler democratic powers. Thus, even though Tito's "deviation" had not been invented until 1948, Monzón's positions, which date from the years 1943-44, are seen through the prism of Titoism, in the dim and indistinct light of the Cominform's Bucharest communiqué. Without knowing it, Monzón was a Titoist five years before Titoism existed. Since Titoists are political degenerates, arrogant individualists, objective agents of the imperialist enemy, Monzón is necessarily, thanks to the retroactive application of the revealed truths of Stalinist theology, a political degenerate, an arrogant individualist, and an objective agent of the enemy.

In this area of relations with the enemy, the damning statements were to become more and more precise. The "light" shed by the Bucharest communiqué against Titoism was to constitute brutal clarification of the question. In the aforementioned report by Carrillo in July 1948, it is stated that Jesús Monzón is "an intellectual of bourgeois background, full of personal ambitions, linked through family ties and education to reactionary elements with whom he has never managed to totally break off." And a little further on Carrillo adds: "Under the pretext of safe-guarding and protecting the cadres of the Party who were being per-secuted, he maintained obscure relations with American diplomats and certain suspect and adventurist elements who came to have more weight in the orientation of the Party than respectable militants."

As can be appreciated from this, the backdrop for a very old farce had already been set in place: the bloody farce of the Stalinist trials. On the one hand, there were the origins and the bourgeois upbringing of Mon-zón; that is to say, original sin. On the other hand, there were his relations with American diplomats—that is to say, the enemies of the proletarian soul—the world, the devil, and the flesh of imperialism. The threads of this sinister plot were to be knotted together later.

In 1950, in fact, *Nuestra Bandera,* no. 4 (February-March 1950), published an unsigned editorial, though it was an open secret that San-tiago Carrillo was the author. This piece was entitled: "We Must Learn to Fight More Effectively Against Provocation." One paragraph of it was specifically devoted to the "Monzón case."

> The Monzón case came to the attention of the Party in 1948. But at that time we lacked certain data, acquired later, that shed more light on certain important aspects . . . . Contravening all the directives of the Central Commit-

tee, Monzón arrogates to himself the direction of the Party in all of France and Spain. Who is behind Monzón? Who is it who inspires his work of falsifying the political line of the Party, bringing it into accord, basically, with that of Quinones, that is, lining the Party up behind reactionary and monarchic forces and bringing about the dissolution of the Party within a National Union directed by capitalists and monarchic landholder? Behind Monzón are the American espionage services, behind him are Spanish Carlist agents. In the Budapest trial [the trial of Laszlo Rajk and other Hungarian Communists], a certain Field was exposed as one of the principal agents of Allan Dulles, the head of American espionage in Europe; this Field was in the "philanthropic" guise of representing, first in France and later in Switzerland, the Unitarian Service, an organization responsible for camouflaging American espionage under the cover of aiding refugees. Field played an enormous role as a recruiter of Hungarian and Yugoslavian spies. The man who has kept in contact with Monzón in France for more than two years is none other than Field; it is he who keeps Monzón in touch with the American espionage services. This explains the vast similarity between Monzón's "policy" and that of the Titoist bandits. This fact throws full light on the "inspiration" motivating Monzón. . . .

What really explains "the vast similarity between Monzón's policy and that of the Titoist bandits" is that both "Monzonism" and "Titoism" were inventions of Stalin's Special Services. Or better stated: from 1948 on, by means of moral pressure, blackmail, torture, spectacular political trials, abject confessions of Communist leaders, Stalin and his police conjured up the themes and the general mechanisms of the supposed Titoist conspiracy and treason. (Since the Twentieth Congress of the Communist Party of the Soviet Union, since the "Prague Spring," there have been sufficient documents and sufficiently exhaustive analyses of all this to shed the brightest possible light on the working of this system of lies and terror.) Against this general background, the leadership of the Spanish Communist Party adapted these themes to fit the concret situation of the Spanish party, inventing, with the personal and decisive participation of Santiago Carrillo, "Monzonism" and "Comoreraism." Ah yes, in this sinister task, the present secretary-general of the Spanish Communist Party did indeed demonstrate "autonomy," "creative initiative," and "political imagination"!

Someday, no doubt, researchers will thoroughly analyze this somber period in the history of the Spanish Communist Party. But I greatly fear that even the most detailed analyses will still lack the terrible flavor and vigor of direct testimony. I am very much afraid that the witnesses of that period will never speak. Jesús Monzón is dead. So is Joan Comorera. Gabriel León Trilla was murdered by order of the Spanish Communist

Party leaders. None of them will ever speak now. And from the other side, the side of the autonomous and inventive executors of Stalin's policy in the Spanish Communist Party, can it reasonably be expected that anyone will speak? La Pasionaria will doubtless die without saying a word. She has not come back to Spain to speak, to tell bloody and miserable truths about the past. She has come back to Spain to die. And she will die without saying a word. In the last analysis, no believer expects the Virgin of Fátima to deliver long speeches. It suffices to parade her image on a raised platform before the prostrate multitude. That is the way the severe and noble image of La Pasionaria will be paraded through Spain, a mute statue still capable, no doubt, of evoking tears of joy and emotion from the masses of faithful militants, but incapable of telling the truth about her own past, or the truths of our own history. Will Santiago Carrillo speak? Will he explain to us that the campaign against "Monzonism" and "Comoreraism" was invented out of the whole cloth? Will he explain to us why, knowing that his accusation was absolutely false, knowing that no document supported it, he dishonored Monzón and Comorera by pinning the damning label of "enemy agents" on them? Will he tell us, once and for all, in a sudden show of sincerity, that he did not need the revelations of the Twentieth Congress to know, in his heart of hearts, what Stalinism was, since he had practiced it, with all its consequences, including the shedding of innocent blood within the Spanish Communist Party? Let us stop dreaming. Santiago Carrillo will never tell us anything about this period in the history of the Spanish Communist Party, nor anything about his personal responsibility in it. Never in the world. Will Manuel Azcárate perhaps speak? Now, there would be an exceptional witness. Manuel Azcárate was, in fact, one of the party leaders in France, along with Jesús Monzón, during the Second World War. Manuel Azcárate was the one who had ties with Noel Field, who was not an agent of the American espionage serives but merely an ingenuous and puritan Yankee anti-Fascist, manipulated by Stalin's Special Services. During the war, from his post with the Unitarian Service, a charitable organization set up to aid stateless persons and refugees, Field helped the cadres of various illegal parties, first from France and then from Switzerland. Later on, at the height of the cold war, Stalin's Special Services made Noel Field the sinister and invisible *deus ex machina* of all the political trials that took place in the "peoples' democracies." Did Field accept this role of agent provocateur of his own free will? Did he fulfill this role only after having been morally and physically destroyed by Stalin's police specialists, by Stalin's Conesa? There is no way of knowing. I mean that for us, simple mortals like us, there is no way of knowing. Noel Field has also disappeared without saying a word.

In 1954, after the death of Stalin, after the physical liquidation of Beria and his principal collaborators, Noel Field and his wife were given their freedom and publicly rehabilitated, in Hungary. But from that moment until the day he died, some years later, Noel Field chose silence. He remained in Budapest, buried alive, without contact with the outside world; as Ramón Mercader, Trotsky's assassin, a former militant of the PSUC, continues to do somewhere in this world. The only thing known about Noel Field since his rehabilitation is that he approved of the Russian intervention in Hungary in the autumn of 1956. This allows us to suppose that even then, even after the terrible experiences he had lived through, with so much blood on his hands, Noel Field continued to be a faithful member of the orthodox militant church. Be that as it may, will Manuel Azcárate tell us some day what he knows about Noel Field, what he knows about this sinister period in the life of the Spanish Communist Party? Will he tell us what sort of "inventive," "autonomous" participation was his in the campaign unleashed to isolate Jesús Monzón by dishonoring him? I doubt it very much.

(But what about you—don't you have anything to tell us?

You were of course not a member of the party leadership in those terrible years. But this does not exempt you from a certain responsibility, even if only a passive one: you too, in fact, never opposed in your neighborhood cell these campaigns of historical falsification and personal calumny. By some good fortune, you were never obliged to participate in any discussion concerning the conduct of a militant in your party cell: you never participated in the ceremony—a purifying one, according to the classics—of punishing some misguided militant or expelling him from your cell. But what would you have done if such a case had come up? Are you certain you would have demanded an objective analysis of the accusations and of the political facts? Are you certain you would have fought the good fight so that the militant facing expulsion would have every possible opportunity to freely set forth his reasons, good or bad? Would you have been capable of listening to him, simply listening to him? You wouldn't dare swear to it of course.

Remember.

When you were still a rank-and-file militant—despite the fact that your status as a Stalinized intellectual permitted you a number of visits to the lofty spheres of Avenue Kléber—in those days when you were that not very assiduous militant, a party comrade, Elena Romo, came to get you one day. There was to be a cell meeting that night that you were to attend without fail. With an air of great mystery the leaders of the radio

93

sector had announced that those absent from the meeting that night without sufficiently valid reasons would be judged harshly. Because she was a good comrade and knew that you weren't as assiduous as you might be, Elena came to tell you about the meeting and beg you not to miss it so as to spare you the severity of the comrades. You did not miss it, not so much because of the threat of possible sanctions, but rather out of curiousity. As it turned out, the long and jumbled communiqué of the Politburo on Comorera's case was read to the militants in this meeting. And you approved this resolution by the party leadership, like all the other comrades, even though you had no facts at your disposal that would have allowed you to form a personal opinion. You approved for no other reason than an almost religious desire to identify with the others. Out of mental torpor. Because of an aberrant conception of what constituted the class struggle. Out of a total lack of clarity regarding the extremely complex aspects of the national problem.

Remember.

In this same period the trial of Laszlo Rajk and other comrades was held in Budapest. One of the false accusations brought against Rajk consisted of the allegation that he had been a police informer since his youth. Concretely, it was alleged that Rajk—who had been a combatant in the International Brigades in Spain and following the Civil War was interned in a concentration camp in the southeast of France—had been liberated from this camp by the German Gestapo, which sent him to Hungary to continue his work as a provocateur and informer in the clandestine apparatus of the Hungarian party. All that was false, as was proved subsequently. At the time, a comrade in your cell, Manuel Tuñón de Lara—who today passes himself off a liberal, objective historian—told you in the course of a personal conversation in which you expressed certain doubts about the Rajk case that all the accusations were true. In order to persuade you of Rajk's guilt, he told you that he had seen with his own eyes photocopies of the card that got Laszlo Rajk out of the French concentration camp, a card that proved the Gestapo had directly intervened in the securing of Rajk's liberation from the camp. You asked him, naturally, who had shown him that card. Tuñón de Lara assumed an air of mystery and whispered that it was Soviet comrades. You shook your head, very impressed. And then, although you didn't discuss it with anyone else, you naturally had to ask yourself what sort of relations Tuñón de Lara could have with "Soviet comrades." But then a series of little things—among them the very fact that Tuñón had fallen away from the Spanish Communist Party without any sort of conflicts so as to take on the role of an objective and liberal historian—made you realize that these relations were special, indeed; or, better put, that they must have been relations with the Special Services. But in any case the essential thing is that in Rajk's case you had again failed to make use of the critical spirit that they say is the hallmark of the revolutionary intellectual. Nonetheless, a mere semantic analysis of the stenographic records of the Rajk trial would have sufficed to make you realize that all those accusations were false. But, as is well known, the first thing that a process of intellectual Stalinization twists and mystifies is one's relation with language.

Go on remembering.

One bad day in the autumn of 1952, you read in *L'Humanité* the summary of the official accusation brought against Rudolf Slansky and the other comrades of the Czechoslovak Communist Party involved in that spectacular trial at which Artur London was also one of the accused. You read that Josef Frank, the assistant secretary-general of the Communist Party of Czechoslovakia, had confessed to having worked under Gestapo orders in the concentration camp at Buchenwald. Your heart skipped a beat, and you were paralyzed for a moment by a strange chill that ran down your spine. Frank had been your comrade in the *Arbeitsstatistik* service at Buchenwald. You had lived side by side with him for two years. You knew immediately that the accusation was false. You knew it with that brutal physical certainty that tangible truths bring with them. When it rains, nobody needs to prove to you that it's raining: the simple fact that you're getting wet is proof enough. The rain itself proves it. It was with this same certainty that you knew Frank had not been a Gestapo agent at Buchenwald. If he had been, you would not be here to tell the tale. If Frank had been a Gestapo agent, you would have become ashes and smoke in the crematory of Buchenwald decades ago. What is more, you had collaborated with Frank on several ultraclandestine party missions at Buchenwald. If Frank had been a Gestapo agent, he would probably have agreed to collaborate with you in those dangerous, secret undertakings, but he would have taken steps to denounce you, if only indirectly so as not to arouse suspicion, to the *Politische Abteilung,* that is to say the Gestapo services at Buchenwald, which were vigilant for any opportunity to dismantle the Communist organization in the camp. But it was 1952 now, in the autumn. You were drinking a cup of coffee and reading *L'Humanité.* You were alive, no doubt of it. And Frank, accused before a People's Tribunal (O bloody farce!), had confessed to having worked for the Gestapo. Josef Frank, your comrade at Buchenwald; a cold, reserved man, on first acquaintance, but one who turned out to be full of tenderness, happiness, serene and tolerant steadfastness once one managed, as you did, to cross the barrier with which he protected his privacy. On that autumn day you suddenly knew that Frank was innocent; you immediately realized that both the accusation against him and his own confession were false. In a sort of nauseated vertigo, you glimpsed the implications of this innocence of Frank's. It was like a drop of acid that corroded all your certainties. Even though you were a Stalinized intellectual, you did not live totally shut up in the ideological universe of the communism of those days. You were acquainted with the works of a few heterodox thinkers. You had read, for instance, the biography of Stalin written by Boris Souvarine, a splendid book that has been recently published in a new edition, the first edition could already be found in your father's library. You also knew something about Trotsky; you were familiar in particular with his work on *Stalin's Crimes* and *The Revolution Betrayed.* But you had always suspended judgment as to the possible truth of some of the demonstrations or analyses by Souvarine and Trotsky, as you waited for better times. You were convinced that Krestinski could not have had that famous interview with Trotsky in Merano, let us say, but you ground this partial truth in the dauntless mill of a pseudo-Hegelian dialectic: the supposed totality of the orthodox truth overcame those mere crumbs of lies or partial errors. In the case of Frank, however, these spiritual exercises would be of no use to you. In the case of Frank, the burning and terrible truth of his innocence contaminated the entire moral environment of your ideological nonsense; because this truth was yours, it welled up from your own experience, from your innermost self. You had not been in Merano, of course, at the time of the supposed interview between Trotsky and Krestinski. You could nonetheless deduce that such an interview had never taken place, despite what had been claimed at the Moscow trial. But you had been in Buchenwald, you had lived side by side with Josef Frank: there was no one, there was nothing that could convince you he had been Gestapo agent. You said nothing, however. Nowhere did you proclaim Frank's innocence, or the falseness of the accusation brought against him. Had you proclaimed that innocence you would no doubt have ended up being expelled from the party. You decided to remain in the party. You preferred living the lie of the accusation against Frank within the party to living the truth of his innocence outside the party. Frank was sentenced to die and met his death on the gallows. Then, in order to blot out all trace of his passage on this earth, his ashes and those of ten of his murdered comrades were scattered along an ice-covered road, somewhere around Prague. The following spring, when it began to thaw and the ashes of the eleven men sent to their death flowed down to mingle with the waters of some river, or the womblike darkness of Mother Earth, Stalin had died. And you made your first clandestine trip to Spain.

Then a new stage in your life began, remember.

In the beginning you had been a revolutionary intellectual. By that you mean you had assumed and accepted the consequences of your ideas, the praxis implied by your theoretical vision. The reading of Hegel, the discovery of Marx and Lukács had led you directly to the Maquis in Burgundy, to the handling of explosives, of a Sten gun, and of a stupendous 43-caliber Smith and Wesson revolver. You were eighteen years old and you were happy; you wouldn't dream of hiding that fact. In those days you were not yet a Stalinized intellectual; that is to say, you had kept your critical spirit, your capacity for negation, that creator of conflicting affirmations. You did not yet have a sacralized vision of the party you had just joined. You thought of it as an instrument of revolutionary struggle, one among others, certain aspects of which could be questioned and were always modifiable. Your Stalinization came later. It came about over the years, within the life of the organization, in daily political practice, to the point of triumphing almost completely—the Party Spirit, that ultimate, degenerate historical incarnation of the Hegelian *Wëltgeist.* Placed in chronological order, your poems of that era would constitute a direct testimonial to the irresistible ascension of the Party Spirit in your moral and ideological firmament, until it reached the aberrant, totally deranged zenith of that poem written in the early fifties, at the very moment you were about to cease being a Stalinized intellectual, a prolix poet, a polemicist fabricating Manicheans, and, in fulfillment of a long-standing and violent desire, turn into a clandestine political leader—that poem that reads:

If my blood is full of happiness
I owe it to the Party;
if my words announce a new day,
I owe it to the Party.

If a banner rustles in the dawn,
I owe it to the Party;
if the world grows giant in my gaze,
I owe it to the Party.

If my hand is joined with so many hands,
I owe it to the Party;
if so many men are more than brothers,
I owe it to the Party.

If each night encloses so much sun,
I owe it to the Party;
if all this earth is home and star,
I owe it to the Party.

If Spain is to be a country born again,
I owe it to the Party;
if I live in peace amid life's urgencies
I owe it to the Party.

If I am on my way, perchance, to be a man,
I owe it to the Party;
a real man, not mere shadow or mere name,
I owe it to the Party.

So in 1953 a new stage in your life began.

You were lucky, remember—it was luck and not merit, remember—to have become a leader of the Spanish Communist Party in the years following Stalin's death. In all truth, your political rise to the maximum responsibilities of leadership can be explained only within the historical context that led to the Twentieth Congress of the Communist Party of the Soviet Union and its aftermath, within the atmosphere of de-Staliniization in those years—a limited development, certainly, coming from the top rather than from a democratic break with the past, and one full of theoretical ambiguities and contradictions; a development incapable, therefore, of really resolving the problems of Russian society and those of the Communist movement, as was soon demonstrated. In the final analysis, your political experience as a leader was decisive in that it enabled you to flee the specters of rigidity of your previous Stalinism, until you again came face to face, ten years after this new stage in your life began, with the Party Spirit, which in the end cast you into outer darkness.

But do not try here to idealize this process by simplifying it. It was a long road, full of pitfalls and contradictions. On the one hand, of course, you can honestly say that your experience and reflection led you to regain the critical values without which Marxism is simply a pragmatic collection of recipes or a hypostasized dialectic. They led you, above all, to cross the barriers of a monolithic, monologizing, monotheistic, and monomaniacal political discourse, of a self-sufficient and self-satisfied logomachy, so as to begin to place yourself in a position to listen to the voices of reality. But along this path, on the other hand, you frequently stumbled across the Church, that is to say, the Party Spirit, before which you still remained awestruck and bedazzled.

Thus, you repeat once and for all, even though you do not share any direct responsibility for the campaigns against "Quiñonism," "Monzonism," "Comoreraism," and "Titoism," you do share responsibility for the fact that since 1956 the leadership of the Spanish Communist Party has refused to engage in any sort of public self-criticism, confining itself to sweeping Stalinist garbage into other people's houses, rejecting any sort of objective historical analysis of its own past. An inhibition due in your case primarily to the particularly painful nature of coming to confront the Party Spirit, a bloody idol that must be demolished if one is to be a true Communist.)

But I was in Pozuelo de Alarcón, in 1969, with Simón Sánchez Montero. We were in a house decorated in very vular taste, with a Technicolor garden. I had just told Simón that the *Aitch En Pee* of ten years before had been a resounding failure.

And that was how our political discussion began.

4 FOR THE EYES OF THE CENTRAL COMMITTEE ONLY

One of the first things Simón said on that afternoon in the last days of the summer of 1969 was that he deplored our expulsion from the party, that he would have liked to see another solution found for the conflict in the Executive Committee, a solution that would have allowed Fernando Claudín and me to remain in the party.

Fine, very good, that was nice of him.

I think Simón was being completely sincere, of course, when he made that statement, but I also think he was inconsistent. The fact is that he knew perfectly well that an organic solution that would have allowed Fernando and me to remain in the party while sticking to our opinions and hence exercising the primary and fundamental right—and duty—of every Communist, which consists precisely in expressing one's opinions and defending them—he knew that such a solution would have required the radical transformation of the party, the liquidation of the democratic centralism then in force. In fact, the major democratic freedom left the dissident militant is to make his self-criticism—or rather, to have others make it—or else leave the party. And the least that democratic centralism demands is not to think with one's own head and to confine oneself to repeating or embroidering on the thoughts of the Leader, whether that leader be called the Secretary General or the Great Helmsman.

Simón, thus, was no doubt sincere, but also inconsistent.

In 1964, when he took part in the discussion following our departure —which in principle was temporary—from the Executive Committee, his attitude was much less inconsistent. That is to say, it was much more consistent with the Stalinist conception of democratic centralism.

FOR THE EYES OF THE CENTRAL COMMITTEE ONLY, it says on the top of the mimeographed document that I have on my work table, OPINIONS ON THE DISCUSSION IN THE EXECUTIVE COMMITTEE. And at the bottom of the page are the words, "Seventh file, number 22."

This seventh file of confidential information contains the opinions of Luis Lucio Lobato, Simón Sánchez Montero, Narciso Julián, Ramón Ormazábal, Pedro Ardiaca, and Miguel Núñez. The first two were in prison in El Dueso, the others in prison in Burgos. In short this file collects the opinions of Central Committee members who were under lock and key at the time.

During these last weeks, I have again been working with the reports and documents related to the 1964 debate that ended with our expulsion from the party. I have read these hundreds of pages over again, and once more I am dumbfounded. I have once more emerged from this reading stunned and demoralized. Every time I have glanced through these documents in these last ten years, the same thing has happened to me. The fact is that it is almost more than I can bear—especially today, a year after Franco's death, when the strategic failure of Santiago Carrillo's policy is now obvious—to reimmerse myself in this ocean of ideological trumpeting of imminent triumph, of idealist blindness, of scandalous intellectual servility displayed by the members of the Central Committee of the Spanish Communist Party.

And one inescapable question arises. I shall formulate it in the words of Fernando Claudín, in the conclusion of his study, entitled *Las divergencias el el Partido (Divergencies in the Party)*, addressed to the Central Committee and dated December 1964. In it Claudín asked himself the following question:

> How is it possible that this overwhelming majority of the Central Committee—comrades who have proven themselves in the struggle, in the life of the Party, and who merit every respect, and in some cases admiration, aside from the unjust and arbitrary attitude that they are now adopting toward Federico Sánchez, toward me, and toward other comrades who concur with our opinions—how is it possible, I repeat, for these comrades to fall unanimously into such astonishing Manicheism? It is not easy to answer this question that will doubtless arise in the minds of all those without preconceived opinions who come to learn of the present discussion.
>
> Behind this chilling fact is the entire formation—or, more exactly, deformation—of the members of the Party that we have forged for ourselves during the Stalinist period. In us, commingled with indisputable determination, combativity, and abnegation, are habits, conceptions, methods that are totally foreign to the spirit of Marxism and Leninism. Under their influence, discussion ceases to be discussion; disagreement becomes heresy; and heresy is to be dealt with following the example of the great zealots of faith in our national history. Marx disappears behind Torquemada [Spanish inquisitor general, 1420–98].

Claudín correctly characterizes here, without polemical exaggeration, the tone and the content of the Central Committee members' written contributions to the discussion. A few instances will suffice to show this.

The first remarks I shall offer in proof, significant both because of the person who offered them and because of the blinding clarity of the alienation evident in their formulation, are those of Irene Falcón, a member of the Central Committee since the Sixth Congress in 1960, and Dolores Ibárruri's secretary.

During the last plenary session of the Executive Committee devoted to the examination of our divergencies, held at the end of March and the beginning of April 1964, in an ancient castle of Bohemian kings on the outskirts of Prague, Irene Falcón was in charge of monitoring the tape-recording of the discussion. We were in a vast salon whose great windows looked out over a very Verlainian park; lonely and chilly. The wires of the microphones that we were speaking into snaked off into a salon next door, where Irene Falcón sat with earphones, seeing to it that the machines were working as they should be. Hence even though she was not physically present at the meeting and thus could not take part in it, Irene Falcón was able to hear everything that was said during the discussion.

One day, toward the end of the long week of plenary meetings—the only persons missing, as I have already mentioned, were Romero Marín and Sánchez Montero—the question of Stalinism came up in the discussion again. That day, in reply to one of my previous remarks, Carrillo declared that the question of Stalinism was now past history, that it did not interest the young militants, that the only ones preoccupied with it were a few party leaders, perhaps because they had guilt feelings and needed to do penance. The principal difficulty, Carrillo said, came from the unhealthy attitude, the morbid pleasure with which certain comrades embraced these questions, moved by some sort of feeling akin to repentance.

And he ended his remarks by shouting, almost beside himself: "*Poking around in this past is masochism typical of the petty-bourgeois intellectual!*"

I asked for the floor again.

As a good petty-bourgeois intellectual—or rather grand-bourgeois, that class does still exist—I began to poke around in the wound of Stalinism again (in my own wound, however; I've never cared much for poking around in the wounds of other people). I recounted to the venerable representatives of the working class gathered there a little personal reminiscence. Personal recollections are not out of place sometimes, even in meetings of the Executive Committee of the Spanish Communist Party.

In the concentration camp at Buchenwald from 1943 to 1945, I had worked—by order of the clandestine leadership of the Spanish Communist Party organization in the camp (I happened to be the only one of the Spanish deportees, moreover, who knew German)—in an internal administrative service, the *Arbeitsstatistik,* along with an international group of Communist comrades.

One of these Communists was Czech. His name was Frank, Josef Frank. Later, after the war, Frank came to be assistant secretary-general of the Czechoslovakian Communist Party. And in 1952 he was one of those involved in the Slansky trial, the last great spectacular trial of the Stalinist era, the same trial in which Artur London was brought to judgment, which he described in his *The Confession*. Frank confessed, as did all the others, to imaginary crimes and was condemned to death.

In 1952 I read in *L'Humanité,* the daily of the French Communist Party, the summary of the accusations against those involved in the Slansky trial. I saw that Josef Frank had been accused, among other things, of having been in the service of the Nazis in Buchenwald. I read this accusation several times in a cold sweat. I thought it wasn't possible, that it must have been an error of transmission. I knew that Frank had not been in the service of the Nazis in Buchenwald, I knew it very well.

I remembered that at the beginning of 1945, when we glimpsed the first signs of the imminent German defeat, the clandestine leaders of the French Communist Party at Buchenwald had asked my aid in organizing the escape of two comrades—Pierre Durand, the present editor-in-chief of *L'Humanité,* and Marcel Paul, the Communist leader of the electricity labor union, at the time a minister in De Gaulle's government, in the era of the tripartite alliance. I agreed to help. My job in the *Arbeitsstatistik* section in fact put me in a position to know which *kommandos* were to work outside the electrified barbed wire fence of the camp to repair roads, railroad tracks, telephone poles and to perform other similar tasks, which were becoming increasingly necessary and urgent as the systematic bombings by the British and American air forces progressively paralyzed the economic life of the Third Reich.

Durand and Paul wanted to be assigned to a *kommando* of this sort so as to be able to study from the outside, concretely, what the possibilities of escape were. So I took on this task

One of those responsible for the distribution of deportee manpower among the various Buchenwald *kommandos* was none other than Josef Frank. I went to see him. It was a winter morning—I remember it now, just as I had remembered it in 1952 when I read the accusation against Frank in the newspaper, just as I remembered it in 1964 in the ancient castle of Bohemian kings. I remember the snow, the white, almost vaporous mass of the thicket of beeches around the camp. I remember the dense smoke from the chimney of the crematory rising up a few yards away from the barracks in which the interior administrative services had been set up, among them that of the *Arbeitsstatistik*. I remember the silence of that winter morning, the great silence of the snow-covered hill, of the beech thickets under their blanket of snow. I remember that in the quarantine camp, beneath canvas field tents, the deportees recently arrived in Buchenwald from all over Europe were dying like dogs. No, worse than dogs. They were dying like men, the way men usually die at the hands of other men. I remember that I was twenty years old and that I was happy. Perhaps this was a first budding-forth of petty-bourgeois masochism, who knows? I was happy because everything was clear. I knew why I was a prisoner. Moreover, the bad guys were on one side and the good guys were on the other, as in a fairy tale. And I was with the good guys. Fascism was Evil and we were fighting against Evil. I was twenty years old, and I was happy. I remember the snow covering Buchenwald, covering the thicket of beeches where Goethe had strolled, chatting with Eckermann, a century before. I remember that a few weeks later spring came, the last spring of that war. The abrupt arrival of spring was the worst moment, no doubt, in the life of a *Kazettler.*

In the slang of the camps, this German word, based on the letters K and Z, *Kazett,* an abbreviation for concentration camp, *Konzentrationslager,* was used as a name for deportees: we were all *Kazettlers,* that is to say inhabitants of the universe denoted by those two letters K and Z, a universe of forced labor and extermination camps that extended from one end of Europe to the other. What we did not know then, in Buchenwald, was that these same two letters, in the reverse order, Z and K, served to designate the similar and parallel universe of Stalin's Gulag, that we were *Kazettlers* whereas the prisoners of the Gulag were *Zeks.*

But spring was the worst moment in the life of the deportee, be he a *Kazettler* or a *Zek,* no doubt because the sudden vital tumult of nature around us underscored in an even more painful way the implacable work of death within the camp itself.

I remember that winter morning, in Buchenwald, my second winter in the camp. I went to see Frank and asked him to find me two work places in a *kommando* that would be going to work outside the barbed wire enclosure of the camp. Two work places for two French comrades. He looked at me intently. He asked me why this request hadn't come to him through the established organizational channels. I told him that these organizational channels, besides being slower, involved letting a certain number of comrades know certain facts: too many comrades in some cases. I laughed and told him that the way that had been chosen was an organizational one too, but a guerrilla-type one. He smiled and shook his head good-naturedly. Frank knew, of course, that I represented the Spanish Communist Party in the *Arbeitsstatistik* office, but the matter I was talking to him about didn't concern the Spanish Communist Party. He looked at me intently and told me he trusted me. He said he would look for two work posts in a *kommando* leaving the camp. He told me he'd let me know when it was all arranged.

In the end the plan for Pierre Durand's and Marcel Paul's escape was abandoned, I don't remember exactly why now. But Frank kept his promise. He found the two work posts that I had asked him for.

I remember the snow on that long-ago day in 1945. I remember the gray smoke of the crematorium. I shook hands with Frank, my comrade. Neither of us could have imagined that seven years later, in the autumn of 1952, Josef Frank would confess to having been a war criminal in Buchenwald, in the service of the Gestapo. We did not know that he would die on the scaffold, murdered by his people—our people—in a country that he had helped liberate. We did not know that his body would be incinerated and that the ashes, along with those of the others put to death, would be scattered on the snow somewhere around Prague, so that not a trace of his passage on earth would remain. Neither of us could have imagined that I would evoke his memory, sadly, desperately, in a sad and despairful month of March in 1964, before a tribunal of representatives of the Spanish working class—O sinister farce!—in an ancient castle of Bohemian kings.

I evoked the memory of Josef Frank before the members of the Executive Committee of the Spanish Communist Party. I had known, in 1952, that he was innocent, and I had said nothing. I had nowhere proclaimed his innocence. I had kept quiet, sacrificing the truth on the altar of the Absolute Spirit, which among us was called the Party Spirit. And this wound of Stalinism on my own skin continued to burn. Never again, whatever the circumstances, whatever the price to be paid, would I sacrifice the truth on the altar of some Pragmatic Reason of State or Party. I told them this.

When I had finished evoking the memory of Josef Frank, my comrade in Buchenwald, when I had finished poking about in the wound of my own Stalinism, there was a silence in the salon where we were gathered together. There was even a temporary adjournment of the session.

Claudín and I went out together, intending to take a short walk around the chilly, lonely park surrounding the ancient castle of Bohemian kings.

Irene Falcón was in the next room.

She was standing there motionless, her face bathed in tears. With her eyes brimming over with tears. This cliché has never seemed more exact. Irene Falcón, standing motionless behind the table on which the tape recorders were set up, with her eyes brimming over with tears.

In the park, as we walked about, Fernando explained the reasons for Irene's intense emotion. The fact was—and I of course did not know this; one can be a member of the Executive Committee of the Spanish Communist Party and not know a good part, or, better said, a bad part of the past of the party; it is almost a commonplace that the secrets of the party are like the corpses of men drowned at sea: they can take years to resurface; some of them in fact will never rise to the surface again: they will remain submerged forever in the memories of our amnesic leaders —the fact was, Claudín told me, that during the emigration after the Civil War Irene had been the companion of Geminder, one of the leaders of the Czech party who had been murdered along with Slansky and Frank. Germinder had been one of those comrades whose ashes had been scattered over the icy snow somewhere around Prague so that not a trace of his passage on this earth would remain. Without knowing it, when I evoked the memory of Frank and the murdered victims of the last great public trial of the Stalinist era, I had been reminding Irene Falcón of terrible moments in her life. Because she had been Germinder's companion at one time, Irene had been kept apart from any sort of political work and had disappeared for a number of years. She had emerged again later, when the discreet posthumous rehabilitation of some of the victims of the Stalinist system had taken place and the few thousands of survivors began to return from the Gulag camps. It was then that Irene had come back to work at Dolores Ibárruri's side.

But a few weeks after that day at the end of March 1964 when I had seen her standing there motionless, drained of her last tear, turned into a mute statue of suffering, Irene Falcón, member of the Central Committee, made a written contribution to the discussion of our positions.

It is a brief text that ignores the real problems that have been presented. After expressing her overall, general agreement with the majority of the members of the Executive Committee, Irene Falcón goes on:

> We have faith, yes, we have faith and confidence in our working class, in our people, in our glorious Party [the capital letter is of course hers, not mine]. And we have reasoned faith and confidence, based on the theoretical analyses and the political practice developed and accumulated by the leadership of our party, based on our own reflection and experience. Precisely because of the great and painful lessons of the time of the personality cult, drawn by the Twentieth and Twenty-First Congresses of the Communist Party of the Soviet Union, we have freed ourselves of blind, anti-scientific faith, *and there has been strengthened in us that faith to which Marx referred when he said that Commu-*

nists are capable of "assaulting the heavens." When this faith grows lukewarm, when one begins to doubt, when one no longer believes, one begins to be a Communist no longer. That is the truth. (The italics, naturally, are mine.)

Is it, indeed, necessary to comment on this paragraph, steeped in an incredible, almost abject religiosity, the same religiosity in which the ideological aberrations of Stalinism took root? Wouldn't it be the sadism typical of a petty-bourgeois intellectual—it is well-known that sadism and masochism are but two sides of the same coin—to root around in it?

In reality, despite a lyrical allusion to Marx, this text exudes a spirit totally contrary to Marxism. I refer, obviously, to the Marxism of Marx, and not to that of his inferior successors, be they Great Helmsmen, Coryphaei of Science, or mere secretaries-general. It has been commonly believed, in fact, that Marxism is, first and foremost, atheistic, in principle and method. Or in other words, that in order to be a communist—and a communist should not be confused with a member of the party: the two things can be quite different—it is necessary to begin by being an unbeliever, even though this is not of course sufficient in and of itself; naturally not. From the empyrean of the New Faith, which is no longer either "blind" or "anti-scientific," Irene Falcón announces the glad tidings to us: in order to be a communist it is necessary to be a believer, the opposite of an unbeliever, and one must have no doubts; in other words, one must believe everything, with all one's heart and soul.

To cap it all, Irene Falcón has the intellectual effrontery (though perhaps it is simply ignorance: supine and divine ignorance) to base her remarks on a quotation from Marx that is distorted and extremely far-fetched in this context. She states that "there has been strengthened in us that faith to which Marx referred when he said that Communists are capable of 'assaulting the heavens.' " These words of Marx's, so overused and pulled out of context until they have been turned into a stick to beat any sort of dog, can be found, as is well known, in a letter that he wrote to Ludwig Kugelmann on April 12, 1871, in connection with the Paris Commune. Marx says in this letter that "the present insurrection in Paris—even though it may succumb before the wolves, the swine, and the rabid dogs of the old society—is the most glorious undertaking of our party since the June insurrection in Paris. These Parisians who are taking heaven by assault *(diesen Himmelsstürmer von Paris)* can be contrasted to the slaves of faith (*Himmelsklaven*) of the Prusso-Germanic Holy Roman Empire, with its posthumous mascarades that stink of the barracks, of the Church, of feudalism, and above all of the Philistine spirit."

The expression that Marx uses, *Himmelsstürmer,* "those who are taking heaven by assault," is a literary allusion. It most probably is taken (at least in my opinion) from the Romantic dramatist Heinrich von Kleist. In this latter's *Penthesilea,* the Queen of the Amazons says:

> Das Glück, gesteh ich, wär mir lieb gewesen;
> Doch fällt es mir aus Wolken nicht herab,
> Den Himmel drum estürmen will ich nicht.

> [Happiness, I confess, would have pleased me;
> But since it is not going to fall to my feet from the clouds,
> I am not for that reason going to assault the heavens.]

But whatever the origin of the expression *Himmelsstürmer* that Marx uses and that forms part of the semantic background of German Romanticism, its meaning is clear. Marx's entire phrase is built around the opposition between *Himmelsstürmer,* "those who are taking heaven by assault," and *Himmelsklaven,* "the slaves of heaven," or more precisely, if we pay close attention to the context, "the slaves of faith." Marx concretely contrasts the revolutionary, Promethean, essentially atheist humanism of the workers and artistans of the Paris Commune to the superstitious, barracks-inspired, bureaucratic faith of the subjects of the holy Empire, of the slaves of faith. In short, Marx contrasts the utopian and humanistic violence of the unbelievers with the abject, stinking, putrefying submissiveness of believers. This attitude can surprise no one who has even a superficial knowledge of Marx's theoretical works. Irene Falcón detracts from and totally alters the meaning of Marx's expression. She uses in favor of faith—the "new faith," the faith that is no longer that of the simple and humble soul, but rather that of the militant of the Glorious Party whose leaders incarnate Universal Wisdom, the faith without which one cannot be a Communist, according to her—a phrase in which Marx proclaims precisely the contrary.

But I prefer to forget this lamentable incursion by Irene Falcón into the quicksands of theory. I prefer to remember her eyes brimming over with tears that afternoon early in April 1964, in an ancient castle of Bohemian kings, after she had heard me speak of the abominable murder of Josef Frank and his comrades, in that last great political trial of the Stalin era.

> Impossible to say,
>   yet it has been said.

Impossible to think
    that a voice has been heard
    announcing it.
Impossible to imagine having read,
    in plain, simple words, that he is dead.
Impossible to write it,
    and yet it is written.
"Stalin's heart
    has failed
has ceased to beat
    it beats no more."
His heart! The breath of the Party!

Impossible to think that this is how it was,
that nothing can be done now, that it has happened,
that every life has been cast in shadow
by this death of Stalin,
    forever;
that time's sound and fury is stilled
by Stalin's silence
    forever.
Forever, think of it, forever.
Never again, never again, never again,
never again Stalin speaking, smiling.
Think of it, forever, forever.

I wrote this, it behooves me to remember.

This is not a bad moment to remember it. One of the last of the long plenary meetings of the Executive Committee of the Spanish Communist Party, in an ancient castle of Bohemian kings, has just recessed for a few minutes. I have just seen Irene Falcón's face, fallen apart with the pain of memory. I have gone out into the damp, cold park, amid the leafless trees, with Fernando Claudín. He is explaining why Irene Falcón's eyes have been filled with tears, why they have brimmed over with pain.

It is not a bad moment to remember the poem that I wrote when Stalin died. I am not going to do what the others did, what almost all the other Communist leaders formed in the Stalin era did. I am not going to wall up my memory.

I wrote this poem in March of 1953, a few hours after the official announcement of Stalin's death. I did not write it because I was ordered to: it was something that came spontaneously from the innermost dephs of my alienated consciousness. The poem was read at the end of a memorial ceremony, before thousands of Spanish political refugees gathered together in the Salle Pleyel, in Paris. The audience was not told who the author was. Mine was an anonymous voice, the voice of the Communists meeting together there. Then it was published, also anonymously, by the party. It was printed on pale green bristol sheets, tied together with a bit of red cord. I claim responsibility for this anonymous poem, naturally, but not for this edition of it, so full of the spirit of small-town vulgarity, of cheap catechism. That edition was put out without my collaboration, without my even knowing anything about it. I have on my work table the only copy of this edition I have left. I look this poem over again with the desperate sadness that it arouses in me nowadays.

The working class is an orphan,
the dockers in Bilbao are orphans,
the steelworkers at Eibar,
the sailors of Ondárroa and Laredo,
the miners of Mieres, of Langreo,
the women of Murcia in the market,
the shepherds of Gredos, the girls
washing clothes in the stream,
the bricklayer is an orphan and his sorrow
gleams in the black lime of the scaffoldings.
The working class is an orphan in Manresa
and in Sabadell. All of Barcelona
is filled with the sound of weeping and a promise:
"Our Stalin has died! We will hoist his banner
till victory!"

Madrid has shuddered.
  No one speaks
on the sad way to work.
Madrid is silent and remembers.
"Our Stalin has died! His Party
will continue along the path he blazed!"

Those who suffer from hunger,
            those who sell
their labor to capital,
those who have nothing to lose
and a world to gain,
            those who saw
that world won and defended,
            from Shanghai to Berlin,

happier each day, made vaster
by the hand of Stalin,
                    all of them are orphans.

Our father has died, our comrade,
our Leader and Master,
Captain of Peoples, Architect
of Communism in giant works.

He has died. He has died. There are no words.
The drums of silence roll.
Our Stalin has died, comrades.
Let us close up the ranks in silence.

It is not a bad moment to remember this poem, doubtless.

Up there in the salon where we were gathered together, Santiago
Carrillo was claiming that the dossier of Stalinism should be closed once
and for all. He was shouting, in a fury, that poking around in that past
was simply proof of the masochism of petty-bourgeois intellectuals. So
be it: I shall continue to poke around in that past in order to uncover
its purulent wounds, in order to cauterize them with the red-hot iron of
memory.

I return to the document that I have on my work table, FOR THE
EYES OF THE CENTRAL COMMITTEE ONLY.

This file contains the opinions of Central Committee members who
were in prison at the time. Narciso Julián, Ramón Ormazábal, Pedro
Ardiaca and Miguel Núñez submitted a collective opinion from the
prison in Burgos. Luis Lucio Lobato and Simón Sánchez Montero submitted individual opinions from El Dueso Prison, in Santona.

The letter from the comrades in prison in Burgos is brief. A flash of
lightning, one might say. It is dated July 14, 1964.

Dear comrade Santiago, dear comrades of the Executive Committee:

We have just received the résumé that Santiago has made for us of the
discussions held at the meetings of the Executive Committee in Paris and
Prague.

As we write you these lines Ramón Ormazábal, Pedro Ardiaca, and Miguel
Núñez are the only ones who have read these documents through a first time.
Because he is in the infirmary, where things are more difficult, Narciso Julián
has not even seen them yet. In any event, we have already exchanged certain

initial impressions among the four of us, and without prejudice to the fact that we will soon send you a letter with our more carefully considered opinions, after proper study and a more ample and profound collective discussion of the documents that you have placed at our disposal, we have decided to advise you immediately of our position regarding what is essential, a position that we sum up for you as follows:

We are in full accord with the majority of the Executive Committee, in particular with the viewpoints expressed by Santiago, Dolores, and Juan Gómez, reaffirming our policy of National Reconciliation, of HGP and HN, of resolute struggle at the head of the working class and the people against the Franco dictatorship and domination by the oligarchy in any form whatsoever, in favor of a democratic solution. We declare ourselves decidedly against the lame "evolutionist" positions set forth by Fernando Claudín and Federico Sánchez, as well as against leftist tendencies, and, of course, against pro-Chinese influences. . . .

This text calls for a few remarks.

It will be noted, first of all, that the comrades did not possess the authentic and complete records of the discussion, but merely a résumé drawn up by Santiago Carrillo. I will be told in reply that it was not possible to send these documents in full to the prisons of Burgos and El Dueso. That is obvious. But the method consisting of putting out only a résumé of a discussion, as drawn up by Carrillo, was not employed exclusively in cases of *force majeure,* as with the comrades in prison. It was very nearly the general rule. And, in certain cases, this was not even a written résumé, but an oral report.

The Central Committee comrades who were living in Latin America, in completely normal conditions, with none of the restrictions and difficulties of life underground, had to be content for instance with a verbal report by Wenceslao Roces. The objectivity of this old professor of Roman Law, who has infested the Hispano-American cultural world with dreadful translations of Marx, can be judged by reading a few extracts from his written contribution to the discussion of the Central Committee.

Roces states that our positions—those of Claudín and Sánchez—"call into question and repudiate not only the Party line and its principles but also the very conception of the world and the ideology that no Communist can renounce so as to profess ideas rooted in the most reactionary philosophies, such as skepticism and agnosticism." And following this first grandiloquent, rhetorical sally, which demonstrates, let it be said in passing, a laughable ignorance of the concrete historical meaning of certain philosophical schools, Roces criticizes the Executive Committee for having been dilatory in dealing with such serious cases, with the result that Fernando Claudín and Federico Sánchez, "encouraged by this *laissez-faire,* came to believe that by toadying to and crudely encouraging—and this for me is what is most reprehensible about their attitude—certain aberrant tendencies of politically immature young people, by stressing the anti-Marxist clichés of the generation gap, senile sclerosis, etc., they would be able to create for themselves a youthful, revivifying platform as fresh as spring based on ideas that are the oldest, most worn out, autumnal, and senile in philosophy as in politics."

As will have been seen, Don Wenceslao imagines that a plethora of adjectives can conceal an absence of ideas and concepts. But without embarking at this point on semiological analysis, it is evident that anyone who expresses himself in this fashion, with all the triumphalist clichés of the Stalinist period, will not be in a position to provide an objective verbal report on the discussions in the Executive Commettee—at which, moreover, he was not present, and heard about only at second hand.

Nonetheless, even though it was not possible to send complete documentation of the discussion to Burgos and Santona, it would have been quite possible to send along with Carrillo's résumé another résumé drawn up by Claudín and Sánchez. This method, moreover, would have been consonant with the principles and norms of Leninism, varied and even partially self-contradictory though they may be.

I, for my part, am not a fanatic or a fetishist of Leninism, but Carrillo for his part is. Or rather he was, or pretended he was, in 1964. At that time, he salivated when he spoke of Leninism, of the return to Leninism, of Leninism as the prime example of revolutionary Marxism. On April 19, 1964, for instance, at the meeting held in Paris to prepare the cadres of the party to accept our expulsion, Carrillo claimed emphatically: "We Spanish Communists will follow Lenin's path, the path of revolutionary Marxism." Today, now that he is in the midst of turning modernist and Bernsteinian, I suppose Carrillo no longer knows quite what to think of Leninism, that is to say, what to think of the theory of Soviet revolution through non-parliamentary means, and of the dictatorship of the proletariat, which are key elements of Leninism. Today, doubtless, Carrillo finds Leninism something of a bother. But in 1964 Carrillo proclaimed himself a Leninist. Leninism was his lodestar, his navigation aid, his Tom Thumb pocket of pebbles, his guide for sinners, or as Don Wenceslao Roces put it in one of the sessions of the Sixth Congress of the Spanish Communist Party, using a daring metaphor that became forever engraved in my memory, Leninism was "the mast to which one must tie oneself and lash oneself, on the tempestuous sea of social life."

And it was in the norms prescribed by Lenin that Carrillo should and could have found inspiration in dealing with the divergencies within the leadership of the party in 1964.

In 1921, during one of the most difficult moments in the history of the young Soviet Republic, when profound divergencies arose in the party concerning the role that labor unions should play, Lenin wrote an article on "The Crisis of the Party," in which he said:

> What must be done to obtain the quickest and most certain cure? It is necessary that *all* the members of the party begin to *study* with absolute sang-froid and the greatest attention (1) the basic issue underlying the divergencies and (2) the evolution of the struggle within the party. The study of both is indispensable, since the basic issue itself underlying the divergencies develops, becomes clear, becomes concrete (and frequently even changes) *in the course of the struggle,* which, as it passes through various phases, reveals to us the *various* implications in the contention, the *various* positions in the struggle, etc. It is necessary to *study* both and not fail to call for the most accurate printed documents for thorough examination. HE WHO TAKES ANOTHER AT HIS WORD IS A PERFECT IMBECILE OF WHOM NOTHING CAN BE EXPECTED. IF THERE ARE NO DOCUMENTS, WITNESSES OF THE TWO PARTIES OR THE DIFFERENT PARTIES THEMSELVES MUST BE QUESTIONED: A THOROUGH INTERRO-GATION, AND IN THE PRESENCE OF WITNESSES, IS ABSO-LUTELY IMPERATIVE. (The italics are Lenin's; the capitals are mine.)

As can be seen, Lenin's opinion is categorical. In an extremely difficult situation, after four years of civil war, economic blockade, and hunger, when the discontent of the masses was being unleashed and workers' strikes and peasant revolts were breaking out in every part of the Soviet Union, Lenin calls anyone who participates in open discussion within the party without studying the basis of the divergencies, without demanding accurate printed documents, without interrogating witnesses on both sides when written documents are unavailable "a perfect imbecile." Anyone who takes another at his word in the course of an open battle of opinions within the party is "a perfect imbecile of whom nothing can be expected," according to Lenin.

It does not seem charitable to judge in the light of these words of Lenin's the attitude of certain leaders who were content with a "first reading" of a unilateral résumé by Carrillo and an exchange of "initial impressions" before setting forth their opinion on the basic issues at stake in a discussion bearing upon anti-Franco strategy in its entirety.

Moreover, by sending the prisoners a résumé entirely of his own making, and one which had not been seen by either Claudín or Sánchez, Carrillo also violated the spirit and the létter of the Statutes of the Spanish Communist Party, which require the presence of the criticized militants at all meetings devoted to their case, a presence which in these circumstances could not be physical but could at least have been a moral one, by way of a document submitted by the two militants in question. And what is more, Carrillo effectively ignored the resolution of the Executive Committee itself, which was approved on April 2, 1964 (with two votes against—those of Claudín and Sánchez, naturally).

This resolution states: "Given the difficulties of calling the Central Committee together at this time—difficulties recognized by comrades Fernando Claudín and Federico Sánchez themselves—and having exhausted the possibilities of overcoming the disagreements of these comrades with the Party line through discussion and an exchange of opinions in the Executive Committee, we consider that the most suitable method for arriving at a solution is TO DISTRIBUTE TO THE MEMBERS OF THE CENTRAL COMMITTEE THE MOST COMPLETE INFORMATION CONCERNING THE PROBLEM, in order that they may come to the proper decision." (The capitalization is mine.)

For the vast majority of the Central Committee members this MOST COMPLETE INFORMATION was reduced to a résumé drawn up by Carrillo, or to a verbal report. And it is not I, but Lenin, who says: "He who takes another at his word is a perfect imbecile of whom nothing can be expected."

But now that I have come to this internal resolution of April 2, I will record for history a minor but significant little incident.

In the last plenary session of the Executive Committee held in the ancient castle of Bohemian kings, the aforementioned resolution was presented by Enrique Líster, who had chaired the small committee appointed to draft it. Following the paragraph that I have just quoted was another that read: "Meanwhile, in view of the express declaration made by comrades Fernando Claudín and Federico Sánchez that they are unable to apply a political line with which they are not in accord— WHICH CONSTITUTES AN EVIDENT INFRACTION OF THE STATUTES OF OUR PARTY—their work on the Executive Committee is rendered impossible."

On arriving at this point in the reading of the resolution, La Pasionaria took the floor, almost wrathfully, to request that the phrase I have quoted in capitals—WHICH CONSTITUTES AN EVIDENT INFRACTION OF THE STATUTES OF OUR PARTY—be stricken from the text. There was a moment of silence. Disconcerted not only by Dolores's request but also by her peremptory tone, Líster and Carrillo looked at each other. I looked at Claudín and he looked at me, and we exchanged fleeting smiles. Líster asked Dolores for an explanation, and she replied categorically that the phrase was not necessary, and moreover did not reflect reality. It would have to be stricken from the text of the resolution.

Carrillo puffed nervously on his cigarette. Líster did not know what to do. It was understandable that he was disconcerted. The fact was that the reference to the party statutes was the key phrase of the resolution. If we had committed an infraction of the statutes, the measures proposed against us were justified. If we had not committed such an infraction, why all the fuss? If the fact of sticking to our opinions and declaring that we would continue to defend them in the party until reality proved us right was not an infraction of the statutes, all the measures proposed against us had no serious basis in fact. If the phrase in question was stricken from the resolution, the entire matter was reduced to a trial of our intentions.

Finally Carrillo, frowning, reluctantly said, all right, very well then, let the phrase be taken out since Dolores so requested. And the little phrase was removed from the text of the resolution. In other words, we had *not* committed an infraction of the party statutes.

I looked at Fernando again. We smiled at each other again.

Nobody asked La Pasionaria to explain the reasons for her almost violent intervention. That was too bad. It would have been interesting to have her reasons recorded in the minutes of the meeting. But whatever these reasons were, the fact is that Dolores was opposed to any mention's being made of the statutes of the party. She was opposed, in short, to there being a legal basis, one might say, for the resolution passed against us, since the statutes are the law of the party.

But I return now to the document here on my work table.

If I have chosen it from among all the material having to do with the 1964 discussion, it is because it contains Simón Sánchez Montero's written opinion. It was the memory of my meeting with Simón in 1969, in that luxurious and vulgar house in Pozuelo de Alarcón, that caused me to search for this document in my files.

Before examining what Simón said in August 1964, however, I would like to dwell for a moment on the opinion offered by Luis Lucio Lobato.

Lobato is no doubt an estimable man. It can even be said that he is an exemplary Communist. I am not referring here to the fact that he spent so many long years in prison. In and of itself, having spent years in prison does not mean anything. One can go to prison, in fact, simply by chance if one happens to have been denounced by an informer or if one has been careless about organizing one's own clandestine labors; this has little merit. The fact that a party member has spent many years in prison must arouse the compassion of the faithful, awaken active, militant solidarity, but in no case is it sufficient proof of political intelligence. I know more than one man who has entered prison a fool and come out an imbecile. From an objectively revolutionary point of view, the mythification of prison is absurd.

Rakosi spent seventeen years in prison, and when he assumed power in Hungary through the will and grace of Stalin and the Russian army, he behaved like a bloodthirsty sectarian fool and was one of those most responsible for the failure of socialism in his country. Thaelmann died, the victim of a cowardly murder in Buchenwald in August 1944, after eleven years of imprisonment by the Nazis, but his death should not obscure his role in the demise of the German revolution and in Hitler's rise to power through his obtuse and unconditional application of the sectarian policy of the Comintern. The Central Committee members of the Communist Party of Portugal, with Cunhal at its head, have spent I don't know how many hundreds of years in prison between them, yet this has not kept the Central Committee from conceiving an adventurist, sectarian, bureaucratic strategy, whose one objective result has been the withdrawal of the Portuguese masses from the revolutionary movement and the subsequent consolidation of the social-democratic and center-right political forces.

Despite all this historical evidence, the mythification of the prison experience is the order of the day in the upper echelons of the Spanish Comminist Party—and to the many long years spent in prison by Simón Sánchez Montero, Luis Lucio Lobato, Horacio Fernández Inguanzo, and so many other comrades there can now be added the seven days spent by Santiago Carrillo in the prison infirmary of Carabanchel. The unquestionable heroism of the Spanish Communist Party is waved like a banner before our eyes as the supreme terrorist argument for silencing doubts and possible criticisms. But even if it runs counter to current fashion, I shall say that the years spent in prison by the leaders of the Spanish Communist Party do not impress me. The fact is that I am not a Christian, but a Marxist. When it comes time to judge the policy of a party, what matters is the strategy that it conceives and executes, not how much suffering its militants have accrued.

When I say, therefore, that Labato has been an exemplary militant, I am not thinking of his years in prison. With a little more luck and a little less ideological trumpeting of imminent party triumphs—which always leads to underestimating the enemy—Lobato could have avoided going back to prison as often as he did, but he would not thereby have ceased to be an exemplary militant. What matters here is the consistency between ideas—an ideal or a body of doctrine—and praxis. The consistency between what one thinks and what one does. It is this stubborn, tenacious, obstinate consistency of his life that to me is the basis of Luis Lucio Lobato's exemplary militancy.

As I write these lines, it has been many years since I have seen Lobato. When he got out of prison after his second incarceration in 1959, I was no longer in the party. But during the first years of my clandestine work in Madrid I saw him very often. At that time, after the Fifth Congress of the Spanish Communist Party in 1954, Simón Sánchez Montero and I were the only members of the Central Committee present in Madrid. Each of us had his specific work sector, but with the aim of generalizing this experience by exchanging information the two of us met from time to time with some of the heads of the different clandestine committees. In these meetings "Miguel"—Lobato's *nom de guerre*—was in the habit of speaking up carefully and reflectively, providing precise facts concerning the workers of Madrid, without excessive rhetorical flourishes.

That was why, when I read Lobato's remarks during the discussion of August 1964, which he had written out beforehand, I was surprised by their grandiloquent tone, their vulgar, downright demagogic flights of oratory.

Lobato begins by regretting the fact that he does not have either the time or the reference materials necessary for a more detailed opinion regarding the situation that had arisen in the Executive Committee. "Because of this," Lobato states, "I find myself obliged to forgo in my opinions quotations, figures, statistical data, or any other references that would have been most appropriate." But this is not too serious a matter, Lobato adds, since "the question being debated is basically ideological and ideology has never needed to call on mathematics. The most inspiring, persuasive, and permanent texts of Marxism-Leninism are free of figures and statistics, yet they shed light on the theoretical, ideological, and political bases that mobilized the pioneers of scientific Communism and continue in our time to mobilize and educate new and successive generations of men and women who see in Communism the superior way of life to which the peoples of the world find themselves destined once the great process of their struggles for liberation have ended."

"Blessed Virgin, what a beginning!" as it says in *Don Juan Tenorio*. But Lobato scarcely gives us time to catch our breath following this introductory paragraph: the particolored warhorses of Lobato's rhetoric are off and running again.

"I naturally do not pretend to compare these notes of mine with such masterworks. If I refer to these latter it is because they serve to anchor my belief that in the final analysis it is ideas that move the world." (Listen carefully! This is being said, however incredible it may appear, by a Communist political leader who claims to be inspired by Marxism!)

"Was it not an idea or a series of ideas, surely rudimentary and perhaps even erroneous, concerning Communism—and not cold figures, however expressive they might have been—that 'filled' each one of us for the first time, that moved our entire being and brought us into the party with an ardent and irrepressible illusion that was a force in and of itself? What gave the Soviet Union, the heroic Soviet peoples during the late war, for example, the indomitable bravery of its first starving, glorious Red Guard, thus enabling them to endure immense calamities as they worked beneath the fury of the elements, with their work tools in one hand and their rifles in the other, if it wasn't the ideas of Communism that made them superior?"

And so on and on, page after page.

In the final analysis, and quite apart from its rhetorical style, Lobato's entire contribution to the discussion is a plea in defense of subjectivism. And the formulations that follow from "it is ideas that move the world" are truly astonishing. Thus, in order to justify his opinion that it is not as necessary as Claudín and Sánchez think to study the realities of capitalist expansion in Spain, Lobato comes round to saying: "What would have happened if the Bolsheviks in Russia between 1904 and 1914 had paid close attention to the statistics of capitalist production, to the indices of its economic development, to stock market quotations? They would have been converted to trade-unionism, and in 1917 their Great Revolution would not have taken place. . . ."

That is to say, in order to transform capitalist reality it is better to have no knowledge of it. In order to wage a revolution, it is better not to know what is at stake. But theory has demonstrated, before history has proved it—without its even being necessary to be a Marxist—that it is only what is known that is transformed, and that the only thing that is known is what is studied, examined, analyzed, so as to reconstruct it in accordance with the concept of a concrete totality. Moreover, history shows us clearly that even before 1904, in the waning years of the last century, Lenin, while in prison or during his deportation to Siberia, devoted himself to studying in the most minute detail all the statistics having to do with the past and future, so as to write a weighty volume entitled— what a coincidence!—*The Development of Capitalism in Russia,* a work abounding in "cold figures." It is a shame that Lobato did not devote his time in prison to a similar labor, even though his ambitions might well have been more modest. It would have profited him more to study statistics than to plunge headlong into expressionist literature.

Simón Sánchez Montero, for his part, maintains that in his remarks he will avoid literature and restrict himself to an analysis of Spanish reality. Unfortunately he doesn't stick to this goal very long, although he starts out very well.

Simón begins, as a matter of fact, by saying: "I believe that there is a great deal of truth in the opinions of Fernando Claudín, which are supported by Federico Sánchez. It is indeed true that in the course of the last few years there has been an obvious development of the economy in Spain and in the principal capitalist countries of Europe and that this development demonstrates the strength and the potentialities of monopoly capitalism, which is not exactly a paper tiger. It is no less true that there has been an improvement in the living conditions of large sectors of the working class and other levels of the population, which has become evident in the increase of every sort of electrical household appliance, television set, motor scooter, automobile, and so on and that this improvement in the standard of living has and will have its repercussions in the political realm. The existence of the Common Market is an obvious reality, as is its economic and political power, which it exerts on other countries, on Spain in particular, and from which Spanish monopoly capitalism can benefit. These and other related facts are evident and demonstrate the enormous strength of monopoly capitalism and the possibilities that it can still count on to prolong its domination."

As Fernando Claudín says in his *Las divergencias en el Partido (The Divergencies within the Party)* in regard to this paragraph of Simón's: "There could scarcely be a better synthesis, in so short a space, of the changes in Spanish reality that I pointed out to the Executive Committee and that must be our point of departure for creating a strategy and a tactic of the party that could have an effect on this reality and guide the fight for Socialism in Spain. All this says a great deal about the political acumen and the sense of reality of Comrade X [as Simón was in prison at the time, Claudín does not mention him by name so as not to create additional problems for him], who in isolation, shut up within four walls, is capable of seeing things much more clearly than almost all the other members of the Executive Committee and the Central Committee."

After this introduction, whose positive character Claudín stresses, it would have been logical to expect Simón to question why the "great deal of truth" contained in our opinions was denied *en bloc* by the majority of the Executive Committee, why we were expelled from this party organization for having expressed opinions in which there was "a great deal of truth." The logical thing would have been for Simón to take this "great deal of truth" as a basis for a thoroughgoing analysis of our positions.

But unfortunately that did not happen. In the next line of the paragraph cited, Simón writes: "A conclusive proof of this force and these possibilities of capitalism is the ideas they created in the heads of comrades such as Fernando Claudín and Federico Sánchez." That's what he wrote, comrades! In other words, there is "a great deal of truth" to our opinions, but according to Simón, this does not stem from an analysis of reality but from the influence on us of capitalism in expansion. That is to say, if the index of annual productive growth of Spanish industry is this or that percent, if the number of tractors has increased by so many thousands of units, saying so is not taking into account a given element of reality so as to know it and eventually transform it, but is, rather, the reflection of the influence on our brains of all-powerful monopoly capitalism. A comparable argument for idealism would not have occurred even to Bishop Berkeley! And here, furthermore, perhaps unwittingly, Simón shifts terrain. He abandons the restrictions of discussion based on facts and situates himself on the dangerous terrain of ideological and moral condemnation. And the reason for this is that, as Simon says a little further on, "we must make the analysis *from the standpoint of* our positions, and the conclusions that result will necessarily be those which, being inscribed in reality, will lead us more directly to the attainment of our objectives."

This process of reasoning, despite the vain attempt to accommodate both the stubborn reality of the facts and the necessary voluntarism involved in all political action, becomes aberrant here. For how can an analysis of capitalist reality in Spain in 1964 be made *from the standpoint of* positions that consist precisely in denying this capitalist development, which Simón, unlike the majority of the Executive Committee, recognized? The analysis of reality implicitly presupposes the criticism of these positions and the conquest of new positions. And this is precisely what the majority of the Executive Committee refused to do in 1964.

Moreover, when Simón says the "conclusions that result will necessarily be those which, being inscribed in reality, will lead us more directly to the attainment of our objectives," this means, despite the sophisticated formulation, a falling back into the most absurd sort of subjectivism— and I deliberately use the word subjectivism rather than voluntarism, which is something quite different. It means, in fact, that we must take account only of those elements of reality that confirm our vision, that are consistent with our objectives. But the fact is that in 1964 our objectives —the *Aitch En Pee;* democratic revolution; the liquidation of the power of the financial bourgeoisie and monopoly industrial capital (all of which were considered inescapable and based on the disappearance of Francoism)—did not reflect the real economic structure or the dynamics of social classes in Spain. They were apparently extremely radical objectives, but since they did not take into account the capitalist transformation of the entire social structure of our country, they became an archaic program that hid the real problems of developing a strategy leading to socialism. In other words, there was no such thing as conclusions actually inscribed in reality that could lead directly to the attainment of these objectives. In short: either we had to modify our strategic objectives, as a function of a concrete analysis of reality, as Claudín and Sánchez maintained in 1964, or cling to our illusory objectives and render analysis impossible. That was the only alternative, despite all of Simón Sánchez Montero's dialectical acrobatics in the remainder of his contribution to the discussion.

A little further on, Simón formulates his opinion on the origin of our divergencies in these words: "I believe I am rather well acquainted with comrades Fernando Claudín and Federico Sánchez, and I believe that they say what they think, being convinced that their ideas are the best for the party. But why do they think this? I find only one valid answer (there are others, but for the moment I refuse to accept them): fleeing from subjectivism, that stumbling block we have tripped over more than once, with grave harm to the party, comrades Claudín and Sánchez have fallen into the extreme opposite, objectivism, which is equally pernicious, and have imperceptibly slid toward positions that in my opinion are no longer ours."

Simón's process of reasoning here is enlightening. It sets in relief all the logical, ideological, and moral vices of a certain Communist tradition that finds succinct expression in what has now come to be called Stalinism, a tradition that needs neither concentration camps nor mass terror to manifest itself: there are, for instance, apparently gentle, apparently inoffensive Stalinisms, clad in slippers, for softly padding about the house.

Simón ends his reflections, in fact, with the above quoted passage on the stumbling block of subjectivism over which the party has repeatedly tripped, with grave harm to its activity. (It might be stated more clearly that the "grave harm" occasioned our party by subjectivism since 1939, to choose a date not too far back in time, is a harm that can be weighed in blood, in deaths: the path of subjectivisn of the Spanish Communist Party is strewn with corpses.) Given this, wouldn't having fallen into the extreme opposite—which happens to be erroneous on all counts: history has already demonstrated that our "objectivism" was pure objectivity— but even admitting this conclusion, wouldn't a small dose of "objectivism" have been beneficial after so much "stumbling" over subjectivism, after so much "grave harm"? But Simón's process of reasoning, by its own internal logic, because it is based on the presumptuous and ill-omened idea of "correct thought," concludes with the remark that we have slid toward positions that are no longer those of the party. If by this is meant positions that are no longer those of the majority of the Executive Committee, that goes without saying. What we wanted was, in fact, to modify the erroneous positions of the Executive Committee. But Simón alludes, in an ecclesiastical tone (that verb "slid" of his is comparable to all the "backsliding" from virtue in all the catechism books) to something more serious: our positions are no longer "those of all the rest of us." In other words, we have strayed from the straight and narrow path of virtue. We have fallen, been abandoned by the hand of God, "slid" into a "deviation," a category that poor Althusser is the only one to continue to consider Marxist.

But what is most serious in Simón's text is not this latter. What is most serious comes before that. When he asks himself why we think as we do, Simón says that he can find only one valid answer, that of "objectivism." But he adds, parenthetically, a short chilling phrase: THERE ARE OTHERS, BUT FOR THE MOMENT I REFUSE TO ACCEPT THEM. The meaning of these words is transparent: the other answer, which FOR THE MOMENT Simón refuses to accept, can only mean that Claudín and Sánchez have capitulated in the face of the enemy, that we are renegades, the more or less conscious agents of this enemy. If this short parenthetic phrase is not pure Stalinism, only God knows what is.

In view of all this, Simon is perfectly consistent when he says at the end of his written contribution to the 1964 discussion: "I am in agreement with the resolution adopted by the Executive Committee with regard to Fernando Claudín and Federico Sánchez. And I believe that it must be broadened to include their suspension from the Central Committee if F. C. and F. S. do not rectify their opinions."

"Rectify" is the decisive word. Return to the "straight and narrow path," to "correct thought." But the problem consists precisely in finding a solution that will permit militants to remain active in the party without "rectifying their opinions" but rather, and quite to the contrary, maintaining and defending them in the regular party structures and the party press. And as long as such a solution has not been found, not only will we not be able to speak of the Communist Party as a democratic party, but it will also be impossible to create a strategy for the real transformation of society. And the second point is even more serious than the first.

Be that as it may, that afternoon in Pozuelo de Alarcón, Simón and I were having a long talk together. We were also listening, each one of us, to the reasons and arguments of the other. Simón mine, and I his. Neither one of us changed the other's mind of course.

Not one afternoon of discussion or a thousand would have enabled us to change each other's minds. However well-reasoned Simón's arguments seemed to me at times to be (it should not be forgotten that this was the summer of 1969, a year after the invasion of Czechoslovakia by the troops of the Russian Imperium, at a moment, therefore, when Carrillo had already initiated his "modernist shift," in the course of which he was to appropriate—in a typically Stalinist form, that is to say by distorting them irremediably, depriving them of their strategic significance and turning them into mere pragmatic, opportunistic elements—some of the ideas Claudín and I had put forth in the discussion five years before, which had been the cause of our expulsion), however sensible some of Simón's points of view were, something already radically separated us: the very conception of the Communist party, of its historical function in the process of transforming society.

"The Party sums up everything. In it are synthesized the dreams of all the revolutionaries throughout our history; in it the ideas, the principles, and the power of the Revolution attain concrete form; in it our individualism disappears and we learn to think in terms of the collectivity; it is our educator, our master, our guide, and our watchful conscience, when we ourselves are incapable of seeing our errors, our defects, and our limitations; in it we are all one and we make each one of us a Spartan soldier for the most just of causes and all of us together an invincible giant; in it the ideas, experience, and legacy of martyrs, the continuity of the great work, the interests of the people, the future of the fatherland and the indestructible ties with the proletarian builders of a new world in every corner of the Earth are guaranteed."

These are the words of Fidel Castro, the First Secretary of the Cuban Communist Party, Prime Minister, Commander-in-Chief of the Armies of Land, Sea, and Air, First Basketball Player, First Specialist in Milchcows, First Agriculturalist and Machete-Wielder, at the First Congress of the Communist Party of Cuba.

They are significant words, doubly significant ones. First of all, because they brilliantly sum up, with a few drops of Castilian rhetoric underlining the almost religious solemnity of the paragraph, the entire tradition of the Stalinist party, whose features were codified in the era of the Comintern. And in the second place, because they were uttered by Fidel Castro, a popular and populist caudillo, a valiant combatant who has ended up, not without fatuity, by making this tradition his own. As a result the Cuban Revolution has progressively lost its original libertarian aims, thus becoming yet another bureaucratic regime of state capitalism, with its own particular features, of course, but essentially a copy of the Soviet and East European social model.

Naturally, as Fidel Castro lyrically sums up what the Party is (the capital letter is his: in this too he follows tradition), as he glorifies it and deifies it, no mention is made of one essential aspect of such a conception of the Communist vanguard: the need to have a Maximum Leader, a Great Helmsman, a Generalísimo, a First Secretary at the very top of the organization. All the virtues that Fidel Castro attributes to the Party are none other than his own personal virtues—real or imagined, but in any case consubstantial with this type of charismatic leader of the revolution: they are none other than his own theological virtues. When he is speaking of the Party, Fidel Castro is painting his imaginary self-portrait: the Party is his ego and his superego. The Party sums it all up and He sums up and assumes the Party and in Him the Party consumes itself —or, in a word, is consumed or consummated at the summit.

(On one of these last few days, you have happened to see a documentary film on the First Congress of the Cuban Communist Party: the delegates are gathered together in a huge theater, martial music is playing; the stage is still invisible, the curtain has not gone up yet: then the music rises in a crescendo and the immense curtain slowly rises: on the stage, as motionless as wax figurines, are the leaders of the Cuban Communist Party; you have never seen, even at the Kremlin or Tien-An-Men, anything as solemn, as imbued with the ritual of authority and hierarchy, as ridiculous: then Fidel Castro Ruz mounts the rostrum, in his brand-new generalísimo's uniform, with his white shirt and a tie that strangles this old and weary guerrilla fighter: then his interminable, biblical peroration begins, flowing on and on like a river: something like the report that God himself might have made on the seventh day of Creation: well, maybe you ought to mention that Fidel Castro has never seemed credible to you, either as an orator or political leader: the first time you heard him speak was in Santiago de Cuba on July 26, 1967: a vast crowd of workers, peasants, and students had been gathered together to hear the words of the Maximum Leader on that anniversary of the assault on the Moncada Barracks: the crowd had been standing for hours beneath a relentless sun, and the Maximum Leader did not appear: sweat was streaming and bottles of rum were being passed from hand to hand: finally, after a long wait, the Maximum Leader appeared: he began his speech and after only ten minutes you had had more than your fill of so much Castilian rhetoric: for Fidel Castro, in a country of peasants and mestizos, spoke the language of the Empire, the language of the Spanish colonial bourgeoisie: you had the impression that you were listening to a speech by your grandfather Antonio Maura or by Manuel Azaña:

begging the pardon of the shades of Antonio Maura and Manuel Azaña, who were better orators, because they were less prolix and set forth their intellectual arguments more eloquently: it was a masterful, distant speech that went over the heads of those congregated there: it was the rhetoric of populist power that could not—and perhaps did not intend to—call forth comprehension from those below, but only fervent loyalty to and admiration for this talented lawyer who spoke so well and so tirelessly in their name, or rather, in their place, in their silence, the only voice authorized to speak in the dark silence of the masses:

you heard Fidel Castro again a few months later, at the closing session of the Cultural Congress, and again you had the same impression: a few days later, Llanusa, who at the time was Minister of Education, informed you that Fidel Castro wanted to have an interview with a certain number of foreign intellectuals who had participated in the Cultural Congress, in order to exchange impressions as to the results: Llanusa informed you that you had been chosen as a member of this select delegation or representation of European intellectuals, along with K. S. Karol and Ralph Miliband: all right, very well, why not?: the next day, all of you were asked not to leave the Habana-Libre as you waited for this interview with Castro: the wait began at nine in the morning: every hour, more or less, urgent messages arrived: patience, the interview is about to begin, right now, this minute: finally, around ten at night, thirteen hours later, Llanusa came to get all of you in a car: he took you to the indoor stadium of the National Sports Institute, he explained to you that on that particular night of the week Fidel Castro was in the habit of playing basketball with a team of captains and majors from the armed forces: that at some time or other during this evening of sports activity he would receive you to exchange impressions: it seemed absurd to you, of course: but then you were all more or less familiar with these work methods proclaimed to be anti-bureaucratic when they were merely disorderly: as though bureaucracy consisted merely in doing one's work in an office: as though the frenetic activity of the leaders, always racing around in a jeep, organizing unscheduled meetings at hours when simple mortals are usually fast asleep after a hard day's work, were a guarantee of democracy: be that as it may, you arrived at the National Sports Institute stadium to find the basketball players also waiting for the Maximum Leader and Top Scorer: time passed and around 11:30 p.m. there was a certain flurry of activity: the men from the State Security Forces stationed themselves strategically around the perimeter of the stadium, for Fidel Castro was arriving: Llanusa introduced all of you to the Maximum Leader, who said you would talk together later, after he'd played basketball, since he needed to relax by getting himself a little physical exercise: okay then, more waiting: you settled down on the benches, alongside Fidel's retinue, as the game began: you then noticed in the distance, on the other side of the stadium, a number of women in a raised box: you asked who they were and it turned out that they were the companions of some of the ministers and military leaders who were playing with Fidel Castro, or accompanying him: you were of course struck by the fact that the women were over there, on the other side, all alone, discriminated against, separated from the men, the lords and masters of the revolution: this isolation of the women seemed significant to you and you made a note of it in your memory: but the basketball game had begun: basketball is a sport with which you are fairly familiar, since you played it for some years in your long-ago youth: after a few minutes you realized that the opposing team's defense was doing nothing to prevent Fidel Castro from sinking basket after basket: when a player dribbles through the other team's defense it is very easy to stop him or make him commit an offensive foul: well, Fidel managed to get through and sink his basket every time, and always in the same way: you noted this little detail too, ironically: it was amusing and interesting to see the personality cult manifest itself during a game of basketball:

you still have some photographs from that night, taken by some diligent court photographer: most of them show Fidel making a basket, triumphant and all-powerful: in the last photo, you are talking with the Maximum Leader, on the edge of the basketball court:

the fact is that you did finally manage to talk: or rather, Fidel managed to talk: around two o'clock in the morning, after having played two entire games, sweating and panting, but visibly relaxed, Castro at last came over to you chosen delegates and deigned to address you: but he did not ask you a single question concerning the Cultural Congress, nor did he allow any from you on the same subject, despite the fact that you had been urgently summoned for that very purpose: he immediately launched into a long discourse on the economic problems of Cuban agriculture and in particular on the need to develop citrus production: you stood there open-mouthed, at least metaphorically speaking, listening to every last word of the simplistic nonsense that popped into Fidel Castro's head: then after forty-five minutes of this peroration delivered at machine-gun speed—which poor "Papito" Serguera was trying to translate for K. S. Karol and Ralph Miliband, something unnecessary for you since Castro was speaking the language of the Empire—Vallejo, the Maximum Leader's personal physician, came over and called his attention to the lateness of the hour and the need to get a bit of rest after so much physical exercise:

and Fidel went off: the Great Man left:

after that, at three in the morning, Llanusa offered the three of you coffee and made you a gift of some books: in the salon where this refreshment was offered, you came across the exhausted, bored ladies waiting for Llanusa and the military or civilian leaders who had stayed around to participate in that final exchange of inconsequential trivialities: but these ladies were very circumspect, very retiring, not saying a word: playing the role expected of them, damn it!

and you do not think it is necessary to complete this faithful account of your one and only interview with Fidel Castro by reporting word for word his ideas on citrus production: really, you do not think that is necessary.)

But this brief wandering down the path of memory is set down here only as a digression on the theme of the ill-omened conception of the Communist Party that Fidel Castro sums up in a masterly way in his report to the First Congress of the Communist Party of Cuba. In the West European countries of Eurocommunism, I have the impression that nobody, not even La Pasionaria, would dare speak of the party that way today, in that tone of enraptured religiosity. Nonetheless this conception of the party, even though repressed, censored, deeply buried in the very depths of the subconscious, continues to obscurely predominate within the entire Communist movement. In the Spanish Communist Party, at any rate, the new generation of militants does not appear to have made a definite break with this conception, which the very structure of the organization tends to reproduce. They apparently accept being made to act like children again, since they seem to like shouting in chorus: "We feel it one and all—Gregorio's [López Raimundo, PSUC head] in the hall!" and you could substitute any name you please for Gregorio: Lobato, Santiago, Dolores, even Christ who started it all. The most clear-sighted, unfortunately, seem to leave the domain of thought, of theoretical and strategic planning to the leaders, limiting themselves to day-to-day militancy, piecemeal, an admirably ardent activism but one incapable of helping to reconstruct a global vision of the revolutionary undertaking.

The reconstruction of a revolutionary movement after forty years of dictatorship must be based on radical criticism of the conception of the party expressed by Fidel Castro and underlying all the formal speeches by the Central Committee members of the Spanish Communist Party during our discussion in 1964. This means that very little can be expected of the Maoist or Trotskyist groups, since all of them have come out of the same matrix, the same mold; since none of them has taken the trouble to rethink the problems of the proletarian vanguard, which are considered to have been historically resolved in the Bolshevik experience. So long as questions concerning the party, its relation with the masses, its conception of the autonomy of workers in the form of labor unions, councils or any other organic structure that history calls forth have not been grappled with at their very "Leninist" roots, we will not have gotten very far. So long as the Party blocks the horizon like a monolith, we will have solved nothing, or rather, we will have formulated none of the problems before us with sufficient clarity.

A good example of this is provided by the "Bandera Roja" ("Red Flag") group. Born of dissidence within the PSUC, specialists in the theoretical reconstruction of Leninist purity and in criticism of Carrilloist revisionism, its principal leaders have returned to the ranks of the Communist party without major difficulties, feeling neither pain nor pleasure, in an overall political situation that has been somewhat modified, and this has been possible precisely because "Bandera Roja" has never asked itself radical questions regarding the theory and practice of the vanguard party. One and the same umbilical cord unites Carrillo and Jordi Solé Tura with the Comintern tradition of the party, and that is what is most important. "The Party sums up everything." Fidel has said so; period.

A clear statement of certain historical truths is therefore in order.

In the first place, it must be understood that the Communist party (and in this context it matters little whether it be Eurocommunist, Trotskyist, or Maoist) cannot be the end, but only a means, an instrument of the revolutionary movement that depends on circumstances and hence is flexible. One instrument among others—such as labor unions, mass organizations, workers' councils, cooperative groups or self-managed groups, neighborhood associations, ecological or libertarian movements, in the domain of private life, of sexuality, of *macho* domination, of the despotic division of social work: in other words, all the organic forms of struggle that permit and favor the broadest possible popular participation. Of all these, the party is distinguished by two principal characteristics, which constitute at once its strength and its weakness (that is to say the possibility of its degeneration). The first is the historical permanence of its organization, through uninterrupted cycles and regardless of the objective difficulties. The second is its predominant dedication to action in the sphere of politics. Now, the permanence of the organization, so necessary on the one hand, is, on the other hand, a source of routines and rites, of mental indolence and submission to authority. And its dedication to action in the political sphere, which is indispensable insofar as there can be no revolutionary undertaking without posing the question of power, is also reductionist and alienating. The political sphere is, in fact, the privileged domain of the dominating classes, and Communist revolution must be the negation of politics insofar as politics is superimposed upon society, an autonomous mediation between men and their own social life. Politics is the state, and Communist revolution makes no sense without the suppression of the state. (And let no one tell me that this posing of the problem is utopian, because I agree. It may very well be utopian, but if so let us stop talking about Communist revolution—that would be more honest.)

All the foregoing means, in a word, that the revolution must not serve the party, but rather that the party must serve the revolution. Thus stated, this appears axiomatic. But a little reflection will prove that this is not altogether so. It will be seen that the Party—with a capital letter, à la Castro—has ended up becoming the supreme aim of the Communist movement. A total inversion of values and historical objectives has taken place. The supreme aim of every revolutionary—however distant and difficult its attainment—no longer appears to be making revolution, but preserving the Party (I purposely continue to use the capital letter): preserving unity, discipline, correct thought—and it is well known that the sole criterion of this latter is to be found in the decisions of the leaders —that almost religious ideology of the Party, whatever its political strategy, even though it is clear that this leads only to an uninterrupted series of disasters.

The Party has been turned into an end in itself, into a devouring metaphysical entity, whose principal vocation is its own preservation. And this implies that elements of acritical loyalty—religious bonds— predominate over rational elements.

As a consequence, I repeat, every step forward that claims to go beyond the obstacles of Stalinism without falling back into the prior tradition of social-democracy (both paths have demonstrated their sterility, and it would be chilling to calculate how many millions of dead each of them in turn has cost the working classes of this century) requires a radical posing, yet again, of the problem of the relation between the working class and its possible vanguard.

The second truth that comes to light by way of the historical experience may appear to be scandalous: in view of the facts, the Communist party is of no use. What I mean is this: it is of no use for the ends that have motivated and justified its creation as an opposition to the social-democratic movement that predominated in the early years of this century. It is of no use either for taking power or for instituting socialism.

Taking power? In the case of the Cuban revolution, for example (the most recent historical case), power was not taken over by the Communist

Party (which was called the Popular Socialist Party), but rather against it, or at least alongside it and despite it. When Fidel Castro proclaims that "the Party sums up everything," that "in it are synthesized the dreams of all revolutionaries," he is not only floating amid the clouds in the heaven of theological virtues but falsifying the history of his own country, of his own revolution.

It will be said that I am mistaking a hawk for a handsaw. It will no doubt be said that the revolution of 1917 in Russia is a classic example of the seizure of power by a Communist party, by the Bolshevik party. But that is not true either.

What is the first thing that Lenin does, in April 1917, on arriving in Petrograd? The first thing he does is dismantle the strategy—the conception of revolution by stages—the organic structure itself, of the party—his party—being led on the spot by a handful of "old Bolsheviks." The accesion of Trotsky and his group to positions of maximum responsibility in the party is the symbol of Lenin's new vision. In fact, the type of party that the conquest of power requires in these months lies at the opposite pole from the party of professional revolutionaries, bound together by ties of steel, that Lenin had previously defended, with pitiless intransigence. The party that sets out to seize power is a party of permanent debates, of theoretical confrontations, of opposing tendencies, and even of splinter groups. It is a party in which freedom of expression is as natural as fish in water. The fact is that what counts are the masses, their presence being increasingly felt in the cities, in the country, and on the battlefronts of the imperialist war. Let there be no doubt about it: the rallying cry of the moment was "all power to the soviets!" and not "all power to the Bolshevik party!" And there would not have been a Russian revolution had it been otherwise. The fact is that the seed of universality contained in "all power to the soviets" was located precisely in the type of relation of the vanguard with the masses where the former was the simple, concentrated, coherent expression of the aspirations of the latter; the seed of universality resided in the soviet forms of a new type of power. When the party ceases in this role, when it begins to devour the entire social texture like a cancer, to homogenize all forms of social life, as a function of a despotic conception of hegemony, even though the party may pretend to be an enlightened hegemony; when the party destroys pluralism and liquidates the forms of soviet power, then the Russian revolution loses its vocation and its universal meaning and becomes nothing more than a particular turn of events in the history of the accumulation of social capital in a backward society.

Let the social systems that predominate in those countries that bear the inappropriate label Socialist be observed in fact without ideological illusions, without mystifications to legitimate them. It will then be noted that these systems—despite their material and social progress, their industrial and military power, which result from the historical development of productive forces, from the valorization of social capital, and do not reflect the political system since the same type of progress has been achieved in Spain for example under Franco's dictatorship, and indeed been achieved even more rapidly and extensively—it will be noted, as I was saying, that these systems have nothing to do with socialism.

It is a question here of original systems, foreseen in none of the sacred texts of Marxism, for which it will be necessary to create new operative concepts.

These systems stand, of course, in violent opposition to those of Western capitalism, where *private appropriation* of surplus value continues to predominate. The fact that in the "Socialist" countries appropriation of surplus value is no longer *private*—resulting in the disappearance of the bourgeoisie as a class—explains the strategic antagonism, on a global scale, of the two predominant systems in the world, an antagonism incarnated in the rivalry of the two superpowers: the USA and the USSR.

In the political sphere, the dominant bourgeoisie will always be ready to make all sorts of concessions and reforms, depending on the relation of forces. The one thing that it cannot permit itself is to abandon the control of the appropriation of surplus value, that is to say, the control of living work, for wages, that sets in motion and gives a value to the enormous mass of dead, accumulated work that constitutes social capital properly speaking. And wresting away from it the control and the *private* appropriation of surplus value is precisely what the victory of the systems under the hegemony of the Communist parties would mean, whether it be in the long or short run (as historical experience teaches the bourgeoisie). It means nothing to the bourgeoisie that it may lose its power for the benefit of a new bureaucratic class, as exploitative and dominating as itself, and not for the benefit of the overall working collectivity. The only thing that matters to the bourgeoisie is not losing power and, more concretely, not losing the possibility of privately appropriating, as a class, the surplus value of work for wages, which is the source of its power.

But on the other hand the fact that the systems of the East and the West—to continue to use a customary though not very precise terminology—are antagonistic; the fact that in the countries of the East the appropriation of surplus value has ceased to be private and become *public* and *bureaucratic* through the politico-productive apparatus of the Party/State does not do away with the reality of surplus value itself, which continues to be extorted from the wage-earning workers of these countries. It does not do away with the reality of exploitation, of oppression, or the alienation of work for wages. Quite to the contrary: it reinforces it by making it more opaque, more difficult for the consciousness of the masses to grasp.

The fact is that in the countries of private monopoly capitalism the working class enjoys some, albeit a minimum of, democratic freedoms —which the bourgeoisie, for its part, is obliged to accept and respect, and which it even needs (outside of the periods of acute crisis of the system) for the valorization of capital—and these freedoms, although limited, are sufficient for the working class not only to become conscious of the exploitation to which it is subjected, but also to organize and fight against it.

On the other hand, in the countries of capitalism within a bureaucratic state—those countries improperly called "Socialist"—the working class does not enjoy these possibilities. It is not allowed to strike. It can organize itself only in labor unions that are mere transmission belts of the state apparatus and the single party, compared to which the vertical unions of the Franco dictatorship were genuine democratic paradises. The working class of these countries has only two ways out of this dilemma. The first is that of the individual solution—backed by no class solidarity—either through dehumanizing piecework or, on the contrary, through absenteeism, work slowdowns, or sabotage: plagues of the relations of production which are endemic in the countries of the East and can only be explained as silent, stubborn, and desperate class struggle. The second way out is revolt, which is almost always sudden, unforeseen, brutal, and ephemeral.

From the workers' insurrection in East Berlin in June 1953—the news of which took me by surprise during the last days of my first clandestine trip to Spain, raising questions in my mind that I tried to sidestep—to the recent proletarian uprisings in Poland in 1976, the history of the "Socialist" countries is marked periodically by this sort of confrontation between the people and the State that calls itself, with cruel and unintended irony, the State-of-all-the-people. Hundreds of workers' deaths mark off the difficult process of becoming aware of realities, one which has not yet managed to lead to a strategy of genuine rupture. For the working class of the Eastern countries must not only confront the repression of a monolithic state, of a one-party system that suppresses all social mediations, but also be prisoner and victim of an ideology that is forced upon it as being its very own: the ideology-of-Socialism. And the ideology-of-Socialism is the opium of the people.

When the Polish workers in the shipyards on the Baltic, let us say, confront the forces of public order in a simple demonstration for workers' rights; when, driven on by the courage of despair, these workers break through all the police lines and parade their dead on stretchers through cities in open rebellion—thus reinventing the time-hallowed gestures and deeds of the workers' movement—when they burn down the party headquarters, which symbolizes a power that is bureaucratic, alienating, and unjust; when they take over the streets and even local power, they do not know what to do with their victory. They can literally do nothing with this victory, for they are unable to generalize it. As they are prisoners, at least in part, of an ideology and of a system of values according to which they are the masters of power, the dominant class, the living incarnation of Socialism on the march, they find themselves disarmed. They no doubt know, in some vague way at least, that all this is false. They are in reality the class-in-itself, but they do not know this. Nobody, almost nobody, reflects with them, among them, on the totality of their social system, because those who endeavor to do so soon end up in prison or a psychiatric hospital. Nobody, almost nobody, explains to them—and the ideology-of-Socialism makes it difficult for them to explain it to themselves, for them to learn it in the overall experience of their struggles—that they are the class-in-itself, the inert and disarmed producer of surplus value, and that it is necessary for them to transform themselves into a class-for-itself. That it is necessary to forge a class consciousness, to learn that they are exploited by a new system of domination, masked behind the bloody tinsel of the ideology-of-Socialism. How could they possibly conceive, or even dare to think, if only in the form of a chilling paradox, that the restoration of capitalism in their country would be necessary for the dynamics of the class struggle to emerge from the lethargic slumber of ideology and begin to function openly again? How could the restoration of capitalism, in other words the restoration of overt, proclaimed, and therefore modifiable violence of the antagonistic relations of class, today concealed and deformed by the mythology of the worker state—how in the world could this be the objective of a proletarian insurrection?

In any event, the failure of de-Stalinization and the liquidation of the Czechoslovakian experiment have now demonstrated that the system of capitalism of a bureaucratic state cannot be reformed from the top, but must instead be destroyed from the base. This latter solution is practically unthinkable, given the relation of forces. And, in reality, thinking through the social situation of the Eastern countries is equivalent to thinking the apparently unthinkable. What I mean to say is in order to think it through new concepts must be forged. The weapons of criticism and the criticism of weapons must be reinvented. I mean by that the weapons of popular violence. Holy, just, destructive, positive popular violence.

In the final analysis, Fidel Castro was right: "the Party sums it all up."

In it are summed up and concentrated all the negative aspects of the situation, all the obstacles standing in the hypothetical way of a solution. We must have done with Communist parties of the Comintern tradition.

Well and good; why not! You have every reason in the world on your side If one coldly analyzes reality you have every reason in the world on your side But can you coldly analyze the reality of the party? Maybe not But know that you have voiced the objective truth At least partially You have voiced a truth that could be supported by argument and historically explained for many pages more You are not going to back away from this truth It has cost you too much time to arrive at this truth It has cost you too much time to conquer it for you to forget it the moment you've uttered it But this objective truth does not cover the entire reality of the party Or in other words the reality of flesh-and-blood Communists You will remember flesh-and-blood Communists You will always remember

You will always remember Communist fraternity You will remember the strangers who opened the door to you and looked at you a Stranger And you gave the password and they opened the door to you and you entered their lives and you brought the risk of the struggle Of prison perhaps You will remember the unknown militants who incarnated Communist freedom

You will remember "César" Twenty years old He worked in a big metallurgy plant in Madrid You will remember your rendezvous with "César" in the Atocha district He came walking down the main sidewalk of the esplanade and you emerged from the shadow and he laughed and called you "Comrade Chronometer" because you were so punctual And "César" went to prison And you have on your work table two photographs taken in the prison at Cáceres And "César" is there in the courtyard of the prison of Cáceres along with several other militants with the same smile he had back then

You will remember Marina in Barcelona Back in 1962 Her adolescent smile Her serenity full of illusory dreams Her ardent sang-froid

You will remember Antonio Pérez and Pilar Claudín in the Concepción district In Madrid You will remember the lunches shared Hope shared They had known prison in the terrible years They told you about Conesa They have burned up their lives in clandestine work They live covered with the ashes of their souls set on fire

You will remember Manolo López who didn't say one word to the police Whose silence permitted you to go on being free You have already spoken of him in *The Long Voyage* But you called him "Alfredo" then so as not to complicate his life You will call him by his real name now Manolo López

You will remember Ángel González A good poet a good comrade You will remember the refuge that his place on San Juan de la Cruz always was

You will remember Pepe Ortega and his study on the Calle de Teruel In Cuatro Caminos

You will remember Amparo and Gabriel and the apartment on Nieremberg

You will remember Nieves Arrazola and number 94 Ramón de la Cruz

You will remember Eduardo and Pilar on Gaztambide

You will remember number 12 Ferraz, yes you will remember

You will remember Eloy Terrón and his house in Ibiza During your first years in Madrid Eloy helped you find your underground places to live You will remember

You will remember José María and Carola

You will remember Antonio and Madeleine

You will remember Communists One by one You will remember those you name here and those you do not name You will remember those who greet you and those who refuse to greet you You will remember those who remember and you will remember those whose memories are short

You will remember Bertolt Brecht and his *In Praise of Work Underground*

"Step forward
for a moment
you the unknown, the ones hiding behind masks, and receive our grateful greeting
... und empfangt
Unsern Dank!"

You will remember the Communists—no doubt of that!

FOR THE EYES OF THE CENTRAL COMMITTEE ONLY

I put this document I have been commenting upon back in the corresponding folder of my personal files. I also put back all the similar documents containing the written opinions of the members of the Central Committee of the Spanish Communist Party regarding the discussion in the Executive Committee. I bury them in my files once again and doubtless I will never take them out of there again.

I will never read them again. I will never again fall into despair at such intellectual poverty, such servility.

Goodbye forever, comrades.

5 INTERLUDE IN AMPURDÁN

On December 10, 1976 we arrived in Barcelona. It was a Friday. The evening before, Colette and I had been in Madrid to hear Raimon, who was giving a series of recitals.

In Barajas that afternoon, José Ángel Ezcurra, the director of *Triunfo,* approached me in the departure lounge at the airport. We had known each other for years, ever since my "Federico Sánchez" period. Ezcurra was all upset. That very day had seen what certain people referred to as "Carrillo's putsch." That is to say, Santiago Carrillo had held his first public press conference since his clandestine return to Spain.

We took our seats in the plane to Barcelona and Ezcurra kept repeating to me what he had been told by César Alonso de los Ríos, who had been present at the famous press conference. Over the next few days, an attentive reading of the preliminary declaration made by Carrillo that day, as well as his replies to journalists' questions, confirmed the impression I received from Ezcurra, even though it was secondhand. Apart from Carrillo's tactical cleverness at manipulating the mass media and his sense of the sensational, the content properly speaking of his declarations was yet another proof of the traditional errors of analysis and perspective that characterized the entire politics of the Spanish Communist Party during those months.

In Barcelona that night, we got together with Ricardo Muñoz Suay.

If I had told this story of Federico Sánchez in chronological order, which is presumably God's own way of writing a story, if we may take the structural model of Genesis as proof of His Divine Will in this respect, Ricardo would have made his appearance in these lines some time ago. For Ricardo was one of Federico Sánchez's oldest comrades underground in Madrid. But I have not written this story in chronological order, perhaps because I am not God, perhaps because nothing bores me so much as biblical models and the fallacious reconstruction of a life from the beginning to the end, perhaps because life has neither a beginning nor an end, even though it has beginnings and ends. In any event, I have begun to write this story by beginning at the end, at the very moment in which the diatribe La Pasionaria is about to deliver will cast Federico Sánchez into the obscure oblivion of outer darkness. That is why Ricardo makes his appearance so late in this story, though he has been familiar with it since its very beginnings.

So then, we were with Ricardo and Nieves that night, deeply involved as usual in disentangling the threads of the tales that memory tells. I do not deny that our conversations may well bear a certain resemblance to a meeting of war veterans. We then went to Alberto Puig Palau's to have a drink.

I don't know if the railroad station in Perpignan is the most important place in the universe, its spiritual epicenter, as poor Salvador Dali one day claimed. But my first meeting with Alberto took place in front of the Perpignan station. It was in February of 1959. There had been a ceremony in homage to Antonio Machado in Collioure. A large group of artists and writers had come from Barcelona and Madrid to attend it. Many others, who were unable to leave Spain, had met together in Segovia, where Pedro Laín Entralgo and Dionisio Ridruejo spoke. It was Dionisio, in fact, who had first spoken to me of Alberto Puig Palau and the days when *Revista* was being published.

So then, we were at Alberto Puig Palau's on that Friday, December 10, and Francesc Vicens had come to join us. When I first met Vicens, many years earlier, in exile in Paris, he was going by the name of Ferrán, or else Joan Berenguer. He was a member of the Excutive Committee of the PSUC.

If we were in a novel, I might be told that the sudden appearance of Vicens is merely a clever narrative device. But we are not in a novel. We are at Alberto Puig Palau's, on December 10, 1976, the day that Carrillo held his first press conference, and it is quite true that the doorbell rang and in came Francesc Vicens. In a novel, of course, such a coincidence would seem odd. It would appear to be just a bit arbitrary that there should enter the room on that very day, at this precise point in the narrative, the one Communist leader who in the year 1964 was not swayed by the campaign launched in the Spanish Communist Party and the PSUC against Claudín and Sánchez. The only leader who held to the norms laid down by Lenin, in 1921 and previously referred to, for moments of dissension and crisis in the party. The only one who dared gather his own information, at his own risk and peril, concerning the real content of the discussions within the leadership of the Spanish Communist Party, the only one who made his decisions on the basis of calm personal study of the basic issues at stake. In other words, if Lenin is right when he says that in periods of dissension and profound crisis within the party "he who takes another at his word is a perfect imbecile of whom nothing can be expected," Vicens (or Ferrán, or Berenguer) was the one Communist leader who was not an imbecile, according to Lenin's definition, for whatever it is worth, though I venture to presume that it is worth as much as a definition by Carrillo.

I have on my work table the document that Joan Berenguer addressed to the Executive Committee of the PSUC on October 15, 1964, with the aim of making his position clear. The last section of this document is entitled "Las divergencias en el Partido y los métodos para su resolución" ("The divergencies in the Party and the methods of resolving them"). It states:

In the meeting of the Executive Committee of the PSUC from the 8th to the 10th of September I expressed my disagreement with the following paragraph of the Declaration on the positions of Fernando Claudín and Federico Sánchez:

The supporters of opportunistic theses merely revive, in other words and in other conditions, the old reformist positions combatted by Lenin when they maintain that the Party must resign itself to the continuation of power in the hands of the oligarchy, board the "train" of "liberalization," adapt themselves to a situation in which workers and bosses are going to "enjoy" together the "advantages" of "modern neocapitalism."

Not only do F. Claudín and F. Sánchez not support this position, but to my knowledge no one in the Party supports it.

In the discussions we had subsequently, at the beginning of October, I added my strongest possible protest against the new tactics being adopted by the Executive Committee of the Spanish Communist Party for informing militants of the divergencies that have arisen.

As an example of the methods being employed, there could be cited the recent meeting of 600 militants, at which Santiago Álvarez read a report. In this meeting, a member of the Secretariat of the Union of Communist Youth said that F. Claudín and F. Sánchez "deny class struggle." Santiago Álvarez not only failed to rectify this untruth but joined in the general applause that greeted this speech. Another comrade (of the Southern Federation) said that FC and FS "disavow the working class and the people" and that they "have betrayed the working class and its courageous sacrifices." In the face of this Santiago Álvarez adopted the same attitude as with the comrade from the Communist Youth. Santiago Álvarez himself, in his final summation, said (referring to the comrades that had been sent to Spain by FC): "I don't know whether the life and the blood of those comrades matters to Claudín," and in answer to the question as to who was paying the expenses of the discussion, he said that objectively the positions of FC and FS aided the enemy and added: "Subjectively, we cannot say that it is Fraga [Manuel Fraga Iribarne, Minister of Information] who is paying them. They have collected their salaries from the party this month, and as yet they don't need to collect from anybody else."

I would like to find a proper word (crude distortions, lies, etc.) to characterize these methods in which the militants are being informed of the positions of FC and FS. I believe that the least that can be said is that this is not a Leninist method.

Vicens, alias Joan Berenguer, then refers in considerable detail to Lenin's texts of 1921 and the era of the Tenth Congress of the Russian party on the methods to be followed in times of crisis. And he concludes in these words:

> Instead of something that would resemble these methods, what has been done among us in response to the present divergencies has been the following:
> • Exclusion from the Executive Committee of the two members who remained in the minority.
> • Publication in the Declaration of June of an odious caricature of their positions.
> • Reports to the militants, at various meetings, on the positions of FC and FS, crudely distorting them.
> • Appeals to the militants, in these meetings, to pronounce themselves in favor of the exclusion of FC and FS from the Central Committee (naturally a pronouncement by the militants under these conditions has no value whatsoever, since they find themselves obliged to express an opinion not on what is said by the leaders in the minority, but on a vastly distorted version of what they say).
> Finally, I wish to allude to the accusation of factional activity leveled against FC and FS. I believe that the facts are these:
> The majority of the Executive Committee distorts the positions of FC and FS to the militants.
> Following this, FC and FS, who remained in the minority on the Executive Committee and were excluded from it, explain their real positions to the militants who question them on the subject.
> Where is the factional activity?
> If the majority of the Executive Committee had correctly explained the positions defended by FC and FS, opening a discussion in accordance with Leninist methods, we would not now find ourselves in the present situation.

With these words Joan Berenguer ended an extensive document of analysis and discussion addressed to the Executive Committee of the PSUC and dated October 15, 1964.

A year later, during an assembly of militants, Gregorio López Raimundo indirectly answered this argument presented by Berenguer, who had meanwhile been expelled from the party.

"The PSU has been," Gregorio López Raimundo said in October 1965, "and still is the target of factional activity undertaken by Fernando Claudín and Federico Sánchez, who have counted from the beginning on the collaboration of Juan Berenguer and certain other militants of the

PSU who, having lost confidence in the inevitability of the victory of Communism, wish the Party to renounce revolutionary struggle, transform its nature, or disappear."

(It will be noted how many inanities poor Gregorio—or rather, Gregori, as he has taken to calling himself, perhaps to reinforce, semantically, the national character of the PSUC—manages to pile up in just a few words. He says that we have lost confidence in the "inevitability of the victory of Communism." But who has any confidence in this inevitability? No Marxist, certainly. The only thing that is inevitable, according to Marxism, is class struggle, but neither the forms nor the results of this struggle are inevitably inscribed in any sacred book. Precisely because the victory of Communism is *not* inevitable, the organization of the proletariat becomes necessary. Consequently, accusing us of wanting to transform the nature of the party, or even to cause it to disappear since we have lost confidence in the inevitability of Communism, is a sign of dangerous mental debility, of an inability, at least, to use language logically. It is in fact only blind confidence in the inevitability of Communism that would explain why the existence of a proletarian party should cease to be considered necessary).

But let us return to López Raimundo's text.

The Executive Committee of the PSU has explained to the Party the factional activities of Juan Berenguer that were responsible for his expulsion. Juan Berenguer, who had been coopted to the Central Committee of the PSU at the Fourth Plenum of the Central Committee, continued to maintain relations of intimate friendship with Fernando Claudín and Federico Sánchez. In personal conversations, outside the regular Party leadership meetings, Fernando Claudín, Federico Sánchez, and Juan Berenguer devoted themselves for some time to setting up a revisionist political platform contrary to the Party. When Claudín and Sánchez went on to openly attack the political line, nature, and discipline of the Party, Juan Berenguer concealed the identity of his views with those of the factionalists, even going so far as to vote for the August 1964 resolution of the Executive Committee of the PSU in which the position adopted by Fernando Claudín and Federico Sánchez was implicitly condemned. But when these latter were formally excluded from the Central Committee of the Spanish Communist Party, Juan Berenguer began to carry on open factional activities against the Party leadership and provoked in the Executive Committee of the PSU the discussion that Claudín and Sánchez had previously provoked in the Executive Committee and in the Central Committee of the Spanish Communist Party.

Once the factional activity of Juan Berenguer was discovered, the Executive Committee suspended him temporarily from his functions and brought the problem before the Central Committee, which unanimously approved the decisions of the Executive Committee and enjoined Juan Berenguer to abandon his factional activity and respect the discipline of the Party. Since Juan Berenguer rejected this exhortation and reaffirmed his decision to continue collaborating with the factional group of Claudín and Sánchez, he was expelled from the Party.

This text, of course, merits a juicy and jocose commentary, for it is typical of a certain political style. I shall limit myself to emphasizing its most curious features. In the first place, Berenguer is accused of having always had "relations of intimate friendship with Fernando Claudín and Federico Sánchez." It is well known that "intimate friendship" between Communists is a crime. Or rather, what is a crime is "intimate friendship" with leaders who are not in accord with the opinions of the majority. If Berenguer had been more cautious and established his relations of "intimate friendship" with Carrillo and Líster, let us say, this "intimate friendship" would not have been a crime, but a proof of Berenguer's sterling Bolshevik character. It is then added—oh horrors!—that Berenguer engaged in "personal conversations" with those who were banned. Personal conversations between Communists! *Vade retro!* Personal conversations are prohibited! But during his years as a leader of the PSUC, Berenguer no doubt had, as is only to be expected, personal conversations with many other leaders of the Spanish Communist Party. But these were not prohibited. These were sacred and all to the good. Let us also observe that if we are to believe López Raimundo's description, Berenguer was a terrible "factional element." In point of fact, he was a babe in the woods when it came to "factional activity." He still had everything to learn in this domain. As it happened, the only thing he could think of was to wait for Claudín and Sánchez to be formally expelled from the Central Committee of the Spanish Communist Party, that is to say to wait until the worst conditions had come about, in order to carry on "open factional activities." It would have been to Berenguer's advantage to take a little course in "factionalism" before plunging into such a mad adventure, such a quixotic undertaking. And I have the impression that Santiago Carrillo and Gregorio López Raimundo would have been good teachers of "factionalism." They are thoroughly acquainted with the mechanisms of this sort of activity. If Comorera had not died, he too could have furnished some interesting lessons in this regard. But to end this long string of false statements in López Raimundo's text on a high note, we are told that "Juan Berenguer's factional activity was discovered." But just a few lines before hadn't it been stated that this factional activity was "open"? How can what is "open" be "discovered"? If Berenguer's activity was open, there was no need for it to be discovered: it was no secret from the very start.

In reality Berenguer's entire process of reflection, which slowly led him to question the statements of the leadership of the Spanish Communist Party regarding our case, began on April 19, 1964.

We were in Calella de Palafrugell on Saturday, December 11, 1976. The beach was deserted, the sea calm. A slightly overcast sky turned the sunshine on the landscape gray.

Then when night fell, after exploring Ampurdán—La Bisbal and Sant Miquel de Cruilles, Peratallada and Ullastret, Pals and Torroella de Montgrí—we shut ourselves up inside Vicens's house, the former rectory of Fontanilles. There, in front of a wood fire, the phantoms of a past that refuses to die began to emerge.

It was Vicens who reminded me of the meeting of April 19, 1964, which he had attended.

That day, before a large group of militants—close to a thousand Communists gathered together there in Stains, one of the municipalities in the Paris suburbs with a French Communist Party administration—Santiago Carrillo gave a speech that caused quite a stir.

The plenary session of the Executive Committee of the Spanish Communist Party in the castle of Bohemian kings had ended a few days before. The two of us, Claudín and Sánchez, had been temporarily suspended from the Executive Committee, as we waited for the Central Committee to render its verdict on the central issues of the discussion after examining the minutes of the plenary session. On April 19, before the members of the Central Committee had even had a chance to receive these minutes, Carrillo launched a general, public offensive against our positions, or rather, against a grossly distorted version of our positions, which were described as "revisionist," "capitulatory," and so on. No doubt Carrillo's attack on certain opinions within the party gave the appearance of being of a general nature: we were not named personally. But the identity of the accused was an open secret. In the first place, we were the only members of the Executive Committee who were not present at the meeting, since we had not been invited to it or even informed that there would be one, so as to avoid, I think, giving us a chance to address the militants and refute Carrillo's false statements. Moreover, the party cadres took it upon themselves to spread the word, to mention by name the anonymous deviationists against whom Carrillo was about to launch forth. In other words, the meeting on April 19 constituted an open violation of what had been stipulated by the majority of the Executive Committee itself.

But even though this was serious enough in itself, it was not the worst part. The worst part was the content of Carrillo's speech.

To attempt to analyze this content immediately presents a problem of textual variation. The fact is that I have in my possession three versions, each of them slightly different. I have, on the one hand, the official version, precisely as it was published, in the form of a brochure for massive distribution to rank-and-file members of the party. I have, secondly, a typed version, with corrections in Carrillo's own hand. As it happened, three days after this meeting of militants, Claudín and I sent, on April 22, a letter of protest to the party leadership, based on information that eyewitnesses had provided us. Moreover, I requested a personal meeting with Carrillo, which he granted me. I went to his house in Champigny and demanded an explanation of the meaning of his speech. Carrillo jesuitically assured me that he had not distorted our positions in any way whatsoever, that he had limited himself to a general exposition of the party's political line. In order to prove his *bona fides,* he gave me the typed copy of his text referred to above. "Read it yourself," he said to me, "and don't listen to what ill-intentioned witnesses may tell you." I read it, of course, and it was even worse than what I had imagined from what the comrades had told me.

Besides these two texts, I have in my possession the magnetic tape containing the original recording of Carrillo's speech. This magnetic tape had been handed over to a young and brilliant university professor—an outstanding member of the PSUC, who was working at the time in the central propaganda bureau—so that he could prepare an LP recording from it to be distributed within the party. Because of the poor quality of the original recording on the tape, it was impossible to make this 33 LP record. Some time later, when that young and brilliant university professor entered into conflict with the leadership of the PSUC—in which he now has important functions again, after having gone through a long period of "leftist" experimentation—he came to me with the original tape, which nobody had ever asked him to return. It is therefore in my personal files and not in the archives of the Spanish Communist Party, owing to this series of fortuitous circumstances.

From time to time during these years, no doubt owing to that "masochism typical of a petty-bourgeois intellectual" of which Carrillo had one day accused me to my face, I have listened to this April 19th speech. Reading a speech and listening to it are two different things of course. The printed page does not reproduce Carrillo's demagogic tone, his sectarian, victory-trumpeting violence, the hatred that certain phrases exude. There is no doubt that this original recording of his speech of April 19, 1964 is an important and significant document. Historians interested in that period in the life of the party may consult it if they wish.

But naturally I am not going to make a complete philological study if the different variants of this speech. I shall limit myself to underlining some of the most curious ones.

On taking up the question of the international relations of Spain and the specific problem of diplomatic relations with the Soviet Union, Carrillo stated: "Spain stands in need of these relations, but what is the obstacle, what is the difficulty? *Mundo Obrero* explained in an editorial a few weeks ago: the obstacle standing in the way of establishing relations with Spain is Francoism. And those who present relations between the Soviet Union and Spain as an accomplished fact are mistaken [*loud applause*]; these relations are not established [*applause*]. And they are not established because there is Franco; and Franco today is an obstacle standing in the way of Spain, in the way of the interests not only of the people, but of all levels of Spanish Society."

And after these lines, which are common to all three versions, including the original direct recording, the variations begin.

The printed text of the official brochure states: "Comrades: the Soviet Union will not take any step that is not an aid to the democratic struggle of the Spanish people . . . [*Loud and prolonged applause that makes the end of the sentence inaudible*]"

As for the typed text that Carrillo himself gave me, it states: "Comrades: I can assure you that the Soviet Union will not establish relations with Spain without consulting the democratic and anti-Franco forces. . . ." But this phrase is struck out in the typed text, and the sentence cited above is inserted.

On listening to the original tape recording, one discovers that Carrillo's actual statement was different from either of the two just quoted. Carrillo can be heard to say the following: "Comrades: I can assure you that the Soviet Union will not establish relations with Spain so long as it is not authorized by the Central Committee of the [Spanish Communist] Party. . . . " And the applause does in fact prevent the end of the sentence from being heard distinctly.

Carrillo's formulation here is, naturally, sheer demagoguery, mere swaggering. But what is more, it is extraordinarily stupid. If it is the Central Committee of the Spanish Communist Party that decides on the relations of the Soviet Union with Spain, if the Brazilian party, let us say, decides on the Russian relations with Brazil, and so on, the result will be that Russian foreign policy will be determined by the central committees of eighty-some Communist parties, which is absurd. The result will be that the Soviet Union will have no foreign policy. But this stupid statement, this demagogic boasting by Carrillo, goes over very well in a mass meeting. It is a striking formula, a resounding bit of rhetoric.

It is well known that despite all the years that have passed, Carrillo is still fond of rhetorical effects. During the press conference on December 10, 1976, in fact, just the day before Vicens and I were harking back on long-ago episodes of our prehistory, Carrillo returned to the theme of diplomatic relations with the Soviet Union. In his preliminary declaration opening the press conference he states: "Our sense of responsibility leads us—and I am here announcing it for the first time—to say through you journalists, to the Communist parties in power in the countries of Eastern Europe, and also to our Mexican friends, that from this moment on the Spanish Communist Party withdraws its opposition to the establishment of diplomatic relations between their countries and ours."

Here, of course, Carrillo reached the height of the ridiculous. His declaration is a real clown act. For at this juncture neither Mexico nor the countries of Eastern Europe were awaiting Carrillo's authorization to establish relations with Spain. Carrillo meant nothing to them, and these relations had already been decided upon or were in the process of being established. Carrillo's clown act reminds me of the well-known phrase of one of Cocteau's characters: *Puisque ces mystères nous dépassent, feignons de les avoir organisés. . . .* " ["Since these mysteries are beyond our understanding, let us pretend that we are the ones who staged them. . . ."]

But we are in Fontanilles, at nightfall, in front of a wood fire burning in the studio fireplace.

Vicens and I have been silent for several long minutes, thinking our own thoughts, lost in the trackless wasteland of memory. The fact is that as we harked back on that meeting of April 19, the memory of Julián Grimau had also come to mind.

The most indecent thing about that meeting of militants on April 19, 1964, in the course of which Carrillo inaugurated the hunt for revisionist witches, was that it was organized so as to fall on the anniversary of Grimau's execution. Carrillo deliberately took advantage of the emotional atmosphere that this anniversary would naturally create among the Communist militants to launch his slanderous attack on us. In order that legitimate feelings of emotion would disturb the militants' capacity for rational thought, Carrillo purposely began his speech by saying: "Comrades: because of the date of this gathering and the political importance of the tragic event that this date evokes, we cannot open this meeting without calling to mind the noble and now historic figure of Julián Grimau, and his martydom and murder by Francoist torturers." Deliberately, indecently, Santiago Carrillo raised on high the death of Grimau, made a banner of his dead body, in order to dull the critical spirit of the militants.

But neither Santiago Carrillo nor any of the other leaders sitting with him on the speakers' platform at this meeting had the right to evoke the memory of Grimau, since they were indirectly responsible for his death.

One year before, on Friday, April 19, 1963, Fernando Claudín telephoned me, around ten p.m. The meeting of the Council of Ministers presided over by Franco had just confirmed the death sentence that had been decreed for Julián Grimau. Fernando was calling me from an office of the Secours populaire français, where he had called together a certain number of comrades in a desperate attempt to alert public opinion one last time and secure some sort of last-minute intervention on the part of personages who had already shown interest in the Grimau case. Fernando told me that he was sending a car for me so that I could go get Carrillo, whose address was known only by a very small handful of comrades. I was one of these.

When I arrived at Champigny-sur-Marne, in front of the little two-story house where Carrillo lived with his family, I found the garden gate closed and all the lights out. It was plain to see that everyone in the house had already gone to bed. I nonetheless rang the doorbell, loudly and repeatedly.

With me was René, the French comrade who at the time was the driver of the party car that had been put at Carrillo's disposal and who also served the latter as his liaison man. He had no official post, he was totally anonymous in the public hierarchy of the French Communist Party, but he had always been entrusted with confidential missions, as a member of that invisible apparatus that works in the shadows even in countries where the party is legal. In the thirties, René had worked with Fried, the Czech comrade delegated by the Comintern to keep an eye on the political activity of the nucleus of French Communist Party leaders. Fried, as is today well known, was one of those men who most effectively contributed to the liquidation in Western Europe of the ultrasectarian and ultraleftist policy of the third period of the Stalinized Comintern, the policy that rendered the victory of Fascism in Germany so much easier. Many of the ideas that eventually crystallized in the strategy of the Popular Front in France, which the French Communists now attribute to Thorez for the sake of appearing as an autonomous party, no doubt came from Fried. During the Second World War Fried installed himself underground in Brussels. He died there in 1943, mysteriously murdered. Someone rang the doorbell of his apartment, he came to the door, and his assassins shot him dead at point-blank range with a machine gun. If his murderers were German Gestapo agents, as a number of Communist historians claim today, their behavior is inexplicable. The Germans would have wanted to take Fried alive in order to interrogate him. Moreover if Fried, or "Clément," to call him by his *nom de guerre,* had been murdered by the Germans, official Communist propaganda would have presented him as a hero after the war. But that was not what happened. In Fried's case, the official Communist propaganda versions of the affair have been so discreet as to border on a game of playing deaf and dumb. All of this leads one to presume that Fried's murderers were most likely agents of Stalin's secret police. This conclusion was solidly argued by Philippe Robrieux in his exciting biography of Maurice Thorez.

Fried's murder, in fact, is perfectly consistent with Stalinist logic. I am referring not only to the logic of Stalin himself, but to the logic of an entire power system in general, of which Stalin was at once the creator and the product. A system of this type needs to remake history constantly so as to adjust it to the tactical necessities of the political moment. Hence the worst enemy of this system is authentic testimony. A lucid and critical memory is the worst enemy of this pragmatic and arbitrary history manufactured by men who have conveniently lost their memories. By assassinating Trotsky—using for the purpose the hand of Ramón Mercader, a young militant of the PSUC, of whom Gregorio López Raimundo will perhaps talk to us someday if and when he wakes up with his memory intact—Stalin not only assassinated a dangerous political adversary. He also assassinated the memory of the revolution. Throughout his death-dealing life, Stalin eliminated possible witnesses, those who would perhaps not have been willing to lose their memories. Fried could well have been one of them.

But Stalin is not an exception. He is, particularly in this regard, the prototype of all Communist leaders. They all have a horror of true memory. To convince oneself of this one need only read their memoirs. Those of the Frenchman Jacques Duclos and of the Spaniard La Pasionaria, let us say. We need only read *Dialogue on Spain,* by Santiago Carrillo, when he takes up historical or biographical problems. There is a difference, nonetheless, between Stalin and these other leaders. It lies in the fact that these latter do not have, and have never had, at their disposal the absolute power that Stalin enjoyed. They are not in a position to liquidate all witnesses, to totally destroy that memory that would allow the historical truth to be reconstructed.

On that warm night of April 19, 1963, as I was insistently ringing the bell at the gate in the fence protecting the little garden of Carrillo's house, I was not thinking about all this, of course. I have just thought of all this now, fourteen years later, on writing of my memory of that warm spring night in April that came back to me at Fontanilles as I was talking with

Francesc Vicens of that night on which the news reached us of the confirmation of the death sentence against Julián Grimau. That night in April, in Champigny-sur-Marne, I was thinking neither of Fried, nor of Stalin, nor of any such thing. I was ringing the bell at Carrillo's garden gate, casting wary glances out of the corner of my eye at the dark, silent Avenue Roger Salengro.

It is common knowledge today that Carrillo lived in that house for many long years. There have been articles, photographs, touching commentaries on it in the mass media of many different countries, of many different political persuasions. We even know how many boxes it took Carmen Menéndez to bring all the books that her husband had in this house back to Madrid. But at the time that I am talking about, there were very few of us who knew where Carrillo's clandestine domicile was. A mere handful of comrades. And that was why I cast wary glances out of the corner of my eye at this deserted, silent stretch of the Avenue Roger Salengro. It would not have been advisable to arouse the attention of some policeman on night duty or some overly curious neighbor.

So I stood there ringing the bell at Carrillo's house, tormented by the idea that we might have been able to avoid Grimau's arrest and consequently the death penalty that hung over his head on this April night that threatened to be endless.

A year before, during the spring and summer of 1962, I had been working, for my last time in Madrid, with Julián Grimau and Romero Marín. Julián, who had lived for a while in the place on Concepción Bahamonde that I had occupied for a little over a year, had already moved in with Manolo and Maria A., two married comrades who had rented an apartment in their name on another street in the same neighborhood, on Pedro Heredia. This was, it will be remembered, the time of the great strike actions that began in Asturias and spread like a tidal wave all over Spain. Exactly the proper moment to realize that the *Aitch En Pee* and the *Aitch Gee Pee* were mythological objectives: if we had not managed to get them under way in the circumstances that obtained in the spring of 1962, the fact was that they were impossible.

In that period I had become aware of a recent, and increasing, propensity of Grimau's toward imprudence and haste in his work methods. He spent too many hours a day outside on the street between one rendezvous and another, for example. In addition to the dangers that this can give rise to when it happens systematically, it was quite likely that Grimau had hardly any time left to reflect on political problems and the lessons to be drawn from his own work, matters to which he had devoted quite a bit more of his time during the first period of his stay in Madrid. Moreover, as though this were not enough, Grimau had the most unfortunate habit of making direct and personal contact with irregular Communist groups, groups that had burned their bridges with the organization for one reason or another and that kept cropping up here and there in fair numbers around that time. The moment someone would point out to Grimau the existence of one or another of these groups and the names and addresses of some of its members, he would be off down the street, presenting himself at the doorstep of these comrades who'd broken with the party. However rash we were, and we were admittedly altogether rash, this was madness, or at any rate utterly unthinking, since Grimau was a member of the Central Committee and therefore responsible for ensuring the continuity of party work. How dangerous this habit of Grimau's was soon became clear: it was an informer who had infiltrated one of these irregular groups who gave him away to the police.

It will be said in reply, perhaps, that this defect of Grimau's was the other side of the coin of his complete dedication to his work, of his combative spirit. Doubtless. But it was above all the direct consequence of the leadership's erroneous conception of the duration and rhythms of the struggle, of the weakness of Franco's dictorship, which according to the party's analyses was always on the verge of falling apart. It was above all the consequence of our overconfidence in imminent triumph, of our vanity, of our subjectivism. Grimau was yet another victim of the subjectivism of the Spanish Communist Party.

On a number of occasions I pointed out to Grimau the need for a radical change in his work methods. I remember one of these times especially.

It was on Manuel Becerra, in front of the church, in the summer of 1962. Ramón Ormazábal and other comrades of the provincial committee of Vizcaya had just been arrested in Bilbao. I had a rendezvous with Julián there on Manuel Becerra: we were to meet at two in the afternoon to discuss some routine matter that could be settled in just a few minutes. I suppose that Grimau, who had chosen the time and the place himself, no doubt planned to go home to his place on Pedro Heredia, quite close by, immediately thereafter. He was no doubt planning to have lunch there. Maria A. would perhaps have made veal scallopini. Perhaps she had prepared a salad with one of her superb dressings. It was now five minutes after two. I changed places, went off to buy a newspaper, and came back to the spot where we were to rendezvous.

I had met Grimau some ten years before, in 1953, when I began to work underground in Spain as head of a mission reporting to the Central Committee. In Paris between trips I took part in the meetings of the Commission of the Interior, headed by Carrillo. Grimau was also a member of this commission, as were Romero Marín, Eduardo García,

Antonio Gros, Miguel Núñez, Abelardo Gimeno, Serrán, Freile, Víctor Velasco and perhaps this or that other comrade whose name I do not remember.

During the meetings of the Commission of the Interior, Grimau would chain-smoke. He seldom spoke up, and when he did it was almost always concerning small details, technical problems of the trips, suitcases with false bottoms, and very seldom concerning the content itself of the political questions raised. I remember that Carrillo was rather hard on him. He never forgave him the least little error, the slightest fault in his work. "If only Julian would stop to think instead of disappearing behind the smoke of that cigarette he's always got in his mouth," I remember Carrillo's often saying. Grimau never said a word in answer to Carrillo's criticisms, frequently expressed in a bitter, personal, almost insulting tone. He would lower his head and give in. I had noticed this strange relation of domination-submission between the two of them. But it never crossed my mind to wonder what the reasons for it were. It had something to do with happenings in the past, I supposed. And the past didn't interest me particularly. Or rather, I had put it between parentheses once and for all. The secrets that all these men must have shared since the Civil War did not interest me. Quite obviously, something like a defensive reflex, a self-defensive reflex, inclined me not to be too interested in what were perhaps murky secrets of the past. Nevertheless I noticed, from the beginning, the strange savageness on Carrillo's part, and the strange submissiveness on Grimau's, which set a very particular seal on their relationship; the odd thing was that this apparently did not strain their friendship, for the two of them were otherwise extremely close.

But on Manuel Becerra it is now 2:10.

Ten minutes is not a long time. But ten minutes can be an eternity. When one is waiting for a comrade, ten minutes can be an eternity of anxiety. I suppose that my reader knows what I mean. It is not that I was afraid of what might happen to me. I think I may safely say, quite objectively, that I have never been afraid of what might happen to me. I think I have enough witnesses of what I am maintaining about myself here, without vanity, so as to make the story I am telling clear. What is agonizing, when one is waiting for a comrade who is late, is the idea of what may have happened to *him.* One imagines the worst. For the worst is always imaginable. It is always possible.

Suddenly I hear a voice right next to me: "Do you have the time, please?" I turn around: it is a very young girl with dark hair. She stares straight at me and the look in her eyes sends a shiver down my spine. It is a piercing, transparent look, an almost inhuman stare, from unblinking eyes. It is a look filled with obscure warnings, awakening very old nocturnal obsessions of mine. It suddenly seems to me that I am the protagonist of one of Gustavo Adolfo Bécquer's stories that my father used to read us when we were little, and that it is death that is staring at me.

But the sun is shining; it is summer. I make the best of an uncomfortable situation, smile, and answer: "It's ten minutes after two, señorita." The "señorita" has been added of course to keep my distance. But the eyes of this dark-haired girl—the green eyes of this girl who in reality looks like most any other relatively pretty young *Madrileña*—drill right through me. She is furious. "What's that you say?" she almost shouts. "That it's ten minutes after two," I repeat, as calmly as possible. "What do you mean?—you haven't even looked at your watch! How do you know what time it is without looking at your watch?" she screams. And it is true that I haven't even glanced at my watch. I can't help laughing —and I can't explain to her that I don't need to look at my watch to know what time it is, that I have the exact minute marked right between my eyebrows, right in my heart, in the pit of my stomach, in every drop of my blood, that every second that goes by without Grimau appearing is like a burning-hot sliver of coal plunging into my veins. I can't tell her why I know what time it is without even looking at my watch. I hold out my left arm so that she can see for herself by my watch that I'm not fooling her, that it is indeed exactly 2:10. Or, rather, 2:12 by now. She looks at my watch, sees that I've told her the right time, and walks on with a shrug of her shoulders, not even thanking me.

I have decided not to wait any longer, and am about to leave. But at that very moment Grimau appears, almost at a run, all out of breath. With a lighted cigarette in his mouth, as usual.

There at the entrance to the Calle Ramón de la Cruz, it seems to me that the dark-haired girl has turned around for a second and is looking at us. But maybe it's just my nerves.

Grimau explains to me that he's just been to another rendezvous, that he's underestimated the time it would take to get from there to here. The usual excuses, in short. But I tell Grimau that I don't accept his excuse. Not so much because he was late, which is not important since nothing has happened, but because of what it signified. I tell him in no uncertain terms that a party leader cannot be out on the street for hours and hours sniffing around between one rendezvous and another like a hound dog. I tell him that I will have to raise the question of his work methods in the Executive Committee, because if he goes on in this way, the day he least expects it he's going to fall into a trap.

Julián nods his head, smiles at me, puts a hand on my shoulder, says don't be mad, don't make such a big thing of it, man, please, Fede; every one of the rendezvous he's had that morning was important. In a word, the usual thing.

In the next meeting the three of us had—Romero Marín, Grimau, and I—at Grimau's place surely, on Pedro Heredia, I brought this question up again. Romero Marín and Julián listened to me without saying a word. They seemed irritated at my having spoken up, and determined not to pay any attention to what I'd said. When you came right down to it, who was I to give them advice? I was Federico Sánchez, yes, a regular member of the Executive Committee, and what was more, responsible for the coordination of our work in Madrid. Romero Marín at the time was an acting member of the Executive Committee. He had not been named a regular member at the Sixth Congress of the Spanish party, in 1960, because of an infraction he had committed of the security rules, no less, a short time before. Through a series of circumstances that are beside the point here, the French police had broken into the apartment of Romero Marín's girl friend in Paris and had found some of his papers, easily decipherable manuscript notes, with certain details on the organization and names of comrades in intellectual circles in Madrid. Romero Marín had no doubt forgotten to destroy these notes after some meeting or other. For that reason he was not made a regular member of the Executive Committee at the Sixth Congress. As for Grimau, he was a member of the Central Committee. In other words, if I may be permitted to use bureaucratic language just this once, simply in order that what I am recounting will make sense, Federico Sánchez was the superior of both of them in the hierarchy of the organization. Fine. But Sánchez had not fought in the Civil War. Sánchez didn't know the secrets of the period of exile. Sánchez had not worked in the clandestine apparatus of the party in the hard, hard years of the guerrilla campaigns. To make a long story short, the two of them listened to Sánchez, not saying a word, and no doubt wondered why I was sticking my nose in their business. They knew more about how to work underground than I did.

They listened to me, they said nothing, they were determined not to pay any attention to my warnings.

Personally, the question of methods of organization had been preying on my mind for some time. More than two years before, at our Sixth Congress in 1960, I had brought up a number of problems regarding the organization of the party. My speech was published in a special issue of *Nuestra Bandera,* in March 1960. In this speech I tried to set forth some of my preoccupations, some of the critical opinions I had with regard to the habitual work system of the clandestine leaders of the party.

I quote word for word what I said at that time:

In these last years, the method of organization and leadership most widely used has been the one that you will permit me to define now as the *system of contacts.*

Around a small group of comrade leaders, many of whom, if not all, are obliged to carry on their activities amid conditions of the most rigorous clandestinity, an entire network of individual contacts has been created, with comrades of various places of employment, neighborhoods, villages. This network of individual contacts has obliged the Communist leaders to keep up a veritable unending chain of rendezvous and interviews.

In times of intense party activity, which are, happily, extremely frequent, this succession of rendezvous, interviews, and contacts could lead to, and in fact has led to, numerous responsible cadres taking on six, eight, and even ten rendezvous per day; this entails risks and more or less prevents the comrade leaders from studying the problems related to their work, from posing the concrete questions of the application of the party's political line to local situations. Furthermore, since the party organization has been growing and broadening, the network of contacts has also been growing and has become self-multiplying.

The drawbacks and negative features of the *system of contacts* seem apparent. In the first place, it is obvious that during the short time of a contact political problems cannot be discussed seriously, in depth. These contacts are limited to a mere interchange of information and opinions, to a simple transmission of general orientations, and, for that very reason, usually abstract ones.

In the second place, the *system of contacts,* independently of the will of the comrades, impedes the development of the organization and the raising of its political level. This is true for various reasons. It makes it difficult for the party to incorporate the young worker revolutionaries, the unorganized young Communists who now number in the tens of thousands in our country. The contacts, being necessarily established with comrades who are already known, are usually those with police records, which restricts, objectively and subjectively, their mobility, their ability to accelerate the massive entry into the party of new revolutionary forces. The *system of contacts* fragments the real possibilities of action by the base; it is not rare to find cases in which we have had, in a given establishment, or in a given geographical location, half a dozen contacts, or even more; this does not mean, however, that we had a real organization.

And above all, the *system of contacts* makes the political life of party groups precarious, both as regards the discussion and study of concrete questions and as regards the continuity of party activity. The *system of contacts* does not stimulate initiative from the base, from the local cadres; it slows down the vivifying, indispensable current that must flow from the base to the summit of the party; it causes this current to be, almost always, unilateral: the contact usually presents himself only to report what information he has and find out what the comrade from "above" is "bringing," and the comrade from "above," however capable he may be, can bring only general, and possibly abstract, orientations, for he knows nothing of concrete questions, because he has no mastery of them.

I have reproduced this long extract from a speech of mine—with its characteristic language, which today impresses me as something of a hodgepodge with its traces of triumphalist jargon—merely to point up my preoccupation then with the role the party cadres ought to play, within the framework of real committees. A preoccupation expressed even more clearly in another passage in my speech: "A Communist leader must not only know how to explain our policy; he must also know how to listen. And knowing how to listen is not as easy as it may appear to be: knowing how to listen to the comrades, knowing how to listen to the masses, knowing how to listen to the voices and the sounds of the social reality of our country." In this attitude of mine toward methodology, formulated in 1960, there is to be found, I think, one of the roots of my later divergencies with Carrillo and the majority of the Executive Committee. The voices and sounds of social reality were growing louder and louder to me to the point of becoming deafening, to the point of drowning out the beatific murmur of our ideological discourse, which was becoming more and more out of phase with reality. I had to choose between the reality of discourse and the discourse of reality. I chose this latter, naturally, as did Fernando Claudín, though he did so by following another path, as a function of other experiences, whereupon he formulated with greater theoretical consistency than I did what we had in the end come to think jointly. But listening to the discourse of reality took us out of the party. Perhaps this is a lesson to be kept in mind.

But to return to what I was saying: the reaction of Romero Marín and Grimau in Madrid when I made them parties to my observations concerning certain of their work methods did not satisfy me, and therefore when I arrived in Paris that summer of 1962, I brought the question up again in the Executive Committee. Or, rather, in what remained of it owing to summer vacations.

Santiago Carrillo and a goodly portion of the party leadership had already left on vacation. All that was left in Paris was a small nucleus of comrades, working under Fernando Claudín, who commonly substituted for Carrillo as head of party activities whenever he was absent. I remember that at the meeting at which I reported on the work of my last months in Madrid, Antonio Mije, Eduardo García, Ignacio Gallego, and perhaps one or two others were present, besides Fernando. At the end of my report, I raised the question of Grimau's methods and asked the Executive Committee to request the secretariat to take the necessary measures to withdraw Grimau from the work in Madrid if he did not immediately change his methods of leadership, which endangered his personal security and hence the continuity of the party effort.

The only one who opposed my remarks on the subject was Eduardo García. This is not surprising. Eduard García has always been insensitive to the problems of security of comrades. This perhaps also applies to his own security, but this remains to be proven in fact. What mattered to García was results. His stay in Russia during the Second World War had left him not only with close ties to the Special Services but also with a sickness or zealotry that I shall call, so that my point will be clear, apparatus Stakhanovism. If one adds to that a *machismo* reminiscent of a lower-class Madrid pimp, no doubt intended to compensate for the many frustrations his very short stature and extremely unprepossessing physical appearance must have caused him, this will give some slight idea of how disastrous Eduardo García's activity was capable of being, especially in view of the fact that he held the key post in the Secretariat of Organization, to which he had been appointed by the grace and favor of Santiago Carrillo. As certain women, it is said, are stricken with *furor uterinus,* so Eduardo Gardía was stricken with *furor ideologicus.* The masses, according to him, were ready for anything in Spain. If the *Aitch En Pee,* or the *Aitch Gee Pee,* or any other confounded sacrosanct mythological action hadn't yet come off, it was purely and simply because we weren't working hard enough, zealously enough, enthusiastically enough. Eduardo García, so far as I know, had been in command of a Republican army unit during the Civil War. And apparently the battle cry of this unit was: "Last one to attack is a dirty fairy!" This strikes me as the perfect expression of the psychopathic moral makeup of Eduardo García and the furious ideological *machismo* that was characteristic of him.

Eduardo García was opposed, at any rate, to my critical remarks. But he was the only one, and it was decided in the course of the meeting to send a letter to Madrid recapitulating the essential points of my argument. This letter is in the party archives. If these archives are opened to the public some day, which at present seems doubtful, researchers will be able to see what this letter has to say.

The answer from Romero Marín and Grimau was not long in coming. They did not back down and in a peevish tone totally rejected all my critical observations. Things remained this way until Carrillo came back from vacation and learned what had happened during his absence. When I saw him he told me that I was no doubt right about the Madrid matter and that the answer from Romero Marín and Grimau was not an appropriate one. He told me he would be obliged to take steps.

Weeks passed, the necessary steps were not taken, and early in November 1962, Julián Grimau was arrested in Madrid.

The memory of all that tormented me that night of April 9, 1963 as I kept ringing the doorbell at Santiago Carrillo's house in Champigny-sur-Marne. Had I really done everything necessary to put my point of view across, persuaded as I was that it was the right one? Wasn't it too easy to chalk up Grimau's arrest to the workings of fate?

Suddenly a light went on in Carrillo's house. A window opened and someone spied René and me. We were perfectly visible in the light of a street lamp. The gate was opened from the house and we entered the garden. Carrillo was waiting for us on the porch; we had obviously gotten him out of bed by ringing the bell so insistently. He was in his pajamas. I gave him the news of the death sentence confirmation, presuming that he didn't know about it yet. But he did: he had heard it over the radio before going to bed. I informed him that Claudín had gathered a few comrades together in the offices of Secours populaire français as a last-ditch effort to alert various personages. Carrillo made no comment. He asked us to wait for him for a few minutes, got dressed, and came with us.

That night from Friday the 19th to Saturday the 20th of April 1963 was a strange one.

We all knew, doubtless, in our heart of hearts, although we refused to admit it, that it was no longer possible to save Grimau's life. We all knew that a decision made by Franco in the Council of Ministers had always been final. In reality, through the steps we took that night—present in the crowded office were a goodly portion of the Executive Committee; Theresa Azcárate, Marcos Ana, Juan Goytisolo, Monique Lange, and others also came—through the steps we took that night, by telephone from the office of the Secours populaire français, what we were trying to do was not to change the course of events, which was already irreversible, but rather, in desperation, to keep Julián Grimau company on that last night of his life. What we were trying to do, amid the tobacco smoke, drinking countless cups of coffee, shouting into telephones, getting word to a prelate at the Vatican Secretariat of State, waking up Monsignor Pla y Deniel's secretary in Toledo, talking with an official at the White House in Washington, who promised to relay the information to Kennedy immediately, gathering round Angela Grimau, who saw the blinding flash of Julián's death arrive with the light of dawn; what we were no doubt trying to do was to spend this last night with the comrade who was going to die, to share these last hours of his life, those first hours beyond his death.

But Colette and I, with Vicens and Françoise Wagener, have left Fontanilles, on the night of December 11, 1976. We are going to the town of Pals, to the house of Enrique Vila and Elena Cordoba.

There is going to be a ratafia contest there. Francesc Vicens and Manolo Vázquez Montalbán are members of the tasting jury.

I have not seen Elena for years. One of the last times was in Paris, around 1960. She called me from L'Aiglon, the hotel where Luis Buñuel usually stays. Domingo "Dominguín" also used to stay there when things were going well for him. When things were going badly, he would sleep at my place. Back then, Elena had just arrived from Madrid, having been sent by Ricardo Muñoz Suay. She was bringing urgent documents with her in a false-bottomed suitcase.

But we are in Pals and the tasting jury has begun to vote on the contestants' ratafias, which have to be homemade. They are being very serious about it, and the guests are flocking around the long table on which the different numbered flasks and bottles of liqueur are set out, and the sound of conversation, of laughter, can be heard, and Franco has been dead a year, and I am submerged in the swamp of memory, all by myself, now that Vicens can no longer converse with me.

With a little more determination, a few more active steps, it would have been possible, then, to get Julián Grimau out of Madrid before he fell into the hands of the police.

But above all, *he should never have been sent to Madrid, never been sent to work underground in Spain.* And I shall explain immediately what I mean.

However strange it may appear to anyone who is unfamiliar with the extremely hierarchical, pyramidal structure of the party, the fact is that I did not know exactly who Grimau was when I worked with him in Madrid. What I mean to say is: I knew that his name was Julián Grimau, I knew some of his virtues and some of his defects. I knew, for instance, because it was obvious, that Grimau was a man totally devoted to the work of the party, religiously faithful to the party. Grimau had no doubt adopted as his own the phrase of Fidel Castro's I have already quoted, the one in which the Maximum Leader says that in the party "our individualism disappears, and we learn to think in terms of the collectivity," when he says that the party is "our educator, our master, our guide, and our watchful conscience." Grimau would no doubt have subscribed to a phrase such as that. But where did Grimau come from? What sort of past did he have? Of this I knew nothing.

Later, immediately after his arrest and above all after his murder, when I participated in the preparation of the book, *Julián Grimau—El hombre—El crimen—La protesta* (Editions Sociales, 1963), that the party devoted to his memory, I came to learn of certain aspects of his life that I had known absolutely nothing of at the time I was working with him in the Madrid underground.

I didn't know, for example, that a few weeks after the Civil War began, when he was still a member of the Federal Republican Party (he did not become a Communist until October 1936), Julián Grimau had joined the Security Corps of the Republic, working first in the Criminal Brigade of the Madrid police department. One day as we were working on the Grimau book, Fernando Claudín, with a rather disconcerted look on his face and plainly upset and disgusted, showed me a testimonial in Grimau's memory that had just been received from Latin America. There was a rather detailed description in it of Grimau's work in Barcelona in the fight against agents of the Francoist Fifth Column and also—and this was what was bothering Claudín—in the fight against the POUM. I do not have a copy of this document and I don't remember the exact details of this latter facet of Grimau's activity, about which the witness from Latin America was quite specific, as though there were nothing particularly questionable about it. All I know is that Grimau's participation in the repression of the POUM was clearly established in this testimonial, the most problematical aspects of which were toned down and censored before being published in the book.

Quite apart from the odd feeling that will never fail to come over me on learning that a political militant is capable of voluntarily joining a police force, of whatever kind or coloration, I am not going to enter at this point into an untimely and scholastic debate as to whether or not there is need for an apparatus of state repression in a revolutionary era such as that from 1936–39. This is not the question I am posing here. The question I am posing is another one. However necessary and sacrosanct the agencies of political repression of the Republic may have been, what is monstrous, what is irresponsible, is to have sent back inside the country, for clandestine activities, a Communist who was a member of these agencies in a struggle-to-the-death period such as the Civil War. What is monstrous is to have run the risk of this Communist being arrested and identified as a member of the Republican Special Police— as was always a very likely possibility—and automatically exposed for that reason to the personal vengeance of the men from Franco's Political-

Social Brigade, those who best remembered the enemy's repressive agencies, since they had often suffered directly at their hands.

When the news of Grimau's arrest in Madrid and his fall from a window of an office of the General Security Headquarters arrived, I remember that all of us on the Executive Committee of the party thought that Julián had been deliberately thrown out the window by functionaries of the Social Brigade in order to hide the traces of torture on his battered body. The only one who did not share this opinion was Santiago Carrillo, who declared that it was possible to conceive, given Grimau's character, that he might have tried to commit suicide. It was not until later that I understood the reason behind this opinion of Carrillo's. The fact was, knowing Grimau's past as he did, knowing Grimau would be subjected, by reason of this past or rather by its unreason, not only to special treatment but also to the vengeance of Social Brigade functionaries, knowing that Grimau also knew all this, it was indeed possible to imagine that he would prefer suicide to a long martyrdom that could end only in death.

I repeat, therefore, measuring my words carefully: a secretary-general who sends a militant with a past such as Julián Grimau's—whatever the judgment of that past—back into a country to work underground, without submitting this decision to any sort of discussion, at least within the Executive Committee, and without making all the pertinent facts available to the members of this committee is an irresponsible leader. Or, better put, he is responsible for what may happen subsequently. But on April 19, 1964 Santiago Carrillo stepped out onto the speakers' platform of the meeting hall at Stains, before a thousand Communists who were no doubt surprised and moved, since for reasons of security such a large meeting had not been held for years in France, and began his speech evoking the "noble and now historic figure of Julián Grimau." So be it: let Santiago Carrillo come to terms with his conscience as he sees fit.

It was also at Stains—where a number of young comrades from Spain who were enrolled in the university militia there compared the meeting to the ceremony of swearing allegiance to the flag—that Carrillo delivered for the first time his unfortunate panegyric on subjectivism.

"To those who accuse us of subjectivism," the secretary-general of the Spanish Communist Party proclaimed, "of not predicting the rhythm of events hour by hour, year by year, I put this question: If in 1939 the Party had said '1964 will come and there will still be Fascism in Spain,' what would have happened?"

It is not worth the trouble to quote the rhetorical answer that Carrillo invented in reply to this question, because if one asks a stupid question one gets a stupid answer. Following a line of reasoning that is a pure sophism, Carrillo here confuses analysis and Marxist prediction with astrology. He makes of the party a collective astrologer, instead of a collective intellectual. No one in fact would expect the leaders of the Spanish Communist Party to have been able to predict in 1939 that there would still be Fascism in Spain in 1964. Such an inanity would never enter the head of any militant, however modest and untutored in Marxist theory he might be. What could be expected of the leaders of the Spanish Communist Party, on the other hand, was that they not continually prophesy, proliferating "objective" analyses of the structure and super-structure of the Franco regime, that this latter was on the point of collapse, that it was actually in the process of collapsing, that its death-throes had begun, that it was a question of weeks or at the most months.

But in addition to being a demogogic sophism, unworthy of a leader claiming to be a Communist, whose words jeopardize the activities and the lives of thousands of militants, Carrillo's pronouncement is a sad innovation of Marxism.

Beginning with Marx himself, nearly all Marxists have doubtless been wrong now and again in their political or economic predictions. This is accountable by the fact that Marxism is a revolutionary praxis, if ever there was one, and every praxis tends to secrete its own ideology—its more or less consistent system of ideas, values, norms, emotions—to justify revolutionary action, and therefore inexorably tends to present its objectives as being close at hand, as being eminently attainable. But the fact that Marxism, precisely because it is a praxis of the masses, if anything is, must bear with this distorting and subjectivist secretion and can never be a pure or exact or natural science does not mean that this aspect should be condoned and even glorified. Quite to the contrary, all serious Marxists, beginning with Marx himself, have spent their lives analyzing, exposing, and criticizing the subjectivist errors of their predictions. Carrillo is the first leader claiming to be a Marxist who, instead of criticizing his own errors of prediction, instead of setting forth the reasons for these errors, boasts of them and goes so far as to state that they are necessary in every revolutionary undertaking.

"Comrades," Carrillo declares in his speech of April 19, 1964, "a certain measure of subjectivism with regard to the rhythm of events—not with regard to their underlying causes or their nature—is doubtless one of the inevitable components of the tactics of every revolutionary force, and all the more so the more difficult the conditions under which the struggle is carried on.

"The subjective, the voluntaristic—I am still referring to the rhythm of events and not to policy, I am speaking of tactics in and of themselves —is a factor that weighs in the balance of historical development."

The confused, awkward, incoherent nature of Carrillo's line of reasoning leaps to the eye, and it is very difficult to reconstitute in conceptual terms. The monumental error of equating "the subjective" and "the voluntaristic," which are two quite different things, also leaps to the eye. Voluntarism is indeed a necessary component of revolutionary activity. Without the will to change society, as incarnated in a force of the masses, even though this will is, obviously, not always articulated in a fully worked-out strategic project, revolutionary action is in fact inconceivable. But subjectivism has nothing whatsoever to do with this will. Subjectivism means that neither the relation of forces nor the real possibilities of action have been correctly analyzed; it means that the forces of the adversary have been underestimated, that wrong objectives have been designated, which on not being attained bring about the demobilization or the demoralization of the revolutionary forces.

"With the vanguard alone, it is impossible to gain victory. It must be recognized that we Spanish Communists have not always kept this teaching sufficiently in mind. Not always, in these years of trying to foment mass actions, have we paid sufficient attention to whether, in addition to the vanguard—our Party—the masses too were prepared, were convinced, on the basis of their own experience, that action was necessary, and whether they were ready to support that action with all their strength. . . . On more than one occasion we have required our militants involved in organizing mass actions to call upon the masses for more than they were in a position to accomplish. . . . Because we forgot this reality we have been confronted in this period with more than one case in which, despite the sympathy with which the masses view our struggle, we have remained the only ones to call for a strike. . . ."

Without the word's ever having been pronounced, this is an excellent critique of subjectivism.

As a matter of fact, these lines come from the pen of Santiago Carrillo himself. They are to be found in an article of his entitled "Sobre las experiencias de dos años de lucha" ("On the Experiences of Two Years of Struggle"), in *Nuestra Bandera,* no. 31 (November-December 1948). In this article there are hints of the results of the discussions within the Spanish Communist Party leadership that involved the abandonment of the guerrilla campaign and the turning toward legally sanctioned activities within the vertical labor unions of the Franco regime—though there is no reference to the origin of the change in party line, that is to say the famous interview with Stalin that I have already mentioned. Contrary to what he was later to say, in 1964, that "the more difficult the situation" the more the subjectivist component of revolutionary tactics must be emphasized—which is utterly absurd if not outright mad—it was precisely because the situation was extraordinarily difficult in that year of 1948 ("the last two years," Carrillo says at the beginning of his article, "have perhaps been the hardest and the most difficult that the organization of our Party has ever endured") that it was urgent, indispensable, vital to correct the grossest subjectivist errors of the moment, even if, alas, only partially and pragmatically. The very survival of the Spanish Communist Party depended, in reality, on so doing.

Other articles, essays, or reports by Santiago Carrillo could be cited in which the criticism of subjectivism is dealt with correctly, permitting one to refute with Carrillo's own arguments, with his own words, the anti-Marxist glorification of this traditional defect of the Spanish Communist Party that he suddenly engaged in at the time of the mass action of 1964, and has continued to engage in ever since.

In this regard, Carrillo's most thoroughgoing and most complete critical effort is doubtless to be found in the report he put before the plenum of the Central Committee in August 1956, on "La situación en la dirección del partido y los problemas del reforzamiento del mismo" ("The Situation within the Party Leadership and the Problems of Strengthening the Party").

(Remember, I remind myself.

I remember that it was in East Germany, not far from Berlin. Deep in the woods. In a School for Cadres of the brother-party, as the expression went. The school bore the name of Edgar André, a Communist murdered by the Hitlerites. I remember that there was a lake.

On the edge of a lake, remember.

This bold presence—motionless eyes of clear water, sometimes bright, sometimes grayish—of difference lakes at different important moments of my life is curious. This presence of primitive, maternal water. Baptismal water?

Remember.

The Fifth Congress of the Spanish Communist Party, at which I was coopted to the Central Committee, in the autumn of 1954, was held in Czechoslovakia on the shores of Lake Majovo. The plenum of the summer of 1956, at which I was coopted regular member of the Politburo, since become the Executive Committee, was held on the shores of a little lake whose name I do not know, in the forest near Berlin, within the ground of the Edgar André School for Cadres of the party of the German Democratic Republic. Late, in 1958, on my first trip to the Soviet Union, on vacation, it was in the Caucasus—that afternoon with Colette—on Lake Ritza that there suddenly came to me the global vision of the archaic, oppressive, hierarchized, fossilized nature of Russian society that had arisen from the bloody history of Bolshevism.

Remember the lake of La Négresse, above all.

I got off the Paris train in Bayonne. Antonio was waiting for me there. He introduced me to the French comrades in whose care I was going to cross the border illegally, once again. We started on our way. There, on the right in my memory, heading for Spain, was the smooth surface of the lake of La Négresse, perhaps made iridescent by a slight puff of wind. It was there, on the left in my memory, returning from Spain, from the realm of dreams. The lake of La Négresse was the frontier-marker of my life, what separated yourself, Sánchez, from me. Or myself from you.

Remember the summer of 1956.

I remember that it was a privileged moment, a moment of maximum illusion, in my political life. In your political life, Federico Sánchez.

Everything had begun a few months before, in Madrid. With a very small group of militants from the university and intellectual circles we had finally managed to embark upon activity that was fairly broad in scope. Plans were under way for the Congress of Young Writers, students were beginning to agitate within the very ranks of the SEU. At the end of 1955, I came to Paris to report on the progress of our work, to discuss perspectives. I had several meetings with Santiago Carrillo and Fernando Claudín. The latter had returned to France a few months before, after a long stay in Moscow. His presence was already making itself felt in the work of the leadership group. The majority of the Politburo members were still in Rumania, staying on, as a sort of vacation, after the gatherings there on the occasion of La Pasionaria's sixtieth birthday.

Spain had just been admitted to the United Nations. The Soviet Union had voted in favor of its admission. It was one step further in implementing the new policy of coexistence of recognizing reality, that had been slowly taking shape since Stalin's death.

In Paris, on analyzing the situation, we had arrived at certain conclusions that were summarized in a text by Carrillo, "Sobre el ingreso de España en la ONU" ("On the Admission of Spain to the United Nations"), published in *Nuestra Bandera,* no. 15, in which the opinion was set forth that the end of the international isolation of Spain would have positive consequences from a democratic point of view.

In this same issue of *Nuestra Bandera,* remember, Federico Sánchez, a brief article of yours was also published: "Ortega y Gasset, o la filosofía de una época de crisis" ("Ortega y Gasset, or the philosophy of a period of crisis"). Remember it and then forget it again: it won't be any great loss.

Simultaneously, the majority of the Politiburo members, who had met together in Bucharest with La Pasionaria, made public a declaration on the admission of Spain to the UN, expressing an opinion contrary to ours. The UN decision was deplored and criticized as an attack on the legality of the Spanish Republic, incarnated in the shadow-institutions created in exile. In other words, a point of view typical of émigrés, a subjectivist inability to analyze the new Spanish situation, continued to predominate in this declaration.

Since Carrillo's text, the result of our discussions in Paris, had already been sent off to the printer's and the declaration of the majority group in Bucharest had been broadcast by Radio España Independiente and reprinted in a party periodical in Mexico, conflict was inevitable.

In view of this, Santiago Carrillo decided to send me to Bucharest to communicate to La Pasionaria the arguments of the Paris group and arrange for another discussion of the problem.

You arrived in Zurich, the first stop on your trip, remember.

It's true, I forgot the Lake of Zurich on my list a while ago. Another lake that was a frontier. Almost always, whenever I went to the East, I passed by way of Zurich. I arrived there with a certain identity and then, with another false passport, took the plane from Zurich to Prague. Occasionally I had a few hours' layover. At such times, if the weather were nice, I would take one of the excursion boats that go around the lake, and contemplate the landscape from the deck.

But on that trip the weather was not nice, remember.

I arrived in Prague and went directly to Manesova Street, where the Spanish Communist Party had its offices. José María Rancaño received me and I explained that I needed to see La Pasionaria as soon as possible, or, if she were not available, Vicente Uribe, who at that time was responsible for the active nucleus of the Politburo in the West.

I had no difficulty getting to see Uribe. He had just returned to Prague with Enrique Líster. Rancaño arranged the meeting by telephone, and a short time afterward I found myself with Uribe and Líster, at Uribe's house, if I am not mistaken.

No, I am not mistaken: the interview took place at Uribe's.

As I went about explaining to Líster and Uribe the reasons for my trip, the opinions of the comrades in Paris—I had brought with me, in a suitcase with a false bottom, not only the notes on our meetings but also the rough draft of Carrillo's article, which permitted me to set forth those opinions in great detail—I saw an expression of shocked surprise come over both their faces. At one point Líster tried to interrupt me with a cutting, threatening phrase. But neither then, nor later, nor at any other time has Líster ever been capable of interrupting me or shutting me up —that would be the last straw! Military men have never impressed me, especially those who lose wars. I answered him curtly and went on explaining what I had to explain. Then after having reproduced as faithfully as possible the arguments of the Paris comrades—along with Carrillo and Claudín, Cristóbal Errandonea and Manuel Delicado also participated in these meetings, though I cannot recall, however hard I try, that they ever contributed anything of the slightest interest or originality to the debate—and in particular the ideas Carrillo was going to expand upon in his article, I spoke up in my own name, basing my remarks on my work experiences in Madrid in the prior months. It was then that their shocked surprise took on major proportions. Líster and Uribe looked at each other as though wondering what could possibly be happening. This was the first time, of course, that they had ever seen a mere member of the Central Committee, coopted by them, especially chosen by the leadership group, dare to criticize them and put forth his own divergent ideas.

Vicente Uribe then put an end to the discussion. He said that Dolores would have to have her say in a matter of such importance. But Dolores was traveling, on the way back to Bucharest from a congress of the German party that had just ended in East Berlin, in a special train of the Rumanian delegation.

So the following day, in the Prague station, you waited with Uribe and Líster for the Rumanian delegation's special train, stopping over on its way back to Bucharest.

The train arrived, there were greetings, bouquets of flowers, and music. Vicente Uribe went to talk with La Pasionaria, who had a parlor car, and came back to tell me that I should get aboard the train immediately, so as to accompany Dolores to Bucharest and report the entire matter to her in detail.

You got aboard that special train, remember.

Why wouldn't I remember it! If I were writing a novel instead of a book that merely bears witness, that relates only what was said and what was done, the grain and the chaff of things, the head and the tail of the naked truth, I would no doubt take advantage of this occasion to show off my literary talents. I could write a marvelous chapter about this trip, just by giving free rein to the stylistic fillips that are the novelist's stock in trade. Just think of the material there for such an undertaking: the closed universe of the special train slowly rolling along the valley of the Danube: and on this train, protected by innumerable agents of the State Security Forces, the official Rumanian delegation returning from East

Berlin, headed by Chivu Stoica, an old labor-union leader who had recently been named president of the Council of Ministers of Rumania; and accompanying Chivu Stoica, a number of Politburo and Rumanian Central Committee members, with their respective aides, secretaries, majordomos, and interpreters, a whole impressive retinue; and then in a parlor car of this special train, La Pasionaria, who had just turned sixty, accompanied not by Irene Falcón, who had not yet emerged from her days in seclusion in some remote spot, accompanied, rather, by a secretary whose name I cannot remember; and finally, I myself—you, Federico Sánchez—just back from Madrid, the happiness of Madrid, that winter: and at lunchtime and dinnertime we all gathered together in the enormous dining car, with its shining copper and mahogany, where waiters in white gloves and with inscrutable gazes served us innumerable dishes, beginning with caviar from the Caspian, herring from the Baltic, plates of ham and sausages, spicy salads, and going on to various smoking-hot soups, meat and fish dishes, and ending with pastries and ice cream, accompanied by countless glasses of vodka, red and white wine, pink champagne from the Caucasus, cognac from Armenia, as the conversation flowed on, amid the respectful attention of the rest, between Chivu Stoica and La Pasionaria, who did not appear to be very much at ease at such long ritual feeds and scarcely touched what was served her, sitting there just sipping mineral water and constantly smoothing back a stray lock of white hair, seemingly coming to life only when calling to mind some memory or other of Spain: and it was only a few weeks before the Twentieth Congress of the Communist Party of the Soviet Union and the shady maneuvers; the sapping and countersapping of the leadership groups of countries that had formed part of Stalin's old empire had already begun, for they were trying their utmost to remain in power: and so naturally I could write a brilliant chapter in a novel, if I were writing a novel.

But you are not writing novel.

And so I shall simply say that the special train had barely pulled out of the Prague station when La Pasionaria invited me to meet with her in one of the compartments of her parlor car. There, with just the two of us present, I reported to her the same things I had already told Líster and Uribe. At the end, I handed Dolores Carrillo's typed outline of the article *Nuestra Bandera* was going to publish. Dolores listened to me with a face as impassive as marble, without making the slightest comment. Then, after having cast a brief glance at Carrillo's text, she told me in a curt tone that she would read it later, that she would reflect during this trip and let me know in Bucharest what answer I should take back to the comrades in Paris. The interview was over.

During the interminable forty-eight hours that it took the special train to make the run from Prague to Bucharest, Dolores never again mentioned the problem. On the other hand, we talked at some length about the situation in Madrid, the work of the party at the university, the comrades she knew, Simón Sánchez Montero, for instance, and those she did not know because they had only recently joined the party. Everything interested her passionately, the least little fact about Madrid, the slightest detail concerning people's daily lives, the changes that had taken place in the city as she had known it. Comparing her memories with the information I had to offer, she told stories about her life in Madrid when the party brought her there from Vizcaya in the thirties.

In Bucharest, where snow was falling, I was lodged in a house in the residential quarter reserved for personages of the ruling bureaucracy and foreign guests of the Rumanian party. I was alone in that house, which was a short distance from the villa occupied by La Pasionaria. The next morning when I came down to have breakfast in the immense dining room on the ground floor, I came upon a silent chambermaid who had set out enough food on the table to feed a dozen persons for a whole day. This comrade, who looked to be about forty, with the face of a peasant and wearing a kerchief tied around her head, stood waiting at one end of the long table covered with viands, ready to serve me. She was heartbroken when she saw that all I wanted was a couple of cups of coffee and a few slices of toast. Worried, murmuring words that I could occasionally catch because they resembled the Church Latin of the Middle Ages, she removed the lids of the soup tureens and the platters of croquettes and meatballs, fish and meat in different sauces, right under my nose so that the good smell would charm me into tucking into them. But gesturing in refusal, I said to her *non possumus,* like a canon of yesteryear.

I spent the first day of that stay in Bucharest alone. Dolores was tired from the trip and sent me a message that she would receive me the following day. A comrade from the Foreign Section of the Rumanian Central Committee came to get me in a car. She accompanied me on a drive through the city that lay paralyzed with cold beneath the winter snow. She showed me the former royal palaces that had been converted into youth hostels or rest homes. She showed me the new low-rent houses that Socialism was building for working people. She provided me with statistics on the literacy campaign, she explained to me how the problem of national minorities had been solved. She listed the advantages of the social security system to me. She spoke in French, with great fluency and an evident mastery of her subject. It was clear that she knew her role as cicerone of the promised land very well. There was only one moment of silence in her long speech. That was when we returned to the house where they had put me up, as we went through the barrier, guarded by soldiers from the Security Forces, which prevented free access to the reserved quarter of the city. The sentinel glanced into the car, doubtless recognized the chauffeur driving, took his cue from that, and pulled the barrier aside. I turned to her then and looked at her; she looked at me and stopped speaking. It was the only moment of silence that came my way all that day.

The following day La Pasionaria received me.

In the study of the villa that she was occupying, she communicated her decision to me. She had prepared what she was going to say in writing. She slowly read the sheet of paper on the desk. In view of the profound divergencies that had come to light and in order not to aggravate them, she had decided that the declaration of the majority group of the Politburo in Bucharest concerning Spain's admission to the UN would be withdrawn. The problem would be discussed again in its entirety at a plenary session of the Politburo that would be called very shortly. Period and amen.

La Pasionaria invited me to dine at her villa that night with the comrades who were working at the time on the editorial staff of Radio España Independiente: Ramón Mendezona, José Antonio Uribes, José Sandoval, and Federico Melchor, if I remember rightly.

You went back to the West, you stayed a few days in Paris, reporting on your trip to Carrillo and Claudín, and returned to Madrid, to the happiness of Madrid that winter. The happiness of Madrid that spring. But there is no need for you to remember this for history: history already remembers it for you. It's written down in books, as Domingo used to say. The student movement in February, the ministerial crisis, the wave of workers' strikes, the Twentieth Congress of the Communist Party of the Soviet Union, Khrushchev's secret report that you read in *Le Monde,* day by day, at José Antonio Hernández's. That is already recorded in history, it *is* history.

And so the August plenum of the Central Committee came round and Santiago Carrillo delivered his report on "The Situation in the Party Leadership and the Problems of Strengthening the Party.")

And no doubt this report is Carrillo's most complete and coherent critical effort to discover the roots of the "subjective appraisals" and "sectarian positions" that had obstructed work of the Spanish Communist Party throughout the Stalinist era. Unfortunately, nothing similar is to be found in Carrillo's later reflections. This report, made under the impetus of the renewal that the Twentieth Congress of the Communist Party of the Soviet Union appeared to usher in, was the swan song of Carrillo's critical capacities. It is also true that at that time he was not yet secretary-general and that his critical capacity was exercised at the expense of others—of Uribe and Mije, principally—and not his own.

"One of the manifestations of the influence of the personality cult in our Party," Carrillo declared in the August plenum, "has been the granting of extraordinary powers to the secretary-general of the Party, thus placing him in a position above the collectivity of leaders. The role played by the secretary-general in the Bolshevik Communist Party in Lenin's time differs substantially from what that role later was in Stalin's time. This practice [of granting extraordinary powers to the secretary-general] was carried over into the life of our Party, in which the secretary-general was considered to be the head of the Party, with discretionary authority to make very important decisions, both as regards political matters and as regards organization, with or without the Politburo's consent. In practice, his opinions or decisions were always considered to be final. To oppose this method, in other eras, would have appeared to be a lack of respect, a grave breach of discipline, an infraction of the norms of leadership. . . ."

How well Santiago Carrillo spoke of this problem when he was not secretary-general, when Dolores Ibárruri was! But in *Dialogue on Spain*, after fourteen years of all-pervading presence in this post, this is what Carrillo has to say: ". . . I believe it useful to add something on the role of personalities, of leaders in the revolutionary workers' movement. Following the condemnation of the 'cult,' a certain tendency toward 'anti-leaderism' developed. This fact may be considered to be the tribute exacted for the excesses of the period of the 'cult.' But this 'anti-leaderism' is also basically idealistic and reactionary. At another level, parties, revolutionary movements have a need of leaders. The popular and working masses do not make up their minds as a scientist is able to do, through precise analysis of concrete reality, nor do they make up their minds on the basis of a revolutionary theory. The masses make up their minds in a simpler way and tend to identify the defense of their interests with a party, with a movement, and with the men who represent it. . . ." The perspective changes radically, as can be seen, depending on whether one is secretary-general or not. It is a commonplace that the post generates an ideology of a legitimating type. Moreover, Carrillo corrects Marx in passing. Marx considered that the emancipation of workers could only be the work of the workers themselves. For Carrillo, however, the popular, working masses must surrender this objective, which is not within their reach, delegating the defense of their interests to parties, movements, and leaders with whom they tend to identify. Religiously, no doubt.

Francesc Vicens does not remember the Edgar André School for Cadres, the little fresh-water lake, the thick woods that surrounded us. He was not at the August plenum of 1956, nor was he at the other one, two years later, in September 1958, which was held in that same spot on the outskirts of Berlin. Present at this enlarged plenum of 1958 were Jordi Solé Tura, Ricardo Muñoz Suay, and Antonio Pérez (Emilio García), among other comrades who were responsible for various work sectors but were not members of the Central Committee.

We are at Foixá, on Sunday afternoon, December 12, 1976.

The castle has been abandoned; its rickety doors torn off their hinges allow free access to the inside. We walk through the spacious halls, the deserted garrets. From the highest window we contemplate the landscape of Ampurdán, beneath a wavering winter light.

Last night, in Pals, at Enrique Vila's and Elena's, the essential problems of the screenplay that I was writing for Joseph Losey, *Les Routes du Sud,* were all at once resolved. It was like a sudden illumination. All the elements necessary for the coherence of the story appeared out of the blue, emerged sharp and clear from the shadow in which they were still hidden. There in Pals, amid the hubbub of the guests, the trips back and forth with dinner plates, and the glasses of homemade liqueur at midnight, after Vicens and Vázquez Montalbán had rendered their verdict —along with a third member of the jury whom I didn't know—as to which was the best ratafia presented in the competition, there, all of a sudden, it became obvious to me that the story should take place between the 27th of September 1975, the day on which the five young ETA and FRAP anti-Fascists had been executed by a firing squad, and the 27th of November, when Juan Carlos de Borbón assumed the royal powers that Franco had bequeathed him.

Well then, that was settled. Now all I had to do was get down to the actual writing.

The same thing had happened to me one Easter Sunday in The Hague, ten years before, in 1966. We were driving down the Alexanderstraat toward Plein 1813, the square on which the building housing the Spanish Legation during the Civil War was located. I wanted to show it to Colette. We had just passed the Alexanderstraat church. I suddenly remembered that other Sunday, thirty years before. Memory, as everyone knows, is like a *babuschka,* one of those Russian painted wooden dolls that can be opened up, inside which is another identical doll, just a bit smaller, and then another and another, until one comes to one last minuscule doll that can't be opened. Well, in Foixá there suddenly appeared the memory of that Easter Sunday ten years before, in The Hague, and inside this memory there appeared another, older one, from

1937, when I was a child and my father was Chargé d'Affaires at the Republican Legation in Holland.

In the last *babuschka* of memory, then, in the one that contained that Sunday in 1937, I had accompanied my father to the Alexanderstraat church. I no longer went to mass at the time, having rid myself of any sort of religious preoccupation—and by that I mean any linked to Catholic faith and doctrine, since my subsequent adhesion to Communism cannot be fully explained without taking into account the diffuse religiosity that played an intimate role in it; it is only today that I can calmly affirm that I have left any sort of religious preoccupation behind. I no longer went to mass in those days, as I was saying, except on occasions such as this one: to keep my father company. I had not yet wanted to, or had not yet dared to, displease him by revealing my recent indifference to religion to him.

We sat in the Alexanderstraat church that Sunday, and the parish priest mounted the pulpit and launched into a long sermon against the enemies of the faith and of the Church, and in particular against the Spanish "Reds," against whom a new crusade had become necessary. My father didn't understand Dutch as well as I did: I had learned it in the classrooms of the Tweede Gymnasium, where I was taking the second year of courses in preparation for the Dutch baccalaureate. But he understood it well enough to gather that the sermon had something to do with Spanish "Reds," that is to say that it was a sermon against *us*.

After mass was over, once outside the church, my father asked me to tell him in detail what the priest had said about Spain. I explained. He turned deathly pale. He asked me to follow him and went back into the church. Inside, in the sacristy, he asked to speak with the priest who had just said mass and delivered the sermon. I translated his request to a sacristan who understood only Dutch. In a little while, the priest who'd given the sermon about a new crusade appeared. My father asked him if he understood French, and the priest replied that he did, more or less. Then for twenty minutes my father explained to that priest that he was unworthy of his ministry, that he was not a good servant of God; he explained to him that the war in Spain was essentially a war of rich against poor, and that if the official Spanish Church had chosen to side with the rich and not with the poor, this was not what the Gospels preached; that the Church of silence, the martyred, evangelical Church, the truly Christian community of Spanish Catholics, however few and however persecuted they were, bore witness for Christ and the future of the Church by siding with the poor, the oppressed, the exploited, the starving; and as he cast severe reproach upon his conscience as a priest and his conscience as a believer, my father's voice resounded with accents of pain and anger, and at times grew hoarse with pain and anger, and the Dutch priest, dumbfounded, his face by turns white and beet-red, listened to this diatribe, this other sermon, this long despairing cry from a believer without a Church, aspiring only to the universality of a religious practice faithful to the message of the Gospels, and blushing now, the Dutch priest murmured something about not realizing, said he had not intended to offend any sincere Catholic, and retreated one step at a time, raising his right hand in a mechanical gesture of benediction, still fleeing however, walking backwards toward a side door of the sacristy through which he suddenly vanished.

And we had driven past the Alexanderstraat church, one Easter Sunday, in 1966, and arrived in front of the Legation building, on Plein 1813, and the iron gate at the entrance was closed and the place seemed to be unoccupied. In any case, it was no longer the Spanish Legation; a plaque alongside the gate indicated that the building was now an annex of the Dutch Ministry of Foreign Affairs. I contemplated the empty house and the deserted grounds, the magnolia without flowers (though perhaps it was not the time of year when magnolias are in bloom), and I explained to Colette what there had been, thirty years before, behind the glass panes of each one of those closed windows.

And there, suddenly, all the bits and pieces that had been floating in my imagination for some weeks, all the obsessions and dreams, crystallized in a silent flash, forming in an absolutely definitive way, down to the very last detail, the plot of a novel that eventually came to be called *The Second Death of Ramón Mercader.* At noon, in a restaurant in Rotterdam, I recounted the narrative line of the novel to Colette. The rest would be easy: all that was left to do was begin. Or, rather, the hardest thing in the world: to make what is evident become evident, in writing.

But we are in Foixá, in December 1976, and Francesc Vicens doesn't remember those woods on the outskirts of Berlin where the School for Cadres of the East German party was located.

Nor can he remember the celebration when the plenum was over. There was a dinner with champagne, and then music and dancing. Though I will be told that a dance among members of the Central Committee of the Spanish Communist Party—with only Margarita Abril ("Maria Lopez") and "Teresa" (Leonor Bornau) available as dancing partners (La Pasionaria did not share the life of the group: she lived in a residence apart, on the other side of the grounds of the Edgar André School)—may appear to be more a nightmare than a party. Or else something that soon turns into something very different. But I immediately censor this obscene and irreverent image of a passionate tango, like those in any sailor's bar in the red-light district of Amsterdam or Barcelona, between Antonio Mije and Eduardito García.

In fact there was music and dancing because among those invited to the party were the service personnel of the School for Cadres, which like all service personnel was made up largely of women. Let it be recorded for history's sake that the liveliest dancer among the members of the Executive Committee turned out to be Ignacio Gallego. I, personally, invited a young chambermaid comrade to dance with me, because she had blue eyes and a supple-looking body. We danced, I spoke to her in German, she was amazed at my good pronunciation, and I explained that I had learned German as a little boy, with Fraülein Grabner, and had practiced it at Buchenwald. Strangely enough, the mention of Buchenwald seemed to make her ill at ease. But anyway, during my second dance with her she held me a little more tightly, which did not particularly surprise me: twenty years ago that seemed quite normal to me. But I immediately fell off the high horse of my masculine vanity, my automasculinatry, because the moment her thighs pressed against mine, she murmured in my ear that she wanted to get to know Paris, life in the West, and asked me if there weren't some way I could help her get out of the country and come to the West. It was a good lesson, both politically and sexually. One never stops learning in life what life is really like.

In any event, as Vicens and I were walking about in Foixá that Sunday in December 1976, history had already settled one of the essential questions of the 1964 discussion that we had been thinking back on all day: the question of the forms of transition from Francoism to democracy, of the liquidation of Francoism.

The document of October 15, 1964 that I have already cited and that Berenguer-Vicens addressed to the Executive Committee to the PSUC contained a paragraph entitled "La liquidación del franquismo" ("The Liquidation of Francoism").

> The liquidation of Francoism is not going to be the Socialist revolution. . . .
> It is going to be an enormous triumph of the struggle of the masses, but not
> a social change, that is to say the revolution.
> I believe that the examination of this problem requires us to take into
> account:
> 1. The Leninist theory of capitalist development of the Prussian type;
> 2. The transformations that Spain has suffered in the last quarter of a
> century;
> 3. The experience of the other Fascist regimes;

4. What is happening at present in Spain, that is to say the high point of the mass movement coinciding with a stage of accelerated economic development.

I have already referred to the first two points above. As for the experience of the other Fascist regimes, it is interesting to recall that in Germany and Italy the power of monopoly capital survived Fascist forms, and this despite the fact that it dragged the country into a gigantic national catastrophe such as that represented by the military defeat at the end of the world war.

The same thing happened in France at the end of the Fascist occupation.

. . . In Spain, the liquidation of Fascism will not be linked with any national catastrophe but rather is coming about gradually within a framework of economic development. The motive forces of this liquidation are the coups carried out by the mass movement and the action of various forces (among which certain crucial centers of monopoly capital must be included).

Vicens thus correctly outlined a key question, as history has subsequently confirmed.

In the discussion within the Executive Committee of the Spanish Communist Party, in March-April of this same year 1964, Claudín and I had presented a similar analysis of the situation.

In his speech opening the discussions of the plenum of the Executive Committee, in the ancient, Kafkaesque castle of Bohemian kings, Claudín put matters as follows:

. . . the possibility of having a democratic political regime of monopoly capital, as is the case in other capitalist countries, seems [to the majority of the Executive Committee, grouped around Carrillo] to be excluded. The democratic solution is linked to a social change, and therefore to the accession to power of nonmonopolistic social powers. Hence it is logically linked to a revolutionary crisis. . . . My opinion is that we are not heading toward a revolutionary situation of this type. We are heading toward a change in the political forms of domination of monopoly capital, which may become more or less democratic in successive phases and inaugurate a new stage in the development of Spanish capitalism. . . . In this stage it is possible that the new political forms will crystallize into a democratic regime which, in order to avoid misunderstanding, I shall call of the Western type, and I emphasize the word *type,* that is to say not identical to that of this or that other European capitalist country. In my judgment the evolution of the situation at present would appear to be tending in that direction.

In the first place, the liquidation of Francoism will inaugurate, is already inaugurating, a constituent period, which will lead to a regime of greater or lesser political freedom; the degree of this freedom, the character of institutions, will depend upon the intensity of action by the masses and other social sectors interested in democracy. Under the pressure of this struggle, the new state regime, even though it is the expression of the power of monopoly capital, may reach the point of having more or less democratic forms. . . . In the course of this process, what should the tactic of the party be, in my opinion? I believe that the first conditions of this tactic should be an objective, scientific understanding of the present process. Of the fact that we are not confronted with a social crisis of the capitalist system, but rather with a crisis of its political forms of domination. . . . We are not heading toward a national revolutionary crisis but we are in a political crisis, which will be resolved by way of the struggles of those from below and the initiatives of those from above, in a series of steps and partial reforms, both political and economical, following a more or less gradual and peaceful path. . . .

Although I have reproduced here only very brief excerpts from Claudin's speech, they are sufficient, I think, to prove that history has borne out, one by one, all the predictions of this 1964 analysis.

But it was against this analysis, which was the central axis of our position, that the ideological fury, the frenetic campaign of the majority of the Executive Committee of that time was unleashed.

In the mass meeting on April 19, 1964, Carrillo declared:

It would be premature at this time to predict the steps, the phases, whereby the transition from dictatorship to democracy will take place. I do not wish to venture into the domain of prophecy. The only thing that can be said, without fear of being badly mistaken, is that this transition will come about through great struggles and popular mobilizations, in which the working class will play the principal role; through an aggravation of the contradictions within the classes and factions governing the country; through a process of closer and closer rapprochement between democratic and anti-Franco forces. In short, it will be a period of severe and acute tensions.

Up to this point there is nothing to object to. Carrillo limits himself to spelling out the abc's of Marxism, one within the reach of anyone and everyone, a kindergarten Marxism. But then the going gets rougher, and the reader would have to hear the original tape I have in my possession to have some idea of the frenzied tone in which the secretary-general of the Spanish Communist Party expresses himself.

If anyone labors under the illusion that this process is going to be a long and imperceptible gradual evolution, with no sudden leaps, with no imbalances and no tensions, it is because he is not dealing realistically with existing conditions.

Some of those who have placidly enjoyed the period of Francoist domination and think of raising their umbrellas only when it starts to thunder have a tendency to imagine this transition as a sort of simple process of "the king is dead, long live the king." [An apt refrain, is it not?]

They are badly mistaken. The elimination or collapse of a Fascist regime, which has triumphed through foreign military intervention, which for twenty-five years has brutally exploited workers and plundered peasants and the middle classes, which has employed the most barbarous methods of terror to reduce every right and every freedom to nothing—such an important historical event is not a simple change of head of state or a modest governmental crisis.

It is something much more profound. Even though it may take place in a peaceful manner, it is a real revolution [*ringing applause; the audience rises to its feet and the applause goes on and on*], it is the beginning of a revolutionary process that cannot help but have profound politico-social consequences.

That sample will suffice, I presume.

Naturally, Carrillo will say that we are still in the first period of the first phase of the first step of this revolutionary process that he proclaimed was inevitable. He will tell us what sort of things we will see: later. Or perhaps he will tell us that the fact that he is the head of a parliamentary microminority is already in and of itself a real revolution. But how to classify the fact that Don Roberto Conesa continues to be head of the political police?

I am not going to cite here all the speeches, reports, articles, interviews in which Carrillo has repeated this idea since 1964. I will simply recall that in September 1975, at the Second National Conference of the Spanish Communist Party, at which the Program-Manifesto was approved, Carrillo persisted in declaring: "Over and against any sort of formula for continuity, the democratic alternative will continue to be our solution. If the succession of Juan Carlos takes place, we will take advantage of the weakening of the entire power structure to impose, with the masses in the streets, the democratic objectives that Spanish society demands, culminating in the political revolution that will put an end to all the holdovers of dictatorial power."

But as it happened the masses did not take to the streets, so as not to alarm the army, so as not to provoke the ultraright, so as not to cause difficulties for Suárez who is doing so well—and what is there left of all the many subjectivist and self-satisfied declarations? There remains the figure of a pragmatic lader, an opportunist of the Left or the Right or the Center, depending on which way the wind is blowing.

The late afternoon is fading, we abandon the hill of Foixá.

This entire discussion with Vicens has brought to mind once more the accursed *Aitch En Pee,* which was the concrete expression of the aberrant strategy of the Spanish Communist Party. As we return to Barcelona now that this interlude in Ampurdán, with its noble and serene landscape in the December light, is over, the place on Concepción Bahamonde, where I lived in 1959 as we were preparing the Peaceful National Strike, comes to mind again.

6 THE LONG VOYAGE

The place at number 5 Concepción Bahamonde was the first clandestine hideout that the party procured for me. Up until then, that is to say from 1953 to 1959, I had hunted up my underground residences in Madrid myself, at my own risk, and with the help of a few comrades: Eloy Terrón in a certain period, Domingo "Dominguín" in another. I was apparently clever enough at it, or lucky enough, I must admit, not to have ever been arrested by the Social Brigade, despite the fact that they spotted me several times, but did not manage to identify me, in the course of one or another of the many dragnets and raids of those years.

One time the Special Tribunal of the Calle del Reloj even published in the press a "Wanted" notice with a rather accurate physical description of me under the name of Federico Artigas, "who claims to be from Santander." I can only presume that one or another of the comrades arrested around that time had talked. Federico Artigas was in fact the name on one of the false Spanish identity cards I had had occasion to use. If memory serves me correctly—and I have an excellent one, thank you very much—Ricardo Muñoz Suay published in *Objectivo* a critical piece he had asked me to write on Luis García Berlanga's *Novio a la vista (Sweetheart in View)*, and I had signed it Federico Artigas. At about this same time, Juan Antonio Bardem called one of the characters in his *Calle Mayor (Main Street)* by the same name, which was going a bit far. But naturally detectives and officers of the Social Brigade have no interest in reviews or screenplays. Hence they never connected the Federico Artigas they were searching for with the Federico Artigas who published articles in *Objectivo* or played a fictitious role in a film by Bardem.

Until 1959, as I was saying, I had organized my clandestine stays in Madrid on my own. But at the beginning of that year the party suggested I occupy the place at number 5 Concepción Bahamonde.

This apartment had been bought, as a matter of fact, for Simón Sánchez Montero's use. It was in the name of two married comrades, Manolo and María Azaustre, who had returned legally from exile in France and had no prison record. Simón moved in there, but a few days later he met one of his wife's cousins, or someone of the sort, on the stairway of the building. Someone his wife's family knew, at any rate. There were the usual greetings, the usual questions. What are you doing here? What about *you*? It turned out that this cousin of Carmen's, or whoever she was, or it might have been Simón's cousin, I don't remember, was living at number 5 Concepción Bahamonde. And so it was impossible for Simón to use that apartment. He would have kept running into her, and she would have begun pondering the reasons for Simón's presence on Concepción Bahamonde and gossiping about it. Could Simón have separated from Carmen? Could he have returned to his dirty political games again? In short, tittle-tattle and tongue-wagging: imminent disaster was more or less a foregone conclusion.

Simón relinquished the apartment, and I moved in at the beginning of 1959; I left it two years later, and Julián Grimau took it over.

It was a very modest apartment. The front door led directly into a hallway. To the left were three rooms overlooking the street. One was a dining room. The other two, both tiny, were those that Manolo and María Azaustre supposedly rented out to their lodger, so as to keep up appearances and comply with the party's security rules. At the end of the hallway were a kitchen and a rather primitive bathroom. Finally, to the right of the hallway was a room opening on the inner courtyard that was Manolo's and María's bedroom.

Neither of them, of course, belonged to any rank-and-file party organization in Madrid. Staying away from all political activity, their sole mission was to keep this apartment at the disposal of the underground apparatus. María took care of the house, and Manolo worked as a chauffeur during most of the time I stayed with them.

There were only three persons who had access to this house: Simón Sánchez Montero, Francisco Romero Marín, and I, since it was where I lived. (Julián Grimau moved in later.) The Azaustres knew neither our real identities nor our official pseudonyms, nor even what posts we held as party leaders. They knew we were militants with responsibilities, and that was all. They knew Simón as "Ángel," Romero Marín as "Aurelio," and me as "Rafael."

When I returned home late at night after the two of them had already gone to bed, María would leave me a cold supper all ready in the dining room. She prepared these meals with great care and affection, varying the meat and fish dishes, making marvelous mixed salads, and so on, since this was the only way she could show that she was participating in the work of the party. It was the only way for her to express her status as a Communist who had agreed to return to her country to perform this humble anonymous task, which for all that was an important one and not without its risks.

In fact, when Grimau was arrested in the autumn of 1962, Manolo and María Azaustre were also arrested and spent several years in prison. At the time of their arrest, they were no longer living at number 5 Concepción Bahamonde. They had bought another apartment a short time before, for the use of the party and at the party's expense, in the same neighborhood, on Pedro Heredia, and had moved into it with Julián Grimau. After being denounced by an informer, Julián Grimau was arrested on the street. But the police discovered his clandestine hideout and arrested Manolo and María Azaustre. No one ever learned the whole story behind their arrest. I have never been able to find out, at any rate, how the Social Brigade found the thread that led them to Grimau's clandestine residence. And Manolo Azaustre, with whom I talked at length in 1972 after his years in prison, couldn't explain it either.

But on nights when I came home in time, I ate dinner with Manolo and María. I tried to take advantage of these opportunities to talk with them and keep them abreast of general political problems, of party activities. As we sat at the table after dinner, Manolo would sometimes summon up his memories of exile. In 1939, as a young soldier in the Republican army seeking refuge in the south of France, he had been interned in the concentration camps there for Spanish refugees. He told me of his experiences at Saint-Cyprien, at the fortress of Collioure, where the French locked him up in solitary because of something that had happened in the camp; I no longer remember what. Then when the Second World War broke out the French formed ex-combatants of the Republican army into militarized work brigades. In 1940, when the Germans wiped out the French army in a matter of a few weeks, many thousands of Spaniards in these work brigades were taken prisoner. When the Germans discovered that they were Spanish "Reds," *Rotspanier,* they transferred them from the prisoner of war camps to Mauthausen, which was an extermination camp. As is common knowledge, some ten thousand Spanish "Reds" died there.

Manolo Azaustre was one of the survivors of Mauthausen. After dinner sometimes, sitting around the table in the evening, Manolo Azaustre would recount his memories of Mauthausen to me.

We were in the dining room of that apartment at number 5 Concepción Bahamonde. Sometimes we'd have a drink together. María would walk in and out of the room, busy at whatever task she was doing. Then if the conversation was still going on, she would go off to bed and Manolo Azaustre would tell me about Mauthausen. He told me about it at length, in great detail, sometimes losing himself in the ins and outs of his story. He did not know, of course, that I had been deported to Buchenwald. The less comrades know of one's life the better. It was necessary to keep in mind at all times the consequences that confidences shared with a comrade in an idle conversation might have if he landed in the hands of the police. Not that it's very pleasant to have to watch everything one says or doesn't say to comrades with whom one works and lives. But in the final analysis that's the way it has to be. So when Manolo Azaustre told me about Mauthausen, I listened without saying a word. He didn't know that I had been in Buchenwald, that I knew more or less what a concentration camp was all about. Manolo Azaustre explained to me what a crematory oven was, and I nodded my head, not saying a word, not telling him that I knew very well what a crematory oven was like. Manolo Azaustre explained to me the work schedule for forced labor, and I nodded my head, perhaps asking him a question or two so as to show I was interested in what he was saying, without being able to tell him that I too had begun my work day at 4:15 a.m. each day, that I too had lined up for evening roll call on the main esplanade of the camp, in the snow perhaps, for a length of time that could be interminable, depending on the whim of the SS officers, after a work day twelve hours long, with nothing at all to eat at noon. Manolo Azaustre told me that there was an orchestra at Mauthausen that accompanied certain moments of camp life with its awkward fiddling and tootling, and I could not interrupt him and tell him that yes, of course, in Buchenwald too, as in all the camps, there was an orchestra made up of prisoners, that they wore extravagant uniforms: high black leather boots, red riding breeches, green jackets with yellow frog-and-braid trimming, like musicians in a circus band. Manolo Azaustre told me of the executions the Nazis organized like a spectacle on the main esplanade of the camp at Mauthausen and I could not interrupt him to tell him of the gallows erected at Buchenwald, on that hillside where Goethe and Eckermann strolled together, a century before, where Napoleon and Alexander had gone hunting together after the Congress of Erfurt.

I didn't say a word. I listened to Manolo Azaustre.

In the end it was his stories, however confused and prolix they may sometimes have appeared to me, that revived my drowsing memories of that entire Buchenwald period. If I had not lived at number 5 Concepción Bahamonde that year, and if I had not met Manolo Azaustre there, it is quite possible I would never have written *The Long Voyage.*

This is how I happened to write it.

In the first months of 1960, around February or March, as I remember, an important mass police raid took place in Madrid. Comrades in various sectors of the organization were taken in by the police dragnet. As the origin of the mass raid and its precise implications and possible consequences were not immediately clear, Romero Marín and I decided to sever temporarily all the ties that linked us, from top to bottom, with the various organizations. We decided to suspend almost all contacts, to cancel most of our rendezvous and meetings, until we had a better idea of the origins of the mass raid and of its repercussions. If we hurriedly reestablished our contacts and organizational ties with the affected sectors, we ran the risk of drawing the attention of the police toward undiscovered comrades. It was better to wait, to determine where to cut into the living flesh so as to keep police infiltration, which was always possible, from proliferating like a cancer in the cellular tissue of the organization. We decided, in short, not to budge from our respective clandestine living quarters, if we could help it, and to wait for more detailed information, which would soon reach us through the most diverse channels. I would hole up on Concepción Bahamonde and Romero Marín on López de Hoyos

(but you are obliged to interrupt yourself at this point. They have just brought the weekly packet of Spanish newspapers that you receive in this country house where you have shut yourself up to write. And it turns out—what a coincidence, it's like a trick of fate, or a literary device—number 172 of *Cuadernos para el Diálogo,* Series II, August 14–20, 1976, contains interviews with Simón Sánchez Montero and Romero Marín. You read them immediately, of course. You learn nothing that you didn't know before, naturally. But once again you are amazed to see how the memory of Communists works. Or rather, their lack of memory. And you are once again amazed to note how selective the memory of Communists is. They remember certain things and forget others. And others they banish entirely from their memory. Communist memory in reality is a way of not remembering: it does not consist of recalling the past but of censoring it. The memory of Communist leaders functions pragmatically, in accordance with the political interests and objectives of the moment. It is not a historical memory, a memory that bears witness, but an ideological memory. Thus Romero Marín tells how, after the loss of Catalonia, in February 1939, he caught a plane in Toulouse and returned to Madrid. He remembers that Hidalgo de Cisneros was also on the plane. But he does not remember that Enrique Líster was on it too. The fact is that Hidalgo de Cisneros died in the odor of sanctity, a member of the Central Committee, and Líster is still alive and expelled from the party. Líster is consequently a non-person. Enrique Líster no longer exists in Romero Marín's memory, since he is no longer a member of the party. Romero Marín looked straight through Líster in those tragic last weeks of the Civil War. He does not remember that Líster was on that plane from Toulouse, he does not remember that Líster was at the meetings at Elda, which he mentions in this autobiographical interview. He remembers Dolores Ibárruri and Palmiro Togliatti, the delegate of the Communist

International in Spain at those Elda meetings. But he remembers neither Enrique Líster nor Fernando Claudín. Claudín was at Elda too. Claudín was with Togliatti, otherwise known as Ercoli or "Alfredo," until his very last hours, his very last minutes, in Spain. Claudín was in the Central-South zone until the very last moments the Communist leaders were there. But Romero Marín naturally did not see him. Outside the Church there is no salvation, nor is there any outside the party. Worse still: outside the party there is neither salvation nor existence. Outside the party one ceases to exist. One turns into a non-being. One becomes transparent, ectoplasmic, nebulous. Without knowing it, Romero Marín is a medieval exorcist. For years he talked about the Peaceful National Strike, the HNP, the *Aitch En Pee,* and ended up believing that some day it would happen, or was happening, or was about to happen, or had actually already happened. Today Romero Marín ceases to mention the names of Enrique Líster and Fernando Claudín, and perhaps he has the impression that by virtue of this magical operation Enrique Líster and Fernando Claudín cease to exist. And for Marín it doesn't matter that the reasons Enrique Líster and Fernando Claudín are outside the party are not only contradictory but diametrically opposed. Radically opposed. It doesn't matter. It is enough for them to be outside the party for them both to cease to exist. In the final analysis, and to simply call a spade a spade: Romero Marín's memory is shitty. It is not a memory that bears witness: it is a memory that bears false witness. Romero Marín remembers only what he finds it convenient to remember. And this is not only a personal problem, or a psychological one, or a moral one. It is a political one. Because it turns out that Romero Marín's memory works exactly like Carrillo's, exactly like Gregorio López Raimundo's, exactly like Marcelino Camacho's. As proof of this, one need only read their autobiographical interviews. Now a party without a memory, without the critical capacity to accept and make itself truly responsible for its own history, is a party incapable of developing a genuinely revolutionary strategy. A party, for example, incapable of critically reflecting upon the experiences of the Civil War, incapable of accepting the truth of the liquidation of the POUM, of the total destruction of the anarcho-syndicalist collectivities, of the Stalinist alliance with reformist and bourgeois forces, of the calumny heaped upon Quiñones, Monzón, Comorera, for instance—such a party will always be incapable of developing the strategic perspectives necessary for the autonomy of the proletariat. Never mind; you light a cigarette and take a break. You are not going to exhaust the theme of the relations between history, memory, ethics, and strategy now. The subject requires much more careful exposition. And you have been unable to contain yourself. This is understandable. You were speaking of Romero Marín, of Simón Sánchez Montero, you were speaking of those years of clandestine work in Madrid, the memory of which you share with them. And it turns out that in fact it is not a memory that you share with them. Or better put: you for your part share this memory with them, but they do not share it with you. You for your part remember them and they do not remember you. It does not suit them to remember you. Thus, for example, you read what Romero Marín says in *Cuadernos para el Diálogo,* which in this case are not so much for dialogue as for monologue, an old Hispanic sickness: *"I came to Madrid for the first time in '56, to prepare my bases for living underground. And in February '57, the day of the streetcar strike, I arrived in Madrid, there to remain, except for occasional brief absences, until '74, when I was arrested."* Did you, Federico Sánchez, pass like a ghostly shadow through the memory of Romero Marín when he made those statements? Perhaps not. Perhaps Romero Marín has censored his memory, like a good political psychopath. Perhaps he has erased from his memory the fact that it was you who welcomed him to Madrid, in '56, in the spring of '56. Perhaps he does not remember that the three of you—Simón Sánchez Montero, he himself, and you—were the ones who together prepared the bases of his clandestine life. Perhaps he does not remember that in February of 1957, the day of the boycott of urban transport— planned and organized by the very small group of comrades led by Simón Sánchez Montero and Luis Lucio Lobato, with the support of the university organizations that you, Federico Sánchez, led—he spent the entire day walking around Madrid with you; perhaps he no longer remembers that long walk up Bravo Murillo to Cuatro Çaminos that the two of you took together, amid the crowd, caught up in the irrepressible joy of the people of Madrid, that day of the streetcar strike. Perhaps Romero Marin, "the Tank," has aged a great deal, perhaps he's lost his memory. That would explain what he says at the end of his interview: *"Nobody in Spain even knew where I lived."* You read that sentence at the very moment that you were speaking of López de Hoyos, the precise street on which Romero Marín's clandestine hideout was located, where he lived until the very last moment of your own stay in Madrid, in December of 1962. Of course you knew this clandestine residence of Romero Marín's. Why wouldn't you know it since you, Federico Sánchez, were the one responsible in Madrid for the delegation from the Executive Committee? You naturally knew all the clandestine hideouts: you had to. Romero Marín's and Sánchez Montero's, Julián Grimau's and Ignacio Gallego's, when this latter worked in Madrid for a few months, and Fernando Claudín's when he came to prepare the damned *Aitch En Pee.* And many times you knew these clandestine living quarters because you had looked for them and got them ready yourself. Perhaps it would be apropos to refresh Romero Marín's memory by reminding him of all this, by reminding him that never, ever, in ten years of clandestine work in Madrid, was there ever the least hitch, the slightest unfortunate incident with respect to the clandestine living places that you prepared, or with respect to the clandestine stays of Executive Committee members that you, Federico Sánchez, organized. Not everyone can claim as much. No one can take that away from you.

And now that you have unburdened yourself and relaxed, you return to your memory of those years, a memory from which no one will be banished, in which there is room for everyone, the foolish along with the wise, cowards as well as heroes, those you respect and those you scorn, the famous and the nameless: all the comrades who have made the party what it is and whom the party has frequently unmade, and you were saying that Romero Marín would hole up on López de Hoyos and that)

I would hole up on Concepción Bahamonde, until we had a better idea of the reasons behind the police raids and their possible consequences.

So all of a sudden, having been temporarily cut off from the obsessive activity of so many years of political work, I found myself alone, immersed in that disconcerting dimension represented by empty hours, endless spare time. It was a strange mental vacation. After two days, without really thinking about it, without deliberately setting it up as a project—or rather, without having stopped and said to myself: I'm going to write a book—I started to write *The Long Voyage*. Or rather, I started to write something that turned out to be *The Long Voyage*. And perhaps it would be more accurate to say that that book wrote itself, as though I had been only the instrument, the translator, of this anonymous work of memory, of the act of writing. As a matter of fact the book came to me with its chronological and narrative structure already all worked out —no doubt unconsciously, I now think, during the long hours I spent listening to Manolo Azaustre's disjointed, repetitive stories of Mauthausen. In any event, I worked all one week, without interruption, scarcely stopping to catch my breath, as that book wrote itself.

Then, naturally, after a little more than a week, I had to abandon that book, to leave it unfinished. I returned to my former life, and forgot it. Or perhaps that book forgot me, that is to say forgot Federico Sánchez. The fact is, it was not easy for Federico Sánchez to be a writer, as is quite understandable. From time to time, however, when I was not in Spain devoting all my time to the clandestine work of the party, I would add a few pages to that manuscript that gave no promise of ever being finished.

Two and a half years later, in the fall of 1962, a series of objective circumstances radically changed the situation.

At that time, following his return from vacation and immediately after Grimau's arrest, Santiago Carrillo informed the Executive Committee of the need to remove me from the clandestine work in Spain, and the committee approved this proposal. For reasons of security, according to Carrillo, it was best that I stop working in Spain. Ten years had gone by since my first clandestine mission, and ten years is a long time underground. Moreover, Carrillo added, by the very fact that I was the one who coordinated the liaison with the other opposition political forces in Madrid, it was inevitable that the existence of a certain Federico Sánchez and his physical description were known to a fair number of people. And certainly to the police as well. Carrillo therefore proposed that Comrade José Sandoval take my place in Madrid.

Sandoval was a member of the Central Committee. Since the end of the Civil War he had lived in exile, in Russia or in one or another of the "people's democracies" in the East. In recent years he had been working in Moscow as a member of a commission headed by Dolores Ibárruri; Manuel Azcárate, Luis Balaguer, Antonio Cordón, and Irene Falcón were also members. This commission had written a very shallow history of the Spanish party and was working on a history of the Civil War, quite unfaithful to the historical truth, of which three volumes were to be published under the title *Guerra y revolución en España, 1936-1939 (War and Revolution in Spain, 1936-1939)*. A few weeks after the Executive Committee had approved Carrillo's proposal to replace me, in December 1962 to be exact, I made my last clandestine trip to Madrid to introduce Sandoval to the comrades with whom he would be working from then on.

I have no objective facts at my disposal, naturally, to cause me to cast doubt on Carrillo's sincerity, his paternal concern for my security at that time. But I nevertheless find it odd that this concern manifested itself only in my own particular case. In the case of Julián Grimau, as we have already seen in detail, security measures that were obviously imperative from every point of view were not applied in any such drastic fashion. Nor in the case of Romero Marín either. Romero Marín continued to work underground in Madrid even after he had very barely escaped falling into a police trap—thanks only to his extraordinary sang froid, his fighting spirit that refuses to accept defeat, however difficult the situation. Even after this incident, Romero Marín continued to work in Madrid, until he finally got himself arrested, as was predictable.

If owing to the absence of tangible facts to prove otherwise, I am obliged to accept Carrillo's word that he withdrew me from Madrid to prevent my falling into the hands of the police, and not in order to neutralize a member of the Executive Committee, Federico Sánchez, since in point of fact a process of political distancing and disagreement with Sánchez had been taking place since the previous spring, ostensibly in connection with a discussion regarding the agrarian policy of the Spanish Communist Party; if I am forced to grant that the security reasons adduced by Carrillo were really the foremost consideration, how to explain the fact that a comrade such as José Sandoval was sent to Madrid?

Sandoval, as I have already said, had lived all his years of exile in Eastern bloc countries. He was a hard-working, cultivated, level-headed comrade, but in Madrid it was going to be impossible for him to be like a fish in water. Everything about him betrayed the fact that he was an outlander: his pronunciation, his manners, his way of lighting a cigarette. Everything. Sandoval, for example, would never be comfortable talking soccer in bars with Madrid locals, who are always falling into conversation with strangers, nor would he be able to comment on Ordóñez's latest bullfight. Working in Madrid under these conditions was difficult, and I say so in all seriousness.

And in fact, just one short year after having taken my place and only a few months after actually beginning work in Madrid, José Sandoval was arrested, along with a whole group of party cadres from the university sector. On that occasion, the Social Brigade also managed to locate a number of clandestine apartments, something that did not happen very often.

From the strict viewpoint of the security of clandestine work, of its continuity, the step taken by Carrillo thus turned out to be a disastrous one. Once again the security of the organization, of the comrades, had been sacrificed to Carrillo's personal policy, for he has always been inclined to keep anyone without unconditional support for him out of leadership positions.

In any event, the decision to remove me from clandestine work in Spain was to have important consequences in my personal life.

In the first place, my situation and role within the party leadership were radically changed. Up until then, my work had been oriented along three principal lines. On the one hand, I was in charge of the specific sector of Communist intellectuals, including university students and professors. And at certain times—particularly after the arrests of Simón Sánchez Montero and Luis Lucio Laboto in 1959—I was also charged with organizing the party in the workers' sector. Hence the first party committees in a number of the most important metallurgy plants in Madrid were organized with my aid. And I shall not forget this experience. Without falling into populism, or into the mythology of the working- class- destined- by- historical- and- metaphysical -vocation-to-transform- the-world, I must say that I learned a great deal from this experience. In addition, I was entrusted with coordinating the work of the permanent nucleus of clandestine party leaders in Madrid, or, to be more precise, until 1959 the nucleus formed by Simón Sánchez Montero, Francisco Romero Marín, and myself, which Julián Grimau joined after Simón's arrest. And, finally, I was responsible for centralizing and politically orienting party relations with the other opposition forces: FLP (Popular Liberation Front), IDC (Christian Democratic Left), PSAD, (Social Party of Democratic Action), ASU (University Socialist Association), PSOE (Spanish Socialist Workers' Party), etc. In this latter branch of my activities, I had the good fortune, from 1956 on, of being able to count on the aid of Javier Pradera, which was inestimable, thanks to his personal qualities and perception of Spanish political realities.

But once I had been removed from my post in Madrid, what did I have left? Only responsibility for the specific work in the intellectual-university sector. But this responsibility very soon became a mere *pro forma* one. (In order to justify having withdrawn the responsibilities assigned me, Carrillo later declared, at the time of our dispute, that these responsibilities had been "withering away." As is well known, everything except the State is capable of "withering away" if it suits Carrillo.)

Given the ultracentralized structure of the party, which caused all decisions and initiatives to come from the summit of the apparatus, the political questions Comrade Sandoval raised from his post in Madrid were examined and resolved by the secretariat of the Central Committee before reaching me, a mere mortal, or, rather, a mere member of the Executive Committee.

Hence the only real responsibility I had left was the work with the intellectuals in exile. Anyone acquainted with Communist intellectuals in exile—with a few notable exceptions, of whom Jesús Izcaray was a very representative example—will understand that my situation was not an enviable one.

In fact, although his function was never clearly formulated in so many words, after I was withdrawn from the work in Spain José Sandoval acted as though he had been coopted to the Executive Committee by the all-powerful secretary-general, attending from that point on all its meetings when he was not in Madrid. Thus it came about that when the reasons behind the political divergencies within the party leadership were taken up in January of 1964, Sandoval participated in the first phase of this discussion in Paris.

As I consult today the official minutes of these meetings, I note that this situation seemed anomalous even to Sandoval. According to the minutes of February 4, 1964, "Costa" (Sandoval's *nom de guerre* among us) admits that the "discussion takes him somewhat by surprise, like a hen caught in a neighbor's chicken yard. Problems are being raised that he finds it difficult to express an opinion about, since he does not know exactly what is taking place." This fact, let it be said in passing, nonetheless did not prevent him from expressing an opinion—in support of Carrillo, naturally.

But along with my having been deliberately shunted aside from all real political responsibility, as jesuitically organized by Carrillo, the decision to remove me from clandestine work in Spain had other consequences for me.

For one thing, it permitted me to have a legal existence in France again. Since 1959, the year in which my papers as a political refugee expired, I had been living illegally in France as well as in Spain.

It would not have been difficult to renew my papers in 1959. But at that time we were preparing the confounded *Aitch En Pee* of June 18. Renewing my papers under these circumstances would have required abandoning my work in Madrid, for a few weeks at least, and appearing in Paris to go through the indispensable bureaucratic procedures. The party secretariat decided that this was not the right time for me to absent myself from Madrid. And besides, weren't we going to bring down the Franco regime in the next few weeks, the next few months? In the face of such a bright prospect, it was really not worth bothering about such a minor detail as a legal existence in France. There is no need for me to say that I was totally in agreement with that decision. In those days I was as mad, as beside myself with excitement, as full of ideological illusions as all the rest of the comrades. In a word, I did not deign to renew my French papers.

Early in 1963, after my last clandestine trip to Madrid, Carrillo pointed out how advantageous it would be for me to regularize my legal situation in France, if only from the viewpoint of reorienting my political work. I therefore took the necessary steps, and despite the years that had passed of not having my papers in order, the Paris Prefecture of Police renewed them without making any really serious inquiries as to why I had been so negligent in the past. A letter of recommendation sufficed to settle the affair. As I had been a member of an anti-Nazi Resistance organization and a deportee to Buchenwald, the functionary (a woman, as it turned out) in charge of the Fourth Section of the Prefecture, which dealt with foreigners, decided to accept my explanations and not open any sort of inquiry. Bourgeois democracy, as is well known, has these humanist and liberal "holes" in the system. In the so-called "Socialist" countries, such bureaucratic insouciance would of course not have come into the picture. In these countries the police do their job as God intended, and God, naturally, is the State.

Along with the decision to remove me from clandestine work in Spain, the other event—the one that "in the final analysis was the decisive factor," as any Althusserian imbecile would put it—within the series of circumstances and happenstances that ended up radically transforming my personal life that winter, was my friendship with Juan Goytisolo.

I had met Juan in the autumn of 1961, at a meeting at Benigno Rodríguez's, in Paris. I had seen him again a couple of times after that. Later, in the summer of 1962, at the time of the great wave of strikes that had begun in Asturias, I had a long conversation with him in Madrid. I remember that we were sitting on one of the terraces of the Castellana. I also remember that this time there began to crystallize between us that strange nebula of feelings that eventually constitutes a friendship, when one goes beyond that frontier marking the boundaries of a mere social relationship and enters another territory, one more difficult to make one's way through, no doubt, yet full of shared surprises, passions, silences, and tears.

. . . it is not easy for you to speak of Juan: this way: out loud: in public: he gives you the impression that you are violating his austere privacy: his natural reserve: but you must speak of Juan: Juan-of-the-land-of-the-landless: Juan-without-a-country: Juan-without-roots: Juan-of-the-dark-womb-of-the-mother-tongue: Juan-rooted-in-the-territory-of-the-mercury-and-sulphur-of-language:

you must speak of Juan, and you are going to speak as though he were never going to read these lines: as though in the very act of writing these verbal-approximations they were disappearing: phrases aimed like darts in Juan's direction:

you have never known anyone as capable as Juan Goytisolo of so much moral rigor applied to the very act of writing: anyone as genuinely involved with the very life-blood of a text: bloody viscera of words pulled up by their roots from the innermost depths of himself: anyone as capable of fiercely questioning his very existence: of beginning everything all over with each dazzling clean sheet of white paper: Juan-Don-Tancred confronting the ferocious bull of the madness of writing: confronting the combat to the death of literature:

perhaps you could compare Juan only with Franz Kafka: but you never knew Kafka: what is certain is that you entered dizzily into his desperate and violent and tender and proud and humble and simple and tortuous conception of life as literature and of literature as the only life possible: like Kafka, no doubt, Juan would say that in the combat between yourself and the world you must choose the world: and in this combat Juan's powers are exhausted and constantly renew themselves: until silence comes to cover with its indecent roaring surge this voice crowned with doves and manure: until the confused clamor of life stifles this stubborn and tireless work of death that the painful giving birth to yourself in bare, spare language is:

and you will tell Juan what you were thinking of telling him in the words of Luis Cernuda:

Down with virtue, order, misery then
Down with everything save defeat
Defeat up to the teeth, up to that chill space
Of a head split in two by solitudes
Knowing only that to live is to be all alone with death.

In August 1962, I met Juan Goytisolo again, in Italy.

That summer, in fact, I had given up the vacation that—hierarchically—I had a right to take in some country of the Eastern bloc. As is well known—or if it isn't, I say it here so that it will be—we leaders and principal cadres of the party had the right, every two years, to a month's vacation with our families in one of the so-called "Socialist" countries.

During the fifties of this century, proletarian internationalism, an old specter that has wandered all over the world, was reduced more or less to bureaucratic arrangements for trips and vacations extended to "brother parties" that were fighting underground, or, more prosaically, were not in power. Internationalism was thus more or less reduced to the function of a travel agency.

In any case, I had taken advantage of this hierarchical right to a vacation in the summer of 1958 and again in 1960. The first time in Sochi, in the Caucasus. The second time in Foros, in the far south of the Crimea. The first time I had had La Pasionaria, Carrillo, and Líster as neighbors and fellow vacationers, and the second time Líster, Carrillo, and La Pasionaria.

But that year, 1962, when I returned from Madrid after the great strike actions that did not lead to the *Aitch En Pee* because the *Aitch En Pee* was not on the map of reality but only on the road to dreamland, I found to my surprise that all the leaders who had the right to vacations had already left for their summer destinations. There was no meeting of the Central Committee scheduled, nor even a plenary session of the Executive Committee, to examine the experiences of that period of active agitation. I was told that Carrillo was in Bulgaria, on a beach on the Black Sea, and that I could leave whenever I chose to join him there and have a rest.

I refused the invitation. I no longer had the strength to endure this sort of official vacation yet another time. Moreover, since the previous spring Carrillo and I had been at loggerheads with each other, and I preferred not to join him. I wrote him a letter expressing my surprise at the fact that no meeting of the Central Committee had been called and teasing him a little about the precipitate haste with which all of them had plunged into the delights of summer vacation. I then went off on vacation on my own.

That was how we met Juan Goytisolo and Monique Lange in Capri, that happy summer of 1962. We were staying with Mario Alicata, an Italian party leader who had invited us to share his house. But we met Juan and Monique each morning at the rockbound bay of I Faraglioni.

(No, don't begin to talk about Capri here. You are not in a novel. If you were in a novel, this chapter would be titled "The Blue Lizard of I Faraglioni." But I will not let you tell about the blue lizard, or about the old gardener of the Via del Tuoro who remembered Lenin, or the Aragonese governor of the fortress of Capri—when Capri belonged to the kingdom of Aragón—whose name just happened to be Sánchez too. I will not let you insert here a graceful digression on Gorki's outing to Damecuta, or recall Lenin's conversations with Gorki and Lunacharski. I will not let you talk; it's out of the question. Not even of Suetonius's *Lives of the Twelve Caesars* and his description of Tiberius's super sophisticated pleasures in his seaside villa, *quasi pueros primae teneritudinis, quos pisciculos uocabat, institueret, ut natanti sibi inter femina uersarentur ac lauderent lingua morsuque sensim adpetentes. . . .*)

Juan, who always seems to have his head in the clouds as he strides absent-mindedly on the heights of Úbeda or Anacapri, proved to have an extraordinary sense of the practical. He made arrangements with a fisherman who had a motor launch and organized marvelous excursions to deserted coves, splendid expeditions to fish for sea urchins, which we ate right there in the launch, drinking countless bottles of a delicious, nearly transparent white wine that he had discovered somewhere and brought with him in a plastic bag full of ice. At night, in the *piazzetta,* we would join Mario and Sara Alicata, Rossana Rossanda and Rodolfo Banfi, Ugo Pirro and Luciana Castellina, and other Italian comrades, and sometimes the discussions would last till dawn.

But as I was saying: I became ever closer friends with Juan all through this period. Later on, in Paris, after it had been decided that I would not be returning to work underground in Spain, one night when we were having dinner at Monique's at that apartment at number 33 rue Poissonnière that we will all remember forever with affection (isn't that right, Carlos Fuentes, Mario Vargas Llosa, José Maria Castellet, Carlos Barral, Octavio Paz, Richard Seaver, Fernando Claudín, Carlos Franqui, Ricardo Bofill, K. S. Karol, Guillermo Cabrera Infante, Heberto Padilla...

[but what have you said? Have you mentioned the name Heberto Padilla? Does Heberto Padilla really exist however? Is the fact that you have in your library a copy of *Fuera del juego* (*Out of the Game*) with a handwritten dedication, "To Jorge Semprún, these pages that have made me diabolical," really sufficient proof that such a person as Heberto Padilla really existed? Is this book sufficient proof that this devil of a poet, this diabolical poet of genius really existed? Perhaps not. Perhaps Heberto Padilla was only the name assumed by a shadow who, one fine day in April 1970, came out of the dungeons of the Cuban Security Police to deliver one of the most abject speeches, one of the most miserable self-criticisms ever delivered, denouncing friends, singing the praises of the State Security men, "the most valiant of comrades who work day and night to bring about moments such as this, to bring about acts of magnanimity such as this, almost unjustifiable gestures of understanding such as this: giving a man such as myself, who fought against the Revolution, the opportunity to rectify his life radically, as I wish to do." And in point of fact he has radically rectified it: he has died. But perhaps that poet who said his name was Heberto Padilla really exists in some wasteland, or in some Hell out of the Hieronymus Bosch, that diabolical poet of genius who described beforehand what would happen to him in "En tiempos dificiles" ("In Difficult Times"), which you are going to quote in its entirety so that young poets of tomorrow may remember it and know it by heart in case someday they are assailed by the dark temptation to give themselves over entirely to collective religiosity or destroy themselves in the service of something that is not their own truth:

They asked this man for his time
to add it to the time of History.
They asked him for his hands
since in difficult times
there is nothing better than a pair of good hands.
They asked him for his eyes
that sometimes brimmed with tears

so that he could look on the good side of things
(especially the good side of life)
because one astonished eye suffices to look on horror.
They asked him for his lips
dry and cracked, to affirm,
to build, with each affirmation, a dream
(the loftiest dream);
they asked him for his legs
hard and gnarled,
(his old legs that were good walkers)
because in difficult times
is there anything better than a pair of legs
for building, for the trenches?
They asked him for the copse that nourished him as a child
with its obedient tree.
They asked him for his breast, his heart, his shoulders.
They told him
this was strictly necessary.
They explained to him later
that all these gifts would be useless
unless he surrendered his tongue as well
because in difficult times
nothing is as useful to stop hatred or silence memory.
And finally they asked him
please to clear out
because in difficult times
this is doubtless the decisive proof,

and yes, this is doubtless the decisive proof that there once existed, in
difficult times, a poet who said his name was Heberto Padilla...])

and at Monique's and Juan's, then, as I was saying, one night
when we had perhaps drunk too much and were talking of literature—
that mixture is always an explosive one—I happened to tell Monique at
one point not to bother me anymore with the problems some poor devil
of a writer was having over something or other that I don't remember,
because I knew about such problems already since I'd written a novel
myself. Monique was skeptical at first, and then enthusiastic, and finally
determined to walk over my dead body if necessary to get, and in the end
got, out of me something that up until then no one else but my wife
Colette had: permission to read the manuscript of my unfinished book,
which at that time was entitled simply *A Voyage,* the book I had begun
to write, two years before, at number 5 Concepción Bahamonde.

Monique liked the book, and since she was working at Gallimard at the time, she gave it to Claude Roy. He liked it too.

A few weeks later, in December 1962, I was walking down General Mola, on the odd-numbered side, between María de Molina and Juan Bravo. These were the last few hours of my last clandestine stay in Madrid. I had already come to this place the night before, to meet the liaison agent arriving from Paris. But he had not shown up. There had been a terrible snowstorm in the north and the Echegarate Pass had been closed for several hours. I presumed that that was why he was late. So the next day I went to the place where we were to meet if he didn't turn up at the first rendezvous. He was there this time, and had indeed been held up by the snowstorm. He also had with him a letter from my wife, telling me that the book had been accepted by Gallimard and that Sartre wanted to publish several chapters from it in his review, *Les Temps Modernes*.

I met with Romero Marín a little later. I gave him the letters I was to pass on to him. We talked about some bit of unsettled business or other and said goodbye. An icy, cutting wind was blowing. That was the last time I was ever to see Romero Marín in the Madrid underground.

It was a sad day for me, really.

I went back to Ángel González's place, on San Juan de la Cruz. I had found refuge there during this last trip to Madrid. I packed my suitcase. At that moment neither the book, nor Gallimard, nor the possibility of a new life, which struck me as a remote, almost unreal possibility, mattered at all to me. The only thing that mattered was that I would no longer be coming to Madrid, no longer be living in Madrid.

I had returned here, to the place where I belonged, to the scene of my childhood dreams, ten years before, in June of 1953. I had arrived by way of Valencia, on a late afternoon train. I had taken up lodgings in a family boarding house on Santa Cruz de Marcenado, and that night I had immediately gone walking in the streets.

(But don't try to touch our hearts with this memory of your first stroll through the streets of Madrid. What is more, you have already described it in another book, *L'évanouissement* (*The Fainting Spell*), and it is not the "in" thing to do to repeat the same sentimental effects. Moreover, at that moment—be sincere—what weighed most heavily on your mind was not the past but the future. You were about to go into exile for the second time. An image that was truly nightmarish exploded in your mind. You saw yourself in meetings of the Executive Committee for months, years—years and years perhaps—doomed to Mije's rhetoric and

hollow perorations; Delicado's interminable, disjointed nonsense; Líster's diatribes when he thought someone was shoving him out of the
limelight or trying to; the mellifluous and repetitive speeches of Santiago
Álvarez, who was in the habit of limiting himself to putting into mourn-
ful tones, like Galician bagpipe music, what Carrillo had said much
better and in fewer words. And the same old stories every day at lunchtime. The same jokes, the same tired anecdotes. "Those of you with a
weak prostate come with me," Mije would inevitably cry when there was
a break in the meetings to go to the rest room.

Yes, everyone knows what exile is like. And if not, so much the better.)

A few months later, on May 3, 1963, Carrillo and I were at a meeting
of delegations of the Western European Communist parties.

It was in a building of a muncipality run by a French Communist
administration, on the outskirts of Paris. It was in Stains. (What a
coincidence! The same place where that confounded meeting was to take
place a year later!) The French delegation was headed by Georges Gosnat, who was responsible for the finances of the French Communist Party
—and I do not mean the revenue from dues, donations, party-aid campaigns, and sale of propaganda, but real finances: the administration of
the considerable movables and immovables and stock certificates that the
French Communist Party possesses. Gosnat had attended our Sixth
Congress in Prague, and his political life had had a certain relation with
Spain almost since its very beginning. Not that Gosnat had been in the
International Brigades, but he had been the very young head of the
France-Navigation company, created with funds of the Spanish Republic
to transport supplies, sanitary material, and also arms to our zone,
whenever possible. In other words, business had been a vocation with
Gosnat from early on.

The Italian delegation was made up of Giancarlo Pajetta and Rossana
Rossanda. I couldn't say who any of the members of the other delegations were. I do know, however, that Jean Blume was not a member of
the Belgian delegation, since I had known Blume in Buchenwald and
wouldn't have been able to forget him. I also know that the delegate from
Luxemburg slept all through the meeting (not that that should reflect
discredit on the militants of the Grand Duchy, who are no doubt as
self-abnegating and committed as those of all the other parties in the
world), waking up only when the noon meeting recessed and the splendid
dishes of the "fraternal luncheon"—the hallowed phrase for this sort of
repast—offered us by the French Communist Party made their appearance.

The purpose of this meeting was to prepare the Conference of Western Europe for amnesty in Spain, scheduled for the following two days, May 4 and 5. This was a step intended to coordinate and prolong the protest demonstrations that the murder of Julián Grimau, some two weeks before, had given rise to all over Europe.

The meeting proceeded as these meetings usually did. Around 12:25 —I remember the time as accurately as witnesses in detective stories: the reader will see why later—Giancarlo Pajetta, a leader of the Italian Communist Party, asked for the floor. Carrillo, who was presiding over the meeting, was about to accede when Georges Gosnat spoke up. He said that it would be better to interrupt the proceedings and have lunch. A bit piqued, Giancarlo replied that what he had to say would not take long, and lunch could no doubt wait a few minutes. No, Gosnat said, the fact was that lunch couldn't wait. There was a roast on the menu that was to be ready at a certain precise time, and if we didn't begin lunch at 12:30 on the dot, the roast would be overdone. Giancarclo Pajetta paled. I know him well enough—that is to say, I used to know him well enough—to realize that he was getting angry, that he was about to have one of those insane fits of temper that sometimes overcame him. He insisted once more, dryly, with a sort of icy irony that is very typical of him. He said that a roast that was just a little overdone wasn't very important, and again asked for the floor, then and there. But Gosnat stuck to his point about the roast, as though it were an affair of state. He came up with a final argument that solved the matter once and for all. "Comrade Giancarlo," Gosnat said, with a deliberate tremor in his voice, "the comrades who have prepared this luncheon in your honor, modest militants who have devoted these extra hours to you, which are not part of their professiona obligations here at the city hall, would not understand if we let the roast be served overdone and ruin this luncheon, which is their humble expression of their solidarity with the cause of Spain." In the face of such an argument, Pajetta opened his mouth, breathed deeply, as though he'd been hit in the solar plexus, and turned ashen. He made a brusque gesture, as though to say, all right, do as you like. Rossana Rossanda, sitting there silent and motionless, had on her face that beautiful, sad, perhaps desperate smile that the peripeteias of the world Communist movement have always brought to her lips ever since I have known her.

So everyone sat down to lunch.

To sociologists, historians, students of politics, Kremlinologists, and other specialists who have been endeavoring for years now to discover and reveal the mechanisms of social life in the USSR, I would recommend that they go out and do what those boring UNESCO documents refer to as a little "field work," to go spend a few weeks in one or another of the municipalities on the outskirts of Paris which have been run by French Communist administrations for several decades now; that they get acquainted with the politico-bureaucratic personnel of these municipalities; that they investigate the behavior, the way of life, and the relations with the rest of the population of those Communists who are the cadres in these sometimes largely populated suburbs. They would thus have an idea, a working model—though no doubt one in some ways particular to this milieu and corresponding to socio-cultural traditions distinct from the Russian ones—in order to understand the functioning of Soviet social institutions. I am referring, naturally, to the *normal* functioning of these institutions, when oppression, hierarchism, the system of values and privileges operate without the need for the open and massive terror of the Gulag era. The French Communist Party, in fact, is not simply a political party. It is also a counter-culture, a microsociety —or a collection of microsocieties proliferating within the tissue of capitalist democracry—a small-scale model of a social laboratory, the study of which, as embarked upon by Annie Kriegal and a few others, is still very far from having been exhaustively pursued to its ultimate conclusion.

In any case, a "fraternal luncheon" such as the one offered us by the French Communist Party on May 3, 1963, constitutes a microcosm that it would be extremely interesting to study in detail.

In any case, the luncheon eventually came to an end. The roast had been at its point of perfection, and delicious. The wines too. Champagne appeared with the dessert. The glasses were filled. Giancarlo Pajetta was looking paler and paler, and had hardly touched his food. Rossana Rossanda had stopped smiling. Then Gosnat rose from his chair, raised his glass, and proposed a toast to comrade Federico Sánchez, who, under the name of Jorge Semprún, had just won the Formentor Prize for Literature, two days before, on May 1.

I sat there open-mouthed, overcome with a sort of indignant embarrassment. What did the Formentor Prize have to do with all this? I looked at Rossana, and she beamed a faint smile my way. The comrade from Luxemburg naturally had no idea what was going on.

Obviously, Gosnat had not taken the initiative of offering this toast to me without having previously consulted Carrillo. As a matter of fact, in those days Carrillo was vastly interested in exploiting my new literary personality. For one thing, it could be beneficial to the Spanish Communist Party to have at its disposal a sort of legal spokesman for its positions who was in exile. In fact, the granting of the prize to my novel provoked the wrath of the Francoist press. *ABC* (the Monarchist right newspaper) devoted a violent editorial to attacking me as a typical representative of the spirit of hatred and rancor that characterized the Red diaspora.

"Who is Jorge Semprún?" *ABC* asked in its editorial of May 13, 1963, "El comunismo y los intelectuales." "He is an exile who abandoned our country in 1939, who fought in the French Resistance, who writes for the Marxist press and militates in the Communist party with activist enthusiasm. Salvador de Madariaga, who can in no way be suspected of totalitarianism, sent a telegram to the Formentor Prize Jury, which met this year in Corfu, with the participation of the unfortunate Einaudi, warning its members against Semprún, whom he described as a Communist agent and an enemy of the Spanish people."

This story of the telegram is true. The Formentor jury did in fact receive such a telegram, sent from Paris and signed Salvador de Madariaga. But Salvador de Madariaga categorically denied being the author of the telegram and demanded an inquiry by the French police to find the party responsible. This inquiry came to nothing. So far as I know, the real author of this telegram was never discovered.

Moreover, Carrillo also thought that the beginning of a literary career for me would smooth over the political problems that had arisen between us and that success would make me forget the way in which Federico Sánchez was being removed from all real responsibility in the party so as to become a mere token writer, a figurehead.

So at the end of that dreary "fraternal luncheon"—being given, let the reader not forget, on the occasion of a meeting devoted to the problems of amnesty in Spain, as a consequence of Grimau's murder—Georges Gosnat raised his glass of champagne and proposed a toast to the Formentor Prize.

Because of all this, when I read *Dialogue on Spain* many years later, in the fall of 1974, "my soul fell to my feet," as we say in Spanish. (If I were writing this book in French, I would say *"les bras m'en sont tombés"* ["my arms fell"] in stupefaction: In French it's not your soul that falls but your arms, all of which demonstrates that Spanish is a more violent language, and also a more metaphysical one; whatever happens, in Spanish our souls are immediately involved.) As I was saying, then, my soul fell to my feet in stupefaction when I read what Carrillo had written:

"The case of Federico Sánchez is somewhat different. I was convinced that party tasks were stifling him, not on the political plane particularly, but because he had not fulfilled his vocation as a writer, as a creator, and that clandestine political work weighed heavily upon him, something I understood very well, and I said to him: 'If you want to write, you can, but it's not worth making a political scandal over.' It may be that he was sincerely persuaded that the Communist movement was reaching a state that had no future and that in order to make his way as a writer it was necessary for him to withdraw from it. He therefore went his own way."

I was of course stupefied!

Everything that Carrillo says in these lines is a lie. In the first place, party tasks were not stifling me because I had not fulfilled my "vocation as a writer." I had abandoned my vocation as a writer, voluntarily, with no regrets, many years before, so as to devote myself to party tasks. Hence it is completely false—as well as being a nasty insinuation—that "clandestine political work weighed heavily" upon me. Everyone who knows anything about me knows very well that clandestine political work is what has most excited, pleased, interested, amused, and passionately attracted me in my entire life. Life has doubtless weighed heavily on me at times, as it does on everyone. Other people's stupidity weighs heavily on me, doubtless. The specters of my own inner life weigh heavily on me, doubtless. But clandestine political work has never weighed heavily on me, above all for the very good reason that it was precisely that: clandestine. And then Carrillo, playing the role of the man who is nothing if not tolerant, says that he understood all that very well and that he said to me "If you want to write, you can. . . ." But I certainly hadn't waited for Carrillo's permission to write—what an absurd idea! I had sat down to write, went back to writing, at number 5 Concepción Bahamonde, without anyone's permission, and there wasn't the slightest conflict with my political work! And as the crowning touch in this series of malicious falsehoods, there was Carrillo's opinion that in order to make my way as a writer it was necessary for me to withdraw from the party. But hadn't I already made my way as a writer, and even won the Formentor Prize, without any need whatsoever of breaking with the party, being in fact a member of the Executive Committee at the time?!

In other words, everything that Carrillo said was false, and he knew it very well. So why did he say it?

When Régis Debray was preparing that book of interviews with Santiago Carrillo, he telephoned me. He wanted to see me, so we got together for dinner one night at a brasserie near the Bastille. Costa Gavras and his wife were also there, I don't remember why. Debray explained to me his plans to write a book with Carrillo, and asked me to draw a verbal portrait of him. I did so. Debray was delighted with this portrait because he has always been facinated by great pragmatic leaders, practitioners of Realpolitik, politicastros: his ideal, it so happens, is none other than Fidel Castro, the great shark in the troubled waters of politicastration.

Debray also asked me to sum up the main subjects of the 1964 debate. This was prehistory to me by that time, but I made an effort and summed them up. And that was it: goodnight.

A few weeks later, Debray came to my place with the endless typed transcription of the interview tapes with Carrillo, before he had done the editing work that is indispensable for this sort of book based on improvised taped conversations, and asked me to read it, which I did. I then went to see him at his country house in Vert, and returned this voluminous manuscript. I gave him my opinion, which he listened to without saying much of anything. I told him that the book was very shaky from the standpoint of theory and mendacious from the standpoint of biography. I demonstrated what I meant through a number of concrete examples.

But that is not the most important thing. The important thing in this particular instance is that in the complete transcription of the very disjointed original recording there was no such paragraph by Carrillo as the one I have just quoted. This paragraph was added later.

And so we come back to the question I posed before. Why did Santiago Carrillo add, at the last minute, this paragraph about me, about my vocation as a writer, and about my decision to withdraw from the party so as to make my way as a writer?

(Let me add incidentally that Jesús Izcaray now knows what he must do to make his way as a writer, he who is so anxious to do so, whose dream is to do so: all he would need to do is withdraw from the party, according to Carrillo's curious theory regarding literary creation.)

I believe that the key to this incident lies in the fact that in talking about me Carrillo uses that forgotten name of Federico Sánchez. In fact, when he is asked a question about me that names me by my name, Jorge Semprún, Carrillo answers by talking about Federico Sánchez.

And in 1974 nobody remembered Federico Sánchez anymore. I myself had forgotten about Federico Sánchez. Why remember him, why bring him back to life again then? I believe that it was for a very simple reason, and one very characteristic of Carrillo. What interested him at that moment was to remind the Communists of the young generations—them especially—and leftist intellectuals in general that Jorge Semprún the writer, the author of such and such books, the scenarist of such and such films that are quite well known, whose influence in Spain might not be negligible in the very near future, or at some more or less imminent point in the future, was none other than that old "revisionist," "capitulator," and "liquidationist," Federico Sánchez. What interested Carrillo, even though it might involve certain downright lies, was to identify Sánchez and Semprún, and jesuitically undermine the prestige of both. Just in case.

Well, then, now that Carrillo has resurrected Federico Sánchez, now that he has conjured up this specter and rescued him from oblivion, now that he has given him a semblance of reality, he is going to be obliged to put up with the consequences. He will be obliged to confront his absence of memory with the memory of Federico Sánchez. He will be obliged to hear the voice of Federico Sánchez. For it certainly is not going to be any easy task to reduce Federico Sánchez to silence.

For one thing, Federico has a few comments to make on the Spanish edition of *Dialogue on Spain,* a book or booklet, or, better yet, a libel, that is at least of some interest in that Carrillo (who no doubt intended to present only his best profile, like an old actor in a western) unwittingly provides a revealing full-length portrait of himself.

If one compares the Spanish edition of the book, published as *Mañana, España* in Barcelona by Editorial Laia, with the original French edition, *Demain, L' Espagne,* a certain discrepancy can be noted. Even though the publisher does not say so—perhaps because he is not a man of good faith, although people say he's full of it—even though the publisher, then, gives no indication of it, provides no footnote at the bottom of the corresponding page to explain the reasons for this discrepancy, such a modification of the original French text does in fact exist. Federico Sánchez naturally spotted it immediately.

In the first Spanish version of the book, published in Paris by Colección Ebro, Carrillo states, after explaining in his own way—that is to say falsifying everything—the principal points of contention in the discussion of 1964 that "reality very soon demonstrated that the path recommended by Claudín and Federico Sánchez was not the right one. And they themselves subsequently took a serious wrong turn that led them to defend positions of an ultraleftist type."

I am not going to discuss this falsehood, since this particular statement has disappeared in the Laia edition. Carrillo himself removed this falsehood. In its place the reader now finds the following lines: "The Party [still with the capital letter that makes it something sacred: there's no teaching an old dog new tricks, as everyone knows!] and the democratic forces had to combat the dictatorship, put their revolutionary will on the line, if they wanted democratic change to become a reality." This is nothing but a platitude of course. Nobody has ever questioned the fact that the party and the democratic forces had to combat the dictatorship. The problem—which was far from being a minor one—lay in deciding how to combat the dictatorship, what strategy to plan and carry out, what objectives to assign the mass movement.

Following these trite lines, a new paragraph is included in the Laia edition that did not appear in the original Colección Ebro edition. It reads:

"In this discussion none of us was probably entirely right [what a sudden attack of unprecedented modesty on Carrillo's part!] I tried to get a solution adopted that would synthesize the various points of view, and in an initial phase of the discussion I appeared to have succeeded. I drew up a text in summation that seemed to meet with everyone's approval; but this outcome was thwarted owing to the intervention of one of the comrades who after the meetings in Czechoslovakia tried to split the Party. The situation became more complicated and there was no longer any way of avoiding the break."

When he read this new paragraph, surreptitiously added to the Laia edition, Federico Sánchez was immediately overcome with a devastating Homeric fury. Then he began to laugh like a madman; he almost died laughing. This Carrillo who pictures himself to us as a political leader of international stature, a true statesman, turns out to be a little village rascal. And what is more, one with no memory, or absent-minded. Because he forgets when he adds these false and farcical lines that minutes of the meetings of the Executive Committee exist, and hence it is an easy task to bring the real truth to light.

And the real truth went like this:

The discussions began on January 24, 1964—if we disregard the preliminary skirmishes in the spring of 1962, when agrarian policy was examined, and in the summer and fall of 1963, when ideological questions arose. On the agenda was a quite routine subject: the examination of an informational note to be sent by the Spanish Communist Party to the four Western European Communist parties that had joined with them in forming a committee of solidarity and support for the anti-Franco campaign. After Juan Gómez (Tomás García) and Ignacio Gallego had spoken, limiting themselves to a few remarks on the subject under discussion and adding a few more precise details here and there, Fernando Claudín then took the floor.

"The informational note is an accurate résumé of a whole series of facts and aspects, to be sure, but it has the defect of being somewhat one-sided in that it does not take into account other aspects of the situation. . . . For instance, as regards the economic situation of the masses, we must keep in mind: the increase in wages since the strikes of '62; the effects of tourism, in that it provides jobs and creates a whole range of new business enterprises; the emigration to other European countries. . . . The improvement in the economic situation of the masses is the result of their own participation in the class struggle, but it is also the result of the practical possibility of making concessions that the bourgeoisie has been confronted with. If on the one hand class struggle is stimulated thereby, on the other hand its extension may be thereby hampered. It affords the oligarchy a greater margin for maneuver. . . ."

This was the line of argument set forth in Fernando's remarks, according to the official (summarized) minutes of this Executive Committee meeting. Then López Raimundo, Líster, Mije, and Delicado spoke without saying anything new (I will send on request to any reader who doubts my objectivity photocopies of the minutes I have mentioned, so that he may be convinced of it). Perhaps a certain note of displeasure at Fernando's observation can be perceived in Mije's remarks. Triumphalist as usual, he states: "Is there any change necessary in the analyses of the situation that we made at the last meeting of the five? No. The hypotheses set forth then have been confirmed. Spain is the weakest link in the chain of European capitalism. It is true that the opposition is not united, but this does not diminish its considerable weight in the balance nor the necessity for changes."

After Delicado, Federico Sánchez took the floor.

"In the informational note there is a certain tendency to stress the positive aspects and not emphasize those related to obstacles and difficulties. For example: the Asturias strike. There is no emphasis put on the series of obstacles that prevented it from spreading: the difference of level between the organization and the political consciousness of the working masses; the economic situation; the international situation, aspects that have permitted the regime to improve its international situation. We are witnessing the acceleration of a process within the monopolist oligarchy. . . . "

Then Manolo (Eduardo García) spoke, with his usual subjectivist frenzy: "The extension and the level of the present struggles by the working class are superior to that of previous periods which preceded large-scale actions. . . . I am more optimistic than ever. We are on the eve of great events. If the informational note has a defect, it is that it is too even-handed. . . . "

As can be seen, two lines of analysis and appreciation of reality were beginning to crystallize, even though as yet in only a veiled form.

The next meeting of the Executive Committee took place on January 29, five days later. At that time, Fernando Claudín, the first to take the floor that day, developed his points of view in greater detail, along the line already mentioned: the need for an objective analysis of reality. In fact, all the opinions that were to be rejected as "revisionist" and "capitulatory" by the majority of the Executive Committee were already there in outline form in Claudín's speech. But when Santiago Carrillo took the floor that day, he began by making the following declaration: "Fernando's speech today is interesting. His political conclusions are correct. They correspond to what we have been doing since the plenum of the Central Committee. . . . " And then after this preliminary statement, Carrillo limited himself to paraphrasing or restating Claudín's positions, though admittedly he toned down some of the latter's more critical formulations.

From that moment on, the Executive Committee members who had listened to Fernando reservedly and suspiciously, and had made their remarks accordingly, immediately took the opposite tack so as to tag after the secretary-general.

The first one to speak after Carrillo was "Costa" (José Sandoval)—who had been attending the Executive Committee meetings ever since my responsibilities as a leader had begun "withering away," according to Carrillo's later phrase, or in other words leading to a "flowering" of Sandoval's responsibilities, the content of which remained identical, the one change being their transfer to a person who enjoyed the secretary-general's complete confidence. Perhaps to justify this confidence, Costa began by saying: "Santiago's remarks have forcefully underscored a series of new elements. Courageously. . . . " This small detail serves as a demonstration of how the "personality cult" works. The fact was that Carrillo had done nothing more than take up the positions Claudín had outlined. It was Claudín who had "forcefully underlined a series of new elements. Courageously. . . . " But these new elements could of course be recognized as such only when it was the secretary-general who took them up and formulated them, even though he had done so in a less cogent, less articulate fashion than Claudín. Anything new, of course, could come forth only from the charismatic hand of the secretary-general.

Ignacio Gallego reacted as Sandoval had. He immediately declared that "Santiago has summed up the worries and concerns that we all have about the situation and the outlook for the future." But if the minutes of the meetings are read carefully, it can be seen that before Carrillo took the floor, Ignacio Gallego had had neither worries nor concerns: the analyses of the party were correct, the outlook for the future radiant; we were proceeding from triumph to triumph and victory to victory, as that comrade of my neighborhood party cell used to say in 1947 when we met in the quarters of the Learned Societies on the Rue Danton.

The last person to take the floor on that 29th of January, 1964, was Federico Sánchez. I am going to cite his words at greater length than those of others. When all is said and done, I am not writing the history of the Spanish Communist Party, nor Carrillo's biography: I am writing the autobiography of Federico Sánchez. Well anyway, his political biography, which has a rather Victorian cast, it must be granted: neither the dreams, nor the sexuality, nor the obsessions of Federico Sánchez figure in this attempt at autobiographical reflection, except obliquely perhaps, by way of some little spark of memory that an attentive reader may discern here and there. And since Federico Sánchez is the protagonist of this narrative, let us allow him to speak exactly as he pleases. If that seems like narcissism, I will say in self-justification that it is the narcissism of the book, of the undertaking itself: it is inscribed before the fact in the very structure of the text.

Be that as it may, the last person to take the floor that day was Federico Sánchez.

I believe that in the remarks made by Fernando and Santiago—aside from a few nuances, a few problematical questions, and others that still remain open —a level of synthesis has been arrived at with which I am in agreement. . . . Implicit in it is an overall conception of the present process which, in my opinion, is the following: the decomposition, on the one hand, of the Fascist forms of power and the recomposition, on the other hand, of the forces of the bourgeoisie. This process will go through a whole series of phases. Some of these may prove even more complicated and difficult than those in the past. . . . We must not link the prospect of the fall of the regime to stagnation or to economic crisis. We must do everything possible to ensure that this remains clear; this is imperative. . . . As to the [government] Development Plan, an observation: it is evident that even if it is carried out, it will not permit the country to reach the European level in the immediate future. Even for a democratic power this would be a long-term task. But the masses—and we ourselves—will judge the social and psychological results of the plan by comparing them, not with an abstract European level, but with the concrete level of the country, which they know from experience. . . . For example, the present level of wages: even though there is only a small increase, it is important for very broad sectors among workers and technicians. Above all, any initial increase in wages is more important than one granted later at a higher level. . . .

As regards the struggle of the masses and the General Political Strike. We must keep in mind that the critical level necessary for a mass action to be politicized and spread tends to become one that is situated higher and higher, given the evolution of the political situation. In '56, at the time of the unrest at the University, in '57 at the time of the streetcar strike in Madrid, important actions were carried out through organizations that were not at all numerous and through propaganda activity that was limited. This would be impossible today. It is not only the working class that is becoming more active. The initiative of the bourgeoisie in general, and of the monopolist bourgeoisie in particular, is increasing, in order to oppose the movement of the masses, an initiative that at times even takes the form of making concessions. This capacity for maneuver is certainly not unlimited, but we have not yet arrived at the limit. No conclusions can be mechanically drawn from the increase in partial actions, as though their generalization and their political content were something that would come about automatically. . . . I wish to express a certain concern regarding the problems that follow from this entire situation, from the passage of time itself, in relation to the orders for a General Political Strike. . . .

I believe that in this whole discussion there has been a serious effort made to put the problems of the situation of the country in realistic focus. To envisage the problems of the prospect before us calmly. This is one way of combatting the danger of subjectivism, which we have had and shall continue to have, given the very conditions of our work and its difficulties. When we read some of our documents of the past, certain economic analyses for instance, we find, alongside accurate appraisals of the overall perspective, certain predictions that were formulated in too categorical a way and that subsequent events did not bear out. If we reread and analyze our own predictions, we see in certain estimations of the rhythm of development a tendency to exaggerate, linked to the need we feel of giving an impression of security, as Santiago has said, linked to the very necessity of mobilizing the masses, which gives this type of exaggeration an objective basis. This is a permanent danger. . . .

The meeting of January 29, 1964 ended with these remarks from the floor by Federico Sánchez.

But it was on the following day, when the discussion was resumed, that events took a most surprising turn.

The first to take the floor was Eduardo García: "I believe that not much light has come from the discussion thus far. It's as though we were engaging in a dialogue between deaf men." Starting from there, brusquely changing terrain, leading the discussion from the analysis of political questions to that of the problems of unity within the group of leaders, Eduardo García launched a systematic attack, a violent one both in form and content, on Claudín and Sánchez.

Shortly thereafter, Enrique Líster made the following statement: "I have had a great deal of difficulty understanding the content of this meeting. When the agenda of these meetings was drawn up, I thought that this question of the unity of the party formed part of the first item. Then I saw that I was wrong. And I failed to understand how what was being discussed could be discussed without first sinking our teeth into this question. When Santiago took the floor, I thought he was going to bring it up. But he didn't. It may be that Santiago preferred to let each one of us bell the cat himself. . . . "

So Eduardo García and Enrique Líster belled the cat; that is to say, they deliberately sidetracked a discussion in which a new, more realistic view of the political situation in Spain was about to emerge, with great difficulty, no doubt, and instead aggressively launched into a whole series of ideological and personal criticisms aimed against Claudín and Sánchez. But as Fernando Claudín later pointed out, this question of the unity within the leadership was not on the agenda of these Executive Committee meetings. Or at any rate it was not on the agenda that had been openly drawn up. It may well be that at some meeting of a dissident group—and let us not forget that a dissident group meeting together may well be a majority—it had been decided to raise this question, without either the knowledge or the assent of two of the members of the party leadership, that is to say, none other than Claudín and Sánchez.

In any case, how did Santiago Carrillo react to this new turn the meetings had suddenly taken? In the paragraph added to the Laia edition of *Dialogue on Spain,* Carrillo states that his attempt at synthesizing the various divergent views "was thwarted owing to the intervention of one of the comrades who after the meetings in Czechoslovakia tried to split the Party. The situation became more complicated and there was no longer any way of avoiding the break." Such a formulation is typical of Carrillo. It in fact contains a grain of truth, for it was indeed Eduardo García's remarks from the floor that sidetracked the discussion. But this grain of truth has been buried beneath a pack of lies. In the first place, Eduardo García did not carry enough weight in the Executive Committee of the Spanish Communist Party to force Carrillo to embark upon a path that he was unwilling to follow. Eduardo García was Carrillo's lap dog (though admittedly one with teeth that could bite), his creation, his factotum carrying out his every wish. And furthermore, what do the minutes of the Executive Committee have to say about all this? The minutes record that when Santiago Carrillo spoke, after Eduardo García and Enrique Líster, he said the following: "I did not bring up the problem of the unity within the party leadership in my earlier remarks because I wanted to restrict myself to political problems. It seems to me to be a very positive development that this question has been posed."

And at the end of his remarks he says again: "When Manolo (Eduardo García) spoke of a dialogue between deaf men, I think he rendered the entire Executive Committee a service by laying on the table the new problems that are present within it."

That was what Santiago Carrillo had to say in 1964. This demonstrates that when he added a new little paragraph to his libel, Santiago Carrillo was lying. If the "break" could not have been prevented it was because this was what he himself wanted, because he himself set loose paranoiacal little Eduardito and poor, vain, old Líster against the two of us, Claudín and Sánchez.

(But you no longer have the courage to go on with this demonstration.

Here, at this point of your book, you had it all nicely planned to insert a few documents that would clarify for the reader all the problems discussed.

Here, for instance, you had thought you would reproduce the memorandum that you prepared for Palmiro Togliatti in July of 1964. It is a complete summary of all points of view, fourteen pages long, written in French. It is entitled "A propos d'une discussion." Rossana Rossanda, who at the time was on the Central Committee of the Italian Communist Party and head of the Cultural Section, informed you that Togliatti wanted complete and objective information on the discussion in the Spanish Communist Party. She suggested that you prepare a note for him on the origins and content of the discussion, a note that she herself could further explicate verbally. And that is what you did. You wrote a report, as succinctly and objectively as possible, reducing your personal comments to a minimum. Rossana Rossanda passed your report on to Togliatti, before he left on vacation. You do not know whether or not he had time to read it. Togliatti died that summer, in the Crimea. You do not know if your report was among the papers Togliatti had with him in the Crimea. Rossana doesn't know either. She passed your memorandum on to Togliatti, and Togliatti died that summer in the Crimea.

You had planned to reproduce that document here. But you are not going to do so. As you call to mind the minutes of those meetings of the Executive Committee, you have just realized that it is all history now. And for you it is already prehistory. Furthermore, even if your demonstration were completely convincing, even if no one could possibly doubt the truth of your argument, this truth would serve no useful purpose whatsoever now. What you mean by that is that young revolutionaries of today who might be on the point of joining the Spanish Communist Party would do so regardless, even though they were convinced of the truth of your demonstration. They would think that all this was past history, that times have changed, that they themselves will change the party. They do not know that the party is going to change them or that they will be obliged to leave the party if they refuse to change. If they want to go on being revolutionaries. But they must go through that experience themselves, as you yourself did. They must either destroy themselves or steel themselves, lose themselves or find themselves, all by themselves, within this experience.

That is why you have just dismantled the plan for this chapter. You have just returned to your personal files the documents that you had been thinking of cleverly inserting here, so as to make your demonstration more brilliant and more effective. You will forget once more the memorandum you prepared for Palmiro Togliatti, a more clearsighted survivor than others of the bloody battles of Stalinism, and that Rossana Rossanda passed on to him and)

Rossana Rossanda is looking at me as Gosnat raises his glass of champagne at the end of the "fraternal luncheon" in Stains, on May 3, 1963.

That night we had dinner with Rossana and Giancarlo Pajetta. Giorgio Fanti, who was then the Paris correspondent of *Paese-Sera*, was also there. Colette and I joined all of them for drinks before going to have dinner at Simone Signoret's.

I had known Simone since the days of the German occupation. I had known her by sight, that is to say. I was in the Café de Flore one day, with some student comrade or other, and a beautiful girl walked in, with eyes like wood-violets and incandescent lava, and a proud, hungry mouth. We stared at this modestly dressed, dazzling girl, and naturally she didn't even so much as glance at us. Then after the war, on my return from Buchenwald, it turned out that Simone Signoret knew almost all my friends of those days. I got to know her too. For a couple of years, back there when I was Federico Sánchez, we never saw each other. But that spring in 1963 two circumstances were responsible for reestablishing a relation that has since become indestructible, with her and with Yves Montand, whom I met that same summer. One of them was the publication of my book *The Long Voyage*. The other, even more important, was the murder of Julián Grimau. His death deeply upset Simone. It was she who, through Pierre Lazareff, then editor-in-chief of the daily *France Soir* and producer of one of the most important news programs on television at that time, "Cinq colonnes à la une," got Ángela Grimau to appear on this program. Ángela's appearance on French television, a few days after Grimau's execution, had an extraordinary impact. All at once, millions of Frenchmen understood what it meant to fight Francoism. This was in April, at the end of April. A few days later, on May 1, we were again at Simone Signoret's when Juan Goytisolo told me the news that *The Long Voyage* had won the Formentor Prize in Corfu. We went to Juan's to celebrate with him. Carlos Franqui was also there that night at the apartment at 33 Rue Poissonnière.

So on May 3, 1963, we found ourselves at Simone Signoret's with Rossana Rossanda and Giancarlo Pajetta. The latter made fun of Georges Gosnat interrupting the meeting for the sake of a perfect roast.

His rendition of the affair was done with that lucid and pitiless irony that is his way of recounting tales of this sort, and made us laugh a lot, though with a touch of sadness, at the expense of Gosnat and the Party Spirit metamorphosed into a roast of beef.

What I did not know that night, of course, was that Rossana Rossanda and Giancarlo Pajetta would appear again a year later in the life of Federico Sánchez, at the very moment when this latter was beginning to fade from existence.

A year later, in fact, early in April of 1964, I arrived in Rome, having come there from Prague. The plenary session of the Executive Committee had just ended. We had had the final luncheon, all together, in the immense vaulted dining room decorated with the hunting trophies of the ancient kings of Bohemia. This last luncheon, like all the others, was served to us by waiters in white jackets and immaculate linen gloves. They went around the table, cermoniously serving the various dishes. It was my last "fraternal luncheon," I knew. It was the last time I would hear La Pasionaria tell some story about her early youth. A false atmosphere of superficial cordiality reigned. Santiago Álvarez, who was usually more prudent and circumspect, put his foot in his mouth by congratulating Fernando Claudín on the fact that an essay of his, "La revolución pictórica de nuestro tiempo" ("The Pictorial Revolution of our Time") had just been reprinted in the review *Cuba Socialista*. Carrillo was not at all pleased at Santiago Álvarez's gaffe, as anyone could see just looking at his face. The fact was that this essay of Fernando's, which had been published in the first issue of *Realidad*, the party's new cultural review that I was head of, had been the object of violent diatribes and outspoken condemnations from the majority of the Executive Committee.

In this essay Claudín criticized the dogmatic positions characterizing "Socialist Realism" and tilted a lance in favor of the freedom of artistic creation. Claudín's last lines in the essay read as follows: "We must fight for realism in art, while at the same time understanding that realism is not restricted to figurative art alone, that a great part of modern Expressionist, Cubist, Abstract painting, and so on is realist, and of the very best sort of realism. And that at the same time there is very little realism, or for that matter art, in a certain sort of figurative painting, even though it may be filled with the very best of intentions."

In this same number of *Realidad* I had published an article entitled "Observaciones a una discusión" ("Remarks on a Discussion"), concerning the debate initiated by the Communist Party of China; my article too was the object of violent attacks from the majority of the Executive Committee. When I recently reread this text of mine, I was struck by the extreme prudence—if not downright timidity—of what I had said. Despite this, a number of points in this article seemed inadmissible to the other leaders of the Spanish Communist Party.

The first inadmissible point had to do with the interpretation of the Twentieth Congress of the Communist Party of the Soviet Union. "From the political point of view," Federico Sánchez said on that occasion, "the Twentieth Congress marks the beginning of the liquidation of the institutional system that has customarily been called (in a rather inappropriate way, more metaphorical than scientific) the system of the personality cult. By this name is meant a system of unipersonal, authoritarian, and bureaucratic leadership of the life of the party and the state in a Socialist society. The most negative characteristics of such a system are reflected in the exaggerated limitation of the functioning of Socialist democracy and the repeated and systematic violation of institutional legality."

As can be seen, this formulation is still situated within the line of postcouncilar reform, that is to say post-Twentieth Congress. But despite its cautious tone, it provoked wrath and scandal. The discussion on my remark about the "institutional system" went on for hours.

The second point that provoked criticism had to do with the history of the Spanish Communist Party itself and the beneficial effect that the liquidation of the Stalinist period had had upon it. Speaking of this period, I had written: "It was no small effort, nor was it easy. Because it was carried out beneath the heavy fire of the concerted repression of the class enemy, at a moment when the democratic movement was on the wane, as a consequence of the unfavorable new international situation and the inner consolidation of the Francoist regime. But it was undoubtedly a decisive period in the formation of the Marxist-Leninist party of the Spanish working class. The period of real, practical liquidation of leftist infantilism, of general and over-simplified formulations; the period of the real conquest—slow, laborious, and obscure—of political hegemony among the new proletarian and student generations formed in the period of Fascism; the period of autonomous theoretical reflection, by way of concrete analysis, on the development of monopoly capitalism in Spain, with the consequent adaptation of tactics conforming to the new configuration and objective regrouping of the various classes and levels of Spanish society."

This passage was held against me as a treacherous attack on the heroic tradition of the Spanish Communist Party. How did I dare say that the "decisive period" in the formation of the party came only with the fifties? Wasn't this an inadmissible underestimation of the activity of the Spanish Communist Party during the Civil War, for instance? What did I mean by my reference to "autonomous theoretical reflection"? Was this not a nasty anti-Soviet way of putting things, or at the very least a criticism of the Comintern?

And finally, there was also violent reaction to what I said concerning the debate in progress within the Communist movement: " . . . the methodological norms of a real and rigorous discussion must be applied, keeping in mind that this is a debate within the Communist movement [which, by its very nature, is] in the process of development, complex and diversified, constituted by parties in power (a situation giving rise to problems between states as regards their mutual relations), by opposition parties situated amid the most diverse circumstances, by Marxist-Leninist currents and tendencies within the most diverse mass movements. What the Communist movement thus offers us is not an image of *monolithism* (nor can it be).

"Hence any attempt to impose from above a single, centralized leadership on the Communist movement would soon come up against the reality of the facts, against the objective necessity of an autonomous diversification of theoretical reflection and the tactical application of the basic principles of Marxism. The entire movement of renewal initiated at the time of the Twentieth Congress of the Communist Party of the Soviet Union leads to the elaboration of new forms of relation and discussion between the Communist parties of the entire world: it leads to the liquidation of the concept of "party-as-guide" and "state-as-guide. . . . "

Today, when Eurocarrilloism is spreading everywhere, these formulations would no longer be found shocking in the Spanish Communist Party. But in 1964 they aroused a storm of protest and criticism. I am not going to cite all these violent negative reactions. I shall restrict myself to transcribing what, according to the official minutes of the Executive Committee, Santiago Carrillo declared in the meeting of February 12, 1964:

"It is probable that for many years to come there will be comrades in the Party leadership whose philosophical preparation is inferior to that of others who are not in positions of party leadership, yet are better political leaders than these latter. . . . I believe that Federico knows much less about philosophy than he would appear to. I am judging by the facts. Let us avoid creating a legend here among ourselves. Federico's philosophical knowledge remains to be proved. . . . And when Federico comes to reduce us to silence with all those words about the "institutional system," many of us get all confused. People may well say: 'What ignoramuses!' But it is ignoramuses who lead the Party and there is no possibility that philosophers could ever come to lead the Party. . . . As for Federico's article in *Realidad*: I share the opinions that have been expressed here by almost all the comrades. The opinions offered by Tomás [García, alias Juan Gómez] are thoroughly reasoned ones, as is his timely reminder that our Italian comrades have abandoned similar positions that were theirs at one time, Togliatti in particular. . . . Not only basically, but also in the explanation that he put forward here, what Federico maintains is that the Socialist system has been replaced by another system, by a Stalinist superstructure. And that is what lies at the very bottom of the disagreement. The entire question is whether what has been called Stalinism was turned into an institutional system (that is to say a system of State) or whether it was an excrescence, an abscess, which did not alter the essence of the Soviet institutional system. We must maintain the Party position with no rectification whatsoever. . . . The system of the dictatorship of the proletariat in the USSR, which was a backward country, with a very small proletariat, subjected to encirclement by all the rest of the world, has had very marked coercive traits for a long time: *there has been a political police, concentration camps, etc., but these institutions were necessary, and I am not certain that they are not necessary in other Socialist revolutions, even though these latter may be carried out under more favorable conditions. What alarms me and repels me is not the fact that police, camps, and so on exist, but the use that Stalin made of them during a given period. . . .*" (The italics, naturally, are mine.)

A few weeks later, on April 19, 1964, during the meeting of militants at Stains that I have already mentioned, Carrillo returned to this question of the relations of the Spanish Communist Party with the Soviet Union, in a digression aimed at attacking the leaders of the Chinese party: ". . . for us it is clear that Marxism-Leninism is one, and that there is not a different Marxism-Leninism for the Chinese, for the Russians, for the Spanish, for the French, and for the Italians. For us it is clear that proletarian internationalism is and must be the golden rule of our conduct! This means that we are going to continue to elaborate our policies autonomously. Ah, but this autonomous elaboration will never lead us to descend to putting forth, to hinting at opinions tinged with anti-Sovietism, in order to give satisfaction to certain "thinkers" who call themselves *independent* and measure their *independence* by the fact that they are critical only of everything that is Soviet; it will not lead us to gibe at the Soviet Union so as to gain the reputation of being "good guys" among the bourgeoisie of our country and among certain intellectuals. We shall not follow that easy road of cheap politics! We shall defend Marxism-Leninism, we shall defend the unity of the international Communist movement side by side with Communist Party of the Soviet

Union, side by side with all Communist parties prepared to. . . . [*Thunderous applause, which drowns out the end of the sentence*]"

As can be seen, considerable water has gone under the bridge since 1964, and Carrillo is doing precisely what he categorically refused to do back then. There are those who will perhaps remind me that since then a crucial event has taken place: the invasion of Czechoslovakia by Russian armies. This is true, but was it impossible to predict that the "institutional system" predominating in the Soviet Union objectively tended toward intervention of exactly this sort? Was it impossible to predict that the involution of the reformist process so timidly inaugurated by the Twentieth and Twenty-First Congresses of the Communist Party of the Soviet Union would inevitably lead to the suppression by force of all attempts at the reconquest of certain forms of politico-social democracy in the countries of the East? The invasion of Czechoslovakia could come as a surprise only to those who had not yet understood the true character of the "institutional system" in the USSR.

But we were in the vaulted dining room of the castle of Bohemian kings. We had reached the end of the last luncheon that Claudín and Sánchez would be sharing with the other members of the Executive Committee. After this last luncheon served by the discreet and diligent waiters with the white jackets and immaculate gloves, beneath the deer antlers that decorated the massive walls of the dining room, we would thereafter be denied so much as bread and salt.

I said goodbye to all of them, knowing perfectly well that it was for the last time. I said goodbye to all of them, one by one. Farewell forever, comrades.

I think I am being perfectly sincere with myself if I say that I was overcome at that moment by two contradictory emotions. On the one hand, the certainty that an essential period of my life, no doubt the most important period of my life, the one that had brought me the greatest adventure and the most experience, was coming to an end. On the other hand, the intimate satisfaction of having been faithful to my most profound convictions to the very last, of not having betrayed that Communist freedom that had brought me to the party at the age of eighteen and that now, in obedience to an identical need for rigor and consistency, was driving me from the party.

Hence amid the uncertainty of these two contradictory certainties, I found myself at the Prague airport, waiting for the plane that would be taking me to Rome.

if you still had time, if you were not already very close to the denouement of this story, if Federico were not about to pass through inspection at the Prague airport, accompanied by a woman comrade from the Foreign Section of the Czech Central Committee, if Federico Sánchez were not about to notice, for the last time, the look of smiling complicity of the functionary from the State Security Bureau who checks, or, rather, deliberately fails to check, your false passport, that look of complicity that is the last dim, bureaucratic manifestation of what proletarian internationalism once was, if you were not already in the departure lounge at the Prague airport, with a plane ticket to Rome, if you were not laughing a little sadly at discovering that this time the comrades of the apparatus hadn't given you the few dollars they usually gave you to continue on your way to Paris from Zurich or Brussels or Milan, intermediate stopovers to blot out your traces, at discovering that the comrades of the apparatus, now that you are about to fall, like Lucifer, into outer darkness, have given you nothing but a one-way ticket straight to Rome, merely that and nothing more,

if you had time, you would speak of Prague, at great length, interminably, of how you would stroll through the little winding streets of the old city, as you had that afternoon in 1958, with Colette, Ricardo Muñoz Suay, and José María Rancaño, you would explain why Prague is the privileged city of your memory and your fantasies, the city dreamed of since those Sunday afternoons in Buchenwald, in the course of your conversations with Herbert Weidlich, the German comrade who had lived in exile in Prague from 1933 to 1939, and who had told you all about Prague, the city of Josef Frank and of Jiri Zak, your comrades at Buchenwald, the city of Kafka and Milena, your comrades on sleepless nights, the city of Kvetoslav Innemann, one of the leaders of the Czech party at Buchenwald, an intelligent little hunchback who used to invent appropriate quotes from Lenin during discussions, or if he didn't invent them at least arranged them in his own way, and one of the improbable quotes from Lenin that he frequently repeated was "the party is not a hen, it doesn't need two wings, a right one and a left one," and later Kvetoslav Innemann was a member of the committees of inquiry charged with investigating the truth of the clever trumped-up trials—and to judge from reports published during the so-called "Prague Spring," in 1968, the Piller Report in particular, his attitude in the years of the slow and laborious process of de-Stalinization was neither very courageous nor very clear; but you would nonetheless speak of Prague, that city which reappears in your dreams—and in your nightmares too sometimes—night after night, which floats in your waking dreams, on the rare occasions you still dare to hope for something in the future, and then you dream of a future of popular plays on Wenceslas Square, a future of a people on the march in the streets of a "denormalized" Prague, that is to say given over once again to the mad undertaking of winning freedom and waging revolution, and Prague floats in your memory like a great ship made of stone and wooded groves, of rivers and statues, like a great phantom sailing vessel that is without a mast now, but will never be abandoned by its crew,

if you still had time, if you were not Federico Sánchez already on the airport tarmac, walking out toward the Alitalia DC 9, you would speak of the two trips you took to Prague later, no longer as Federico Sánchez but as yourself, that is to say myself....

The first time, in fact, I didn't go to Prague, but only to the Prague airport. It was in July of 1966, the middle of July. A film I had written for Alain Resnais, *La guerre est finie*, had been officially selected for showing at the Karlovy Vary Festival. The film had already been selected a few weeks before for the Cannes Festival, but had been withdrawn from the list of official French entries at the last moment by the festival board, no doubt so as to avoid any problems with Spain (that is to say with the Spanish authorities).

Then the same thing happened at Karlovy Vary, though for different reasons and under different pressures. When Alain Resnais and I arrived at the Prague airport, the producer of the film, Catherine Winter, told us *La guerre est finie* had been withdrawn from official competition. In this case it had been the Central Committee of the Czech party, at the express and peremptory request of the Spanish party, that had demanded the withdrawal of the film.

Resnais and I were driven directly to Karlovy Vary, where we were received by Podleniak, the director of the festival. Visibly unhappy and upset, like someone obliged—in a system where there can be no discussion—to obey orders from above with which he does not personally agree, Podleniak informed us that *La guerre est finie* could not participate in the competition properly speaking. Turning to me then, he hinted that the reasons behind this could be laid at a Spanish doorstep. But the film would be projected outside of competition at one of the regular festival showings.

That was what happened, and the showing was a resounding success. People from the Czech film world—critics, scenarists, actors, and directors—urged on primarily by Miloš Forman and Antonin Liehm (do you remember? of course I remember! do you remember that it was in the United States, when you went there to present *The Confession* with

Costa Gavras and Yves Montand, where you saw comrade Liehm again, who had had to go into exile when the "normalization" began in Czechoslovakia? It was your third trip to the United States. You had made the first one a year before, in the fall of 1969, for the premiere of *Z* in New York. You had just won the Fémina Prize for *The Second Death of Ramón Mercader*. You went to the American consulate in Paris to pick up your visa. The clerk who took care of you asked you to fill out a card. "It's merely a formality," she said to you with a smile. So you filled out the card that was merely a formality. When you came to the question that is on all these forms concerning whether the visa applicant has ever been a drug addict, a homosexual, or a member of the Communist party or any of its front organizations, you answered yes. And in the corresponding space you provided the information that you had indeed been a Communist, though as yet you were neither a drug addict nor a homosexual. When the clerk read your card, she gave a start. "Why did you say that?" she asked in surprise. "Because it's true," you told her. "Is it absolutely necessary to remember that?" she asked. "Absolutely," you replied. "It's public knowledge that I cannot and do not wish to hide." The clerk shook her head, disconcerted. She told you she would have to go see someone higher up about it. You didn't mind. She came back in a few minutes and told you that you would have to fill out another special form. After that you would be interviewed by Miss Bryant. The name amused you, since in *The Second Death of Ramón Mercader* one of the characters belonging to the CIA was named Bryant. In any case, you supposed that Miss Bryant was somebody higher up. You filled out the special form for former members of Communist parties. And you were then taken to Miss Bryant's office. She was tall and blonde and rather angular, in the Anglo-Saxon manner, yet not without a certain suave charm. She spoke softly and very politely. She invited you to sit down in front of her desk, and began to read the special form. On it you were to answer a series of questions, almost all of them without any real importance. How long were you a member of the Communist party? What party? When did you cease to be a member of the Communist party? Where did you live during those years? You had answered this latter question by saying that you'd lived in Paris, adding that after 1939 your stay in Paris had been interrupted for two years, which you spent in the concentration camp at Buchenwald. When she reached this point, Miss Bryant raised her head and stared at you for a second. Something stirred in the depths of her gaze. But she said nothing and went on with her reading. Finally she arrived at the one question that you hadn't answered, that you'd left blank. It was the one referring to the responsibilities that you had had in the Communist organization, your precise activities therein, and the leaders that you might have known in these circumstances. She raised her head again and pointed out to you, with exquisite courtesy, that you had forgotten to answer one question. "I didn't forget," you said to her. She looked at you, waiting for an explanation. You gave it to her. "Look, Miss Bryant, the Spanish Communist Party is illegal here in France. It's even more illegal in Spain. I can't answer any questions about its organization. I won't answer here or anywhere else. It's a matter of principle." Miss Bryant looked at you intently. Something stirred again in her blue eyes. You had the confused impression that your reply had, paradoxically, given her great satisfaction. As though the motives you had given for not answering seemed admirable to her. A brief smile crossed her face. "It's all right," she said. And she stamped the visa in your Spanish passport, adding a whole series of handwritten observations. It was naturally a very specific and highly restricted visa. It permitted you to enter the US only once—ONE ENTRY—for a period of eight days. Underneath the visa, a series of numbers added in Miss Bryant's hand no doubt indicated, cabalistically, your political antecedents. In the group going to New York that time for the premiere of *Z*, Yves Montand, Simone Signoret, and you all had the same type of visa. Though Yves and Simone had never been members of the Communist party, in the fifties they had signed texts of the Peace Movement, which was considered to be a front organization of the party. And this was the first trip to the United States. The second, early in April 1970, with an identical new visa obtained by means of the same ritual, had been a trip to Hollywood. *Z* had been in the running for several Oscars. In the end it won two. On April 7, after the announcement of the results, there was a supper at the Beverly Hilton, with an orchestra and dancing. You still have the menu of that supper. It is in French, as required by the cosmopolitan gods of international gastronomy. To begin with, *Fruits de Mer Neptune*. Then *Contre-Filet "Cordon Bleu" Rôti*, with the following accompaniments of side dishes: *Fonds d'Artichauts Clamart*, *Petits Pois*, and *Pommes Champs-Elysées*. For dessert, *Bombe Glacée Martinique*, and to end with *Café Mayan* with *Petits Fours*. During supper, you were first served a Pouilly Fuissé and then a Bordeaux red, Château de Rouffiac Saint-Emilion. Perfect, all very amusing. You saw Fred Astaire dance, you spoke briefly with Liz Taylor and Gregory Peck. Very amusing. But the third trip, early in the winter of 1970, was to present *The Confession* in New York and at Yale University. It was on this occasion that you saw Antonin Liehm again: he was a visiting professor in New York and was living on Staten Island. It was bitter cold on Staten Island the day you went to see Antonin Liehm there. You remembered the days in Karlovy Vary, naturally), and in

Karlovy Vary, a few years before, in July 1966, people from the Czech film world, urged on by Miloš Forman and Antonin Liehm, had created a special prize that was awarded to *La guerre est finie*.

The second, and last, time I had been in Prague after my expulsion from the party was at the end of spring, 1969. I was in Prague two days, with Costa Gavras. At the time we thought that *The Confession* could be filmed in Prague, and the heads of Czech cinema agreed. The invasion had already taken place, the country was already occupied by foreign troops, but the conquests of 1968 had not yet been totally liquidated through the process of "normalization". The director of Czech cinema, who was none other than Podleniak, the person who had explained to me in Karlovy Vary that *La guerre est finie* would have to be projected outside of competition, received Costa and me. A protocol of agreement for the filming of *The Confession* in Prague was signed with Podleniak. But within a few weeks Dubcek was expelled from the government and Podleniak himself lost his post after being accused of the most diverse and most absurd transgressions. I will not return to Prague again until Prague is the free capital of a new spring.

But you were in the Alitalia DC 9, early in April 1964, on a flight from Prague to Rome.

In Rome you had a series of political interviews with leaders of the Italian Communist Party. You spoke with Mario Alicata, in his office as editor-in-chief of *L'Unità*. You spoke with Giancarlo Pajetta too, at the headquarters of the Central Committee of the Italian Communist Party, on Botthege Oscure. You spent the evening before your return to Paris with Rossana Rossanda and Bruno Trentin.

In his office on Botthege Oscure, Giancarlo had listened attentively to your report on the discussion in the Executive Committee of the Spanish Communist Party. He finally told you that perhaps you and Claudín had been right, that most probably you had been right, insofar as essentials were concerned at least, but that it was useless to be right outside the party. With or without a proper strategic view of things, the party would continue to be the only political instrument capable of keeping avant-garde groups together, of maintaining the spirit and the continuity of the struggle. What good would it be to be outside the party under these circumstances? What would all your reason weigh in the balance compared to the enormous weight of the organization? Hence Giancarlo advised you to give in to the party, to make whatever concessions were necessary in order to keep yourself at the highest possible level within the leadership of the party, even though you had to keep your opinions to yourself so as to be in a position to lend impetus to the rectification of strategy when events themselves would make this latter imperative.

You did not reject this advice of Giancarlo Pajetta's outright. You pondered the possibilities for several days, and measured their consequences. But then the mass meeting of April 19 took place, in which Carrillo launched his slanderous attacks against you and Claudín, grossly distorting your positions and riding roughshod over the pronouncements of the Executive Committee itself. It was clear that it was not possible to follow Giancarlo Pajetta's advice. It may well be that you would not have followed it in any case, but Carrillo's speech burned the bridges, barred every possible path to understanding and cast you into outer darkness.

A few days later, on May 1, 1964, you were in Salzburg.

You were there for the ceremony officially awarding you the Formentor Prize of the year before, which you had won for *The Long Voyage*. In the vast salon of another castle, not that of the Bohemian kings, but that of some Hapsburg or Hohenlohe perhaps, the publishers who had constituted the jury for the prize rose from their chairs just before the gala dinner was served. They came over to your table to present you with the first copy of the thirteen translations that were to be published simultaneously. Ledig Rowohlt got up and handed you the German edition of your book. Weidenfeld got up and handed you the English edition. Giulio Einaudi got up and handed you the Italian edition. Finally, Carlos Barral got up and you rose to your feet too and went to meet Carlos, and Carlos could not hand you a printed book because the censors had prohibited its publication in Spain, and Carlos handed you instead a book with blank pages, and this virgin book, dazzling with words not yet written, seemed stupendous to you, as though *The Long Voyage* had not yet been finished, as though everything still remained to be done, still remained to be written, and Carlos Barral embraced you as he handed you this stupendous book, this book still to come and still to be written, this waking dream of a book, and then you remembered once more the place at number 5 Concepción Bahamonde, you remembered the comrades, you remembered the fraternity of Madrid, you remembered that this book surely would not have been what it was had you not written it on Concepción Bahamonde, in the apartment you had passed that night of June 17, 1959, sure of yourself, or, rather, sure of him, sure that Simón Sánchez Montero would not talk in the basement of the Social Brigade.

7 A NUMBER OF DEATHS, THE DEATH...

In the years that followed I used to see Simón Sánchez Montero every once in a while. The last time there again loomed up between us the specter of the mythological strike, the *Aitch En Pee,* which had now metamorphosed into the National Democratic Action. Simón seemed convinced of the concrete possibility it would come off in the weeks to come, and tried fruitlessly to convince me as well during a luncheon at the Hotel Suecia in Madrid.

This was in November 1975, during Francisco Franco's interminable death throes, a few days before the political police again arrested Simón, for the nth time.

Madrid was keeping quiet, as though the city were holding its breath. Madrid was living this death watch passively, with a sort of agreeable internalized terror, a strangely joyful, masochistic terror. It was already obvious, except to the leaders of the Spanish Communist Party who continued to be obsessed by the possibilities of apocalyptic action, that nobody was going to lift a finger, as though the paralysis that had overcome the dying Franco were gradually spreading throughout the entire city, as though the long-ago poetic pronouncement by Dámaso Alonso were about to come true at last: Madrid in those weeks was indeed a city of I don't know how many million corpses.

A few days before, on Monday, October 20, 1975, I was in Brussels. The Belgian television was showing *La Guerre est finie* that night. One of the principal themes of the film, as the reader may know, is in fact the critique of the orders for a General Strike that is conceived of as a mere ideological expedient, destined to unify the consciousness of the militants religiously rather than to have any effect on reality. *La guerre est finie* sets forth the impossibility, which today has been confirmed to the point of tedium, of coldly organizing a mass action on a national scale on a fixed date and directing it by remote control from abroad, through a clandestine apparatus. The film advances the view that mass action is autonomous, and that even though the party may play a certain role in it as a leavening and as a temporary *ad hoc* structure it can never be a substitute for it.

In any event, after the showing of the film there was to be a debate on its current significance, and the Belgian television network had invited me and a number of journalists and representatives of Spanish political groups to participate in it. The debate bored me, I must confess, perhaps because it was not well led by the moderator, or perhaps because, like many debates, it was nothing but a succession of monologues. The only participant who said sensible things was Edouard de Blaye, who had been a correspondent in Spain for years and was the author of a historical essay on *Franco, O el reino sin rey* (*Franco, or the Kingdom without a King*).

Finally the moderator asked all of us to say a few words in conclusion. This bored me as much as the rest. When my turn came, I answered brusquely that the fact of the matter was that Franco had died in July of 1974, but Spaniards hadn't yet realized it, perhaps because they didn't want to. I said that we had to become fully aware of Franco's death if we were ever to begin to get rid of his political corpse.

A few minutes later, once the debate was over, a Belgian journalist approached me. His newspaper had just received a press agency bulletin announcing that Franco had just had an extremely severe heart attack.

On Tuesday, October 21, the news of Francisco Franco's death began making the rounds. An American television network had interrupted its programs to announce it, citing official sources at the State Department. In Paris, Carrillo confirmed the news. Fernando Claudín had telephoned Carmen, his wife, from Madrid to tell her the same thing. But in spite of all this information from such apparently reliable sources, I didn't believe it. Irrationally, I was convinced that Franco could not die that way, all of a sudden, in such a nice clean way. Since his life and his absolute power had been the terrifying symbolic representation of so many hundreds of thousands of Spanish deaths, I was convinced, without being able to explain it in any rational terms, that he would arrange his death too in such a way as to poison our lives.

I remembered a book by Max Aub, a book that had been around a long time, the title of which was *La verdadera historia de la muerte de Francisco Franco* (*The True Story of the Death of Francisco Franco*), from the title of the first story in the book, a very amusing tale. I went to look for it in my library. It was there. Published in 1960 by Libro Mex-Editores (Apartado postal 12196, México 1, D. F.). I opened the book and saw it had a handwritten dedication in it. Not to me, of course. The dedication read: "To So-and-So, we'll see whether or not. . . . Max Aub." I write "So-and-So" here because I don't consider myself authorized to put the real name of the Spanish writer to whom Max had dedicated his stories, a name that had made a fair splash before the "boom" of the

Latin-American novel, at the time of the mini-boom (no, less than a mini-boom, a micro-one) of the Spanish social novel. It was not difficult to figure out how this book had come into my possession. I had had a close relationship with that writer in the old days when I was Federico Sánchez. He no doubt lent it to me one day, and I had forgotten to return it. But it was years now since this writer had abandoned literature to devote himself professionally to politics. Among my friends, there had been a difference of opinion in regard to this change of his. Some of them thought that Spanish literature had lost nothing as a result of this change. Others agreed, but added that it was politics which had lost something with the intrusion of this ex-writer into its domain. And of course the discussion always ended up with all of us considering the following question: Which is most fatal for a country, bad literature or bad politics? We never arrived at any definite conclusion, I must confess.

Anyway, on that October day in 1975, now that Max Aub had died, in Mexico, of a heart attack—what can an exile die of but heart trouble? —now that Max had died before even having time to unpack his suitcases after just returning from a trip to Europe (I had seen him in Barcelona at Ricardo Muñoz Suay's) I felt a twinge of bitterness reading that dedication: "we'll see whether or not. . . ." We'll see whether or not what happened in the story really does happen, or something like it, whether or not the fabricated story of Francisco Franco's death comes true. And in fact it did seem as though it was finally going to come true. But Max Aub was dead now and that truth would be of no interest to him at this point.

I put Max's book back in the library. I remembered the other dead of that summer and autumn. The last bloody autumn of the patriarch. At that precise moment the telephone rang. It was Edouard de Blaye. We had arranged in Brussels to have lunch together at the end of the week in Paris. He was calling me to cancel this lunch date. He was leaving for Madrid, where his press agency was sending him as a special correspondent. I told him we'd see each other there. For as it happened I had just that minute decided to go to Madrid myself. Immediately after hanging up, I dialed the airlines and reserved seats on the first plane I could catch. I called the Hotel Suecia and reserved a room. And finally, I called Javier Pradera, told him I was arriving, and at what time. Javier told me he'd be waiting for me in Barajas.

And he was.

I was going to Madrid to be present at the death of Francisco Franco Bahamonde. I was going as a spectator, but there was nothing special about this. We were all going to be spectators, passive spectators at the end of a regime that it had proven impossible to bring down. But perhaps

Fascist regimes cannot be brought down except in periods of historical crisis on a world scale.

Then I remembered all the deaths of that summer. Of that bloody autumn.

The beginning of that summer found me in Greece, in Lagonisi.

On Saturday, June 28, we were at Cape Sunion. Like every tourist, I suppose, we were searching among the Doric ruins of the temple of Poseidon for an inscription on Byron. The dry heat had left us with parched throats. We went off to have a few beers without having found among the innumerable graffiti the least inscription that would prove Bryon had passed that way. Nor, for that matter, that Julio Cortázar, the Argentine novelist, had. Cortázar has some wicked things to say about his trip from Athens to Cape Sunion in his *Vuelta al día en ochenta mundos* (*Around the Day in Eighty Worlds*). But I found no proof of his passage through Sunion recorded in stone. It remains to be seen however whether the beard Julio has grown in these last few years may not be an indirect proof of a certain infernal contact with Poseidon, the handsome, hirsute god of the ocean depths.

Sunday, June 29, dawned, a perfect day. But then at mid-morning a windstorm came up, and it soon became impossible to stay on the Lagonisi beaches. The usually smooth surface of the gulf became very rough. We were obliged to shut ourselves up in our hotel rooms.

This unexpected howling windstorm did not surprise me too much. I had been reading Gabriel García Márquez's *The Autumn of the Patriarch* at the time, and had brought it with me to Lagonisi along with Alejo Carpentier's *El recurso del método* (*Reasons of State*), Roa Bastos's *Yo, el Supremo*, and Valle-Inclán's *Tirano Banderas,* the ironic predecessor of all these others; all were related to the theme of a novel I was planning whose structure I was blocking out. It was going to be my first book written in Spanish. Hence, buried in García Márquez's story of the interminable death of the fabulous patriarch, I was not too surprised when the violent windstorm suddenly came up. It seemed like simply another episode in the book I was reading.

But the following day, Monday, June 30, with everything calm once again, as I sat facing the mirror of this ancient, original sea, this mother-sea, become smooth and gleaming once again, I came across the news of the death of Dionisio Ridruejo in a German newspaper. I understood the real meaning of that sudden storm then. Dionisio had died early in the morning on Sunday, June 29, between 1:30 and 2 a.m. A few hours later the windstorm began lashing the Greek coast of Lagonisi, between

Athens and Cape Sunion. A windstorm blowing in from the west, of course.

(LAGONISI: June 30, 1975:

I am reading a German newspaper, or perhaps a Swiss-German one, I don't remember whether it was the *Frankfurter Allgemeine* or the *Neue Züricher,* and I mention this not so that I can boast of being a polyglot but simply because, given the huge numbers of German tourists there are along these beaches and amid these groves and vineyards, it is newspapers in this language that arrive here soonest: I am reading the paper distractedly, in a semi-sleep of salt and sun; and then I suddenly come across the news of the death of Dionisio Ridruejo in Madrid; I call to Colette, who is with me, and tell her that Dionisio Ridruejo has died in Madrid; there is a moment of silence between us, and in the silence the death of Dionisio begins to be real, begins to take on the opacity of the irremediable:

it was in a cafeteria on the Calle de Goya, in 1956: Dionisio had agreed to an interview with a representative of the Spanish Communist Party leadership: Javier Pradera had organized this interview, of course: Javier Pradera was in fact the organizer, under my direction, of most of the party's contacts with other political groups during this period: Javier Pradera introduced me to Francisco Bustelo and Vicente Girbau, of the ASU (University Socialist Association); to Julio Ceron of the FLP (Popular Liberation Front); to Barros de Lis and Jaime Cortezo, of the IDC (Christian Democratic Left). During this period Javier Pradera also set up contacts with Giménez Fernández and José María Gil Robles in the name of the Spanish Communist Party. What would we have done, I wonder, if Javier Pradera had not existed?

it was on the Calle de Goya, on the mezzanine of a cafeteria; when I arrived Javier and Dionisio were already there, sitting at a table somewhat apart from the rest; Dionisio and I began to talk that day, and since then we've never stopped talking; only death could have interrupted this dialogue:

unfortunately, the memoirs that Dionisio wrote do not go up to this period in 1956 or the following years; all that we have left of this period in Dionisio's *Casi unas memorias* (*Almost Memoirs*) is what goes to make up the "almost," that is to say the documents, letters, and articles that Dionisio would no doubt have used to put his memoirs in finished literary form; for this reason, I cannot, alas, continue my dialogue here with Dionisio's memory, with his memories of that period, as I continue my dialogue with him beyond the silence of death:

it was on the Calle de Goya that I had my first interview with Dionisio Ridruejo; in a cafeteria; later there were many, many interviews, in cafeterias, in restaurants, in houses of friends; when Federico Sánchez disappeared, when all that remained of our political relations was the essential, that is to say friendship in the form of dialogue, we saw each other in his house on the Calle Ibiza or in one or another of the neighborhood bars that he frequented;

the last time I spoke with Dionisio, we had a long conversation in the garden of Faustino Lastra's little private mansion, in the park of the Count of Orgaz; fortunately I can relive this conversation whenever I want to; all I have to do is go to a projection room and look at the long interview I filmed with Dionisio Ridruejo in July of 1972, of which I used only a very small, minimal part in my documentary film *Les Deux Memoires* (*The Two Memories*); in a certain way it is a consolation to know that any day I might feel the need to go on listening to Dionisio, to go on having a dialogue with him, to hear his precise, quiet voice, his perfectly articulated speech, all I would have to do is have someone project for me this interview with Dionisio, brought back from the dead with his weary smile, with the clarity of his mind, an inimitable conversationalist, much more real and alive in the trembling light of summer in Madrid, on the illusory screen of what does not exist, than so many dull-witted supreme egotists of today's politics; whenever I like, whenever I need to, I can listen to Dionisio again, I can be the absorbed spectator of my last stroll with him, my last dialogue with him:

but in Lagonisi, on June 30, 1975, death began to grow like a creeping vine over the broken marble columns of summer)

That day, curiously enough, after long weeks of proceeding by trial and error, of hesitating, of weaving and unweaving the warp and woof of my planned novel, there suddenly came to me not only its overall structure, but also the detailed plot line linking together the principal episodes and events of the narrative.

It was as though there existed an obscure relationship between the reality of Dionisio's death and the fictitious death of Franco that I was planning to tell the story of. And such a relationship doubtless existed.

Two weeks later, on my return to France, I joyously began to write.

This unfinished novel was called

THE PALACE OF AYETE

and this was how it began:

At precisely the appointed hour, the General appears on the veranda of his summer palace.

Wait a minute, he's not a General. He's a Generalísimo. And if you think about it, the last Generalísimo still alive in the whole and entire world. Alive? Not for long. A fleeting smile crosses Juan Lorenzo Larrea's face. He picks up his rifle and aims it at the last Generalísimo still alive in the whole and entire world.

The very last one, no doubt about it.

Not the last marshal. No, there were still a few marshals left. In Africa, in Europe, in Asia, under every regime, in every latitude. Black marshals, yellow ones, white ones. Jacks of all trades. As useful for a commemorative ceremony as for a coup d'état. And captains-general too. Quite a few. Too many, even in this country. But not a single Generalísimo outside of this one of ours. Because Stalin had died, more than twenty years ago now. Even though it sometimes wasn't very evident, Stalin had died. This was the rumor at least that had gone about, around the year 1953: that Stalin, the Generalísimo of the celestial armies of land, sea, and air, had died.

A fleeting smile again crossed his face.

He observes through the telescopic sight of his rifle the frail silhouette of the last living Generalísimo. Because Chiang Kai-shek has died too. There had been no front-page headlines about it, but Chiang Kai-shek had died, in Taiwan, a bad death he'd been a long time dying.

There is no doubt about it: what he is observing, through the telescopic sight of his high-powered big-game hunting rifle, is the slow, cautious movement of the last existing Generalísimo. It's good for a laugh. And in fact he begins to laugh, a brief, wan laugh.

As he aimed the weapon, he had pushed the button that started the photographic mechanism. The fact is that the telephoto lens of the rifle was mounted on a miniaturized super-8 movie camera. A little technical marvel. Japanese, no doubt. Or so one might suppose, though there was no trademark on the apparatus.

The camera began turning with a barely perceptible sound that might be mistaken for the murmur of a faint breeze in the leaves of the trees.

The film would be projected, the fragile silhouette of General Ísimo would be seen to appear on the veranda of his summer palace. He smiles again at his own bon mot: he's in good form today. Ísimo is dressed in gray flannel trousers and a blue blazer. Knotted in the open collar of the Ísimo's immaculate white shirt is a silk scarf with red and gold ornamental motifs. From the scarf there emerges a bare, wattled throat, like that of a gargoyle or an ancient tortoise. A gleaming yacht captain's cap tops the Ísimo's skull.

The film would be projected and show things in blue and white and green and red and gold, because it was in color. The Organization had foreseen everything, down to the very last detail. It was also true that the film could be sold for its weight in gold to any of the Yankee television networks. The spectator would see the pontifical glow—white and yellow —and the blue shadows of summer. The green leaves of the trees in the park of the Palace of Ayete would move. The General would be seen on the veranda of the Palace of Ayete, overlooking the greenery of the park. He would be seen to lift his head, as he is doing now, to gaze at the sky. The deep indigo of the sky would be seen.

Everything would be seen, down to the smallest detail. The death of the Generalísimo as a spectacle, from the front row of box seats.

He is in that first row.

He follows with the barrel of his rifle the slow movements of the old dictator as he walks along the veranda of the summer palace. With little staccato, somewhat mechanical steps, the old man with the wattled parchment-like neck of a tortoise several hundred years old begins to walk down the steps of the veranda.

Just a few steps more, just a few seconds more.

He adjusts the back sight slide of the telephoto lense of his rifle. Sixty meters, there you are. Some shooting gallery, comrades! Simultaneously, the camera's zoom mechanism has functioned electronically. The image has moved up so close that it seems to him that the rifle barrel is touching the Generalísimo's body.

Then for the first time he is frightened. For the first time his blood begins to pound, in his temples, in his chest, in all the dark meanders where blood usually pounds. He takes a deep breath, gets hold of himself, curbs his pulse, quiets the pounding of his blood, aiming again, placing the dictator's skull in the very center of the crosshairs of the sight.

He is about to shoot.

But at the very instant he is about to press the trigger, why does he remember that bit of black humor the people in Madrid would mock the AVIACO company [Spanish domestic airlines] with: "You furnish the corpse, and the company will furnish the rest?" He doesn't know why he remembers that, but he does. He presses the trigger and thinks: "You furnish the corpse and the company will furnish the rest. . . ."

But I am not going to insert here the rest of this never to be finished novel. There are some hundred pages more, and the device of the collage can be amusing if it is short, and terribly boring if it is carried too far. *Omnis saturatio mala,* as the doctor on Barataria Island used to say. Moreover, however perverse and sophisticated this reconstruction of the autobiography of Federico Sánchez may be, it is best not to lose the thread of the narrative.

Back to that thread, then.

During the month of July and early August 1975, I was writing in a house I own in the Ile-de-France, in a hamlet just on the edge of the Gâtinais, a region long famous for its good harvest weather and its good honey. The house, with a blind northeast façade, opens onto a private inner courtyard, oriented south-southwest. Through the window of my study I can contemplate the waters of a pond and the trees of a little grove behind the house. It was there that I was writing *Palacio de Ayete,* a fictional work about Franco's death that the reality of his death-agony interrupted.

One night at the end of July we were having dinner in Burcy, a hamlet not far from mine, at Jean-Michel Folon's, with Julio Silva and Alberto Gironella. Julio had prepared a marvelous grilled rabbit *a la criolla.* The wine flowed freely. Gironella gave me a present, the lithograph he had made for the frontispiece of Carlos Fuentes's *Terra Nostra.* I told them about the novel I had begun to write. Naturally I didn't recount all the events of the book to them, but instead restricted myself to the essential, the central axis of Juan Lorenzo Larrea's novelistic adventure, that is to say, the attempt on Franco's life in the garden of the Palace of Ayete and its fantastic consequences.

A little later, around the middle of August, we took a trip by car down to Santander and Euzkadi. This trip had a twofold purpose behind it: on the one hand to recapture the scenes and memories of my childhood and, on the other, to have a clearer picture of the places the Juan Lorenzo Larrea, my imaginary character, would be visiting after the successful attempt on the Generalísimo's life.

A very relative and fleeting success, to make a long story short.

Two days after having shot at Franco in the gardens of the Palace of Ayete and seeing him fall to the ground, Larrea, who has holed up with Isabel in a hotel in Santander—I know I haven't explained who Isabel is; it doesn't matter, there's no time left for that—would see on television a festival of songs and dances, broadcast direct from San Sebastián, presided over by the Generalísimo in person. Dumbfounded, Larrea realizes then why there has been no official announcement of Franco's death, and sits there watching the Generalísimo offer on this occasion a few words of thanks and congratulations to the organizers of the festival, in his famous cracked, falsetto voice.

And it goes without saying that at that point Juan Lorenzo Larrea's heart sank or, if you prefer, his soul fell to his feet, Spanish-style.

But I am not going to reveal here the surprising plot of this unfinished novel. I am not going to relate, or even summarize, the well-nigh incredible events that took place after the apparently successful attempt on

Francisco Franco Bahamonde's life, followed by his fabulous resurrection.

As I was saying, then, we set off by car to Santander,

(but don't tell me you're going to continue speaking in this way, in this impersonal tone, as though you were only the chronicler of this trip; don't tell me you're going to speak in this way about that first morning in Santander: it was very early, you went out on the balcony of your room at the Real Hotel; it was a splendid day; you contemplated the bay, the Magdalena, the sands of Pedreña; the tip of Cabo Menor; the beaches of El Sardinero; you closed your eyes and began to tremble; not only on account of the incredible beauty of the view, in the light of this early autumn morning; but because it seemed that merely by opening your eyes, merely by gazing on this landscape, merely by absorbing the light of the briny horizon, you were canceling out time past, the years away from your homeland, the long exile from your own self; you opened your eyes again and you had returned to your childhood, gone back forty-five years, to that summer of 1930: it was the same landscape, intact, identical to the one you remembered; in 1930 you were seven years old, you were going down to the beach at La Concha with your brothers; beyond Piquío, a rope marked off the stretch of sand reserved for the royal family; the tents set up for these Bourbon vacationers had red and gold stripes; and it suddenly seemed to you that all the time past, lost, destroyed, was unfolding once again before you; you closed your eyes, you opened them again; everything was still in its place, reality coincided with dreams, with the images of your memory, with the evocative images always summoned up in your mind by a poem of Jaime Gil de Biedma's, a marvelous poem that you know by heart, which begins like this:

Entonces, los dos eran muy jóvenes
y tenían el Chrysler amarillo y negro,

[They were both very young then
and had the yellow and black Chrysler,]

and even though your parents never had a Chrysler, even though you remember only a De Dion Bouton, several Hispano Suizas, and above all a fabulous red Oldsmobile convertible, even though you don't remember any Chrysler, it *is* true that your parents too were very young then; it even so happens that they are younger every day in your memory, as though death had stripped them of all the indispositions of middle age, as though their death had restored to them that proud bearing, that tall and elegant stature and that youthful smile of one of your memories, a faded one, and dangerously encircled by a halo of oblivion, that memory that must date back to El Sardinero, around 1930, near Piquío, alongside that very same red Oldsmobile; but perhaps it is not their death that restores to them that exultant, youthful appearance, perhaps it is the fact that you yourself have grown older, perhaps it is the inexorable journeying toward your own death that resuscitates those evanescent images of their youth that float in your memory, because you have no photograph of the two of them when they were young, when they had the red Oldsmobile, when the Cantabrian breeze set the long silk scarf in the hand of your mother, Susana Maura, to fluttering, near Piquío, because you have no tangible proof left of those summers in El Sardinero, because that house of yesteryear no longer exists, with its garden abloom with azaleas and hydrangeas, with its veranda from which you could catch a glimpse of the sea, and)

in Santander, the first thing I did was to drag my wife and the two married friends who were with us in search of the house that for many years we used to rent in El Sardinero during the summers, until my mother died, shortly after the proclamation of the Republic.

But I did not find it.

Real estate promoters had developed the slope that gently rises behind La Concha, to the left of the Casino. We went walking down the streets of this new housing development with bungalows huddled one right next to the other, surrounded by ridiculous little garden plots. In the days of my summer vacations here as a child, the only buildings were a few villas, with spacious grounds all around them. So I didn't find our house of long ago. Perhaps it still existed, perhaps it had not been torn down, but I could not locate it in the labyrinth of new construction that confused all the perspectives, all the reference points of memory. It was a good-sized house, with a garden full of flowers. I remember every corner of that garden. I remember the house perfectly, as seen from the garden, with its terraces and verandas. But all I remember of the inside of the house is the big living room on the downstairs floor, with its veranda facing the ocean horizon and its terrace overlooking the entire garden. I remember the flight of steps leading to the upper floors, and that is all: the rest of the house has been blotted out by the mist of oblivion.

And I know very well why. There is no need for anyone to explain why.

I know very well that all that I remember of the house in El Sardinero are the places where I used to see my mother. I remember the garden, and the hydrangeas in the garden, because she would walk about in the garden protecting the perfect whiteness of her face with a round wide-brimmed straw hat that at times she would hold down with her hand if a puff of wind rose off the sea. I remember the veranda because we would join her there in the late afternoon, when we were tired out from the long walks to the lighthouse, to the village of Cueto, to the mysterious solitary tomb on the promontory. We were all there for a nice cool drink, gathered round this mother who was so young and so extraordinarily beautiful, listening to her questions about the least little adventure that the afternoon had brought, bending our heads beneath her hand as it caressed the foreheads of her children. I know very well that I remember the house in El Sardinero only because I cling to the memory of a beautiful, serene mother, passionate and gentle, tender and strong-willed, that very young mother who abandoned us a short time later and whom death has immobilized at the most perfect moment of her life, whereas I have continued to grow older, finally reaching the age at which Susana Maura could now be my daughter, the daughter of my infinitely sad and solitary reverie.

But I did not find the house in El Sardinero that day in August 1975. The silhouette of my mother, dressed in white, did not reappear like a plantom amid the azaleas and the hydrangeas in the garden. In *The Second Death of Ramón Mercader* I had evoked her memory in these very same places, and now as I walked among them again, after so many years, an immeasurable sadness accompanied me.

At San Vicente de la Barquera, however, everything seemed to be in its proper place. What I mean is, everything was in the place it had in my memory. We had lunch in a tavern on the wharf and I decided that Juan Lorenzo Larrea would also have lunch here, with Isabel, two days after having shot at the Generalísimo in the park of the Palace of Ayete.

I should doubtless explain here who Isabel is. This is the second time I have mentioned her and if only out of courtesy I ought to explain Isabel's antecedents to the reader.

In *Palacio de Ayete*, the novel that I was writing that summer, and the main reason for my trip through the north of Spain, Isabel was Juan Lorenzo Larrea's companion. The Organization, in fact, had planned things so that Larrea would hide out in Spain after the attempt on the Generalísimo's life rather than trying to cross the border immediately thereafter. And in order to hide the best thing was not to hide at all, that is to say, to pretend that he and Isabel were a French couple making the normal rounds of the tourist sights in the province of Santander.

I must add, however, that Isabel had been selected in a most unusual way. The second chapter of *Palacio de Ayete* tells how this came about.

The companion's name was Isabel, this time. He himself had chosen her, with Xaviera's help.

In June, in Madrid, they had stuck him with a companion who was unbearable. A hothead, a semi-hysterical type who spent her time politicizing sexuality and sexualizing politics. With a libido in all-out imperialist expansion, proliferating anarchically like a cancer. [A pleonasm, that.] In any event, on his return from the failure of "Operation Corrida for Charity," he had decided to select the companions for his next attempts himself.

He had gone to seek Xaviera's advice, in the little private mansion in Neuilly, at the far end of a huge garden that was invisible from the street. He had gone through a first door, that of a vulgar apartment house, then entered a narrow courtyard and passed through a second door, and on the other side of it, at the end of a vaulted corridor, he had come out on an immense garden planted with chestnut trees, walnut trees, and willows, a garden in which there was not even lacking the touch of several sculptures of Maillolesque nymphs, shamelessly covered with moss at the very spot, a maleficent triangle, where the Victorian decency of the era in which these statues had been sculpted decreed that only the incredibly smooth, and therefore equally disquieting, polished surface of asexual stone be shown.

Xaviera had installed herself in a little three-story private mansion at the back of the garden. Larrea was one of the three members of the Board of Directors of the Organization authorized to consult with Xaviera concerning the problems of selecting not only companions but all the cadres of various operations. Some of those in the Organization, on hearing the name Xaviera, perhaps imagined a human being, though of the female sex. The initiates—who were three in number, as has been said—naturally did nothing to disabuse the naïve of this notion. They could not have cared less that these latter might believe Xaviera was possibly a redoubtable blonde, a mysterious Amazonic muse of the Organization. In reality Xaviera, comfortably installed in a salon on the ground floor of the discreet little mansion in Neuilly, was the nickname of an IBM-Omega 666 electronic computer. Xaviera was the infallible memory of the Organization.

The decision to make use of Xaviera's services despite the extravagant price of such devices—the Organization had pulled off several coups in these last few years that had greatly enriched its coffers—instead of having a Secretariat of the Organization and a Committee of Cadres (the etymological and even semiological history of this latter word "cadres" had been the object of a very pithy recent study by Professor López Riego, whom Larrea had met at the University of Vincennes, late in the spring, during a seminar on Fascism and dictatorship—attended by Macciochi, Poulantzas, and Balibar, among other specialists quite at home amid the mirror-like universe of Althusserian concepts—and this essay by Professor López Riego, an assistant lecturer at the École pratique des Hautes Études in Paris, had been published, in French, in the review Annales, *since López Riego was bilingual, as are the majority of the protagonists of this true and prodigious story), but, as we were saying, the decision to use the electronic services of Xaviera rather than the human, all too human ones of a Committee of Cadres, had no doubt been the result of a political choice. In point of fact, in the Organization, where everything was capable of being an object of discussion and criticism—the divine and the human, the supernatural and the subhuman, the diabolical and the miraculous, the ordinary and the extraordinary—one and only one thing remained beyond the reach of the dialectic of the pro and the con, of the delightful play between the "positive aspect" and the "negative aspect" of phenomena, and this one and only thing, this unquestionable certainty was the intimate conviction, shared by all, that Secretariats of the Organization and Committees of Cadres engendered Stalinism as the liver secretes bile.*

Every being tends in fact to persevere in its being, but the specific being of Secretariats of the Organization and Committees of Cadres possesses this tendency in the highest possible degree. Hence, since the being of such bodies is none other than power, the possibility of doing and undoing, commanding by fiat because that's the way God does it (God here being nothing more than the allegorical figure of Supreme Power), these bodies, Secretariats, or Committees, in order to persevere in their being, need to be surrounded by mere factotums, simple yes-men, people who enjoy shouting: "At your service, Mr. Secretary!" who walk all over each other so as to be on the spot to shout: "At your service, Commander-in-Chief!" for example.

Cadres, consequently, if one thinks about it, or at least those cadres usually selected as members of Committees of Cadres, are the sort of militants who like to toe a straight line. Ad hoc *Committees are accustomed to select those militants who need (as they need water to drink and air to breathe) to have everything crystal-clear: the good over here, the bad over there, and forward march, straight ahead, without stepping one inch out of line or looking one inch to the right or left, toward the radiant future of the Future.*

That is why Committees of Cadres and Secretariats of the Organization had been done away with. Xaviera was a recourse—admittedly an imperfect one, but as everyone knows, in this vale of tears nothing is ever perfect

—against the natural, visceral, spontaneous, irreversible, congenital, en-slaving and cancerous Stalinism of Committees and Secretariats of the Organization. "Let's hope however," one of the comrades on the Board of Directors had said one day, "let's hope that Xaviera doesn't escape our control or cut loose and start acting on her own, surreptitiously foisting militants on us who suit her own particular dissident strategy." Everybody laughed, of course, but then they'd suddenly felt a bit edgy, and a sort of cold shiver went up their spines: the fact was that the idea of a progressive, malevolent autonomy on the part of the IBM-Omega 666 couldn't help but terrify them.

But in any event, when the possibilities of a new operation, which was immediately given the code name of "Operation Ayete," began to jell, Larrea had decided to choose his companion for this expedition himself, with the inestimable help of Xaviera's memory.

He had shut himself up in the little mansion in Neuilly. Through the open windows on the ground floor there came wafting the cool fragrance of the garden, patiently and skillfully watered and tended by an old deaf-mute gardener. There for several days in the month of July, an extremely warm one in that year of grace 1975, he had minutely pro-grammed the search for a companion for "Operation Ayete."

He had more or less ignored the classic questions concerning "political awareness," "social origins," "Marxist training," and other foolishness of this sort listed on the master questionnaire. He was not looking for a companion capable of discoursing on Lenin's errors in the twenties, or the brilliant intuitions of Rosa Luxemburg, or even the precise content of the program of the Kronstadt Commune. He had had his fill of such discus-sions. On the other hand, he had carefully and minutely described certain unusual requirements regarding the ideal companion's reading. She would have to have read Malcolm Lowry's Under the Volcano, *Kafka's* Letters to Milena, *and Alexander Solzhenitsyn's* One Day in the Life of Ivan Denisovitch. *These books constituted a minimum requisite, a* sine qua non. *Any girl in the Organization whose name was stored in Xaviera's electronic memory would be eliminated if she had not read these three books. For those who got past this elimination, Larrea had programmed another series of subsidiary questions. In view of the final selection, he had included Gabriel García Marquez's* The Autumn of the Patriarch, *Alejo Carpentier's* Reasons of State, *and Luis Goytisolo's* Inventory.

Once Xaviera's search was programmed, Larrea pressed the various keys setting the electronic mechanism in motion. The process lasted no more than thirty seconds. Larrea had just time enough to light a cigarette, turn his head toward the greenery of that private garden in Neuilly, where the deaf-mute gardener, dressed in blue cotton overalls, was pruning rosebushes, before the light went on announcing the positive result of Xaviera's investigation. Larrea now had the ideal companion for "Operation Ayete."

Or so he thought.

Through already-established organizational channels he summoned the girl chosen by Xaviera to an initial interview. He had word sent to her that they should meet late in the afternoon in the gardens at the far end of the Champs-Élysées, where he presumed that the suffocating heat of this month of July would be more bearable. But when Milagros—that was the name of the ideal companion Xaviera had come up with—came walking toward him, or rather, when she came walking toward the stranger who was to be at such and such a place, dressed in such and such a way, wearing dark glasses and holding a copy of the weekly Triunfo *in his right hand, when Milagros came walking toward him and he saw that she had the specified multicolor sun umbrella under her arm, he was suddenly overcome with irrepressible laughter. He tried to control himself, but he choked with laughter till tears came to his eyes.*

Milagros stood there in front of him looking at him, a bit surprised and disconcerted. In a very disciplined way, however, she uttered the prearranged password. And he, also in a very disciplined way, but still doubled over with laughter, gave the required answer. Then the two of them fell silent for a moment and looked at each other.

Larrea had finally managed to choke back his laughter. He looked at Milagros and thought what a shame it was that the girl could not be his companion on this next expedition. Xaviera had done her work most efficiently, and Milagros would have been an ideal companion, there was no doubt of that. All he needed to do was look at her to be convinced of it. And Larrea continued to look at her, drawn to her and at the same time disappointed. Milagros was exceptionally beautiful. A beautiful body, and no doubt a beautiful soul as well. As for the body, one needed only to look at it—supple, well-proportioned, warmly sensual. Bodies have one advantage over souls: they are as they appear to be, a body doesn't lie. But Milagros's soul was also apparent in her gaze—intelligent and affectionate, full of mischievous charm, full of cool water. A soul of water to quench a thirst for water.

Larrea looked at her and thought what shame it was that he couldn't have a companion like this with him. And Milagros looked at him too, but it is impossible, or at least premature, to reveal what she thought. The fact is—as will not have escaped the reader familiar with the complexities of the contemporary novel, now that critical terrorism has demolished the original innocence of every story, narration, and hence Narrator—that we cannot yet abandon Larrea's point of view: we must continue to observe everything that happens through the prism of his subjectivity. We already know that Larrea is a character in this novel, but we do not yet know who the Narrator is, who the astute and perhaps perverse little god is who is recounting all of this to us. Hence we cannot yet naively abandon ourselves to the delightful and occasionally dizzying shift back and forth from one subjectivity to another, as though we were not only the more or less captivated readers of this book that is taking shape before our eyes, but also its creators, capable of listening at once to the deep, desperate pounding of Larrea's heart and the dark desire that is mounting in Milagros from the most intimate depths of her flesh, like a wild, succulent plant with the fragrance of tropical rain.

Larrea looked at Milagros and gave a slight shrug. "I'm sorry," he said. Milagros's eyes blinked briefly in disappointment. "I won't do?" she asked, looking at him. He laughed, reached out his right hand and fleetingly caressed the girl's earlobe, her cheek, the soft curve of her chin. "Not for what I had in mind, no," Larrea answered. "You're too conspicuous." She hung her head and hid her eyes.

The fact is that Milagros was a mulatta. Not a blond, café-au-lait mulatta, shy and diffident. Nothing like that. A dark-skinned mulatta, regal, proud, pure black coffee. Larrea imagined himself with her on the road in Spain, at the hotel in San Sebastián, in Lekeitio, in Santander and San Vicente de la Barquera, after the "Operation." Everybody would remember a couple like them. Everyone, doubtless: hotel receptionists, waiters in restaurants, motorcycle cops on the highway, the Guardia Civil patrolling by twos. Everybody in creation would remember them, because of Milagros's exotic, provocative, incredible beauty.

"So I won't be seeing you again then?" she said. And her voice trembled, as though the idea of not seeing him again were truly painful.

They had been walking since their conversation first began, and now had reached that stretch of the Avenue Gabriel where on certain days of the week philatelists meet to exchange, buy, and sell stamps. But this wasn't one of the philatelists' days.

They were walking slowly beneath the shade of the trees. Lorenzo—that was what people usually called him, instead of Juan Lorenzo, or rather Jean-Laurent, which was his real name—Lorenzo, then, looked at the girl again. "Who knows?" he said. "Maybe some day, in some African or South American country, where nobody will notice you're a mulatta." She smiled and gazed into his eyes. "Oh, I do hope so!" she said. "Meanwhile I'll be hungry for you," Lorenzo murmured, looking straight into her eyes too, drowning in her gaze of liquid emerald.

They stopped and furtively took each other's hand. He felt Milagros's haunch against his thigh. He closed his eyes for an instant.

238

Lorenzo knew of a discreet, luxurious maison de rendezvous *close by, on the Rue Ponthieu. A labyrinth of corridors, with thick carpets and dim lights, for avoiding embarrassing encounters, leading to spacious rooms that were cool in summer, for they looked out over an inner patio in the Moorish style with fountains and glazed tiles. The bathrooms were immense, full of mirrors, marble facings, gilded faucets with griffons' heads. To stimulate flagging or frankly defunct imaginations, a closed-circuit television system was available for watching erotic films on a screen concealed by a large mirror.*

Lorenzo had closed his eyes.

He imagined Milagros for an instant in one of those rooms that he knew well. He imagined her gestures, their purity, their violence. He opened his eyes, looked at Milagros, smiled slightly. The thought crossed his mind that there would be no need to call upon the resources of the closed-circuit television system, which were multiple and all calculated to stimulate what Pavlov calls "the second signaling system."

They had reached the end of the Avenue Gabriel, the end of the shade of the trees. He was about to cross over in the direction of the Rue Ponthieu, holding Milagros by the hand, when the traffic light changed, stopping them and letting cars go by. Then just to be saying something, to break the silence full of vague presentiments, of whirling images, a turbulent and promising silence within which Milagros appeared to have docilely immured herself, just to be saying something Lorenzo asked what she had thought of Luis Goytisolo's novel Inventory.

"Did you like Luis Goytisolo's book?" he asked.

She looked at him in mild surprise. "How do you know I've read it?" she said. "I'm not the one who tracked down that information—it was Xaviera," he replied.

Milagros blinked and her cheeks unexpectedly flushed. "Xaviera!" she exclaimed in a trembling, almost choking voice. A sort of ecstasy seemed to envelop her. "Xaviera!" she repeated, in a lower, more fervent voice. Lorenzo looked at her, suddenly irritated. "Do you know Xaviera?" the girl asked, in the same tone that a believer would have used to ask: "Do you know God?," in precisely the same manner in which certain people, even today, announce that they know Fidel, for instance. Lorenzo looked at her in irritation, thinking that he was witnessing the advent of a new phenomenon in the already long history of political aberrations: the curious phenomenon of the personality cult of an electronic computer. So it was not enough to do away with secretaries of the Organization to cut off religious fetishism, fawning toadyism, alienating identification at their very roots. "Of course I know Xaviera," Lorenzo said curtly. He was not obliged to pass this confidential information on to Milagros, but he hadn't been able to contain himself. "And what do you know about her?" he inquired inquisitively. Milagros's eyes lighted up again, and her voice cooed: "That she's the brains of the Organization. A woman! Can you imagine!" the girl exclaimed in a triumphant, pleased tone of voice. "And do you know what she looks like?" Lorenzo went on. Milagros closed her eyes, as though unable to bear the blinding, dazzling vision of Xaviera. "Don't make fun of me," she said sadly. "You know I don't. But I can imagine." And doubtless she could. One could see the chimerical image of a protean and preternatural wonder-working Xaviera quivering in her fascinated gaze.

Meanwhile the traffic light on the Avenue Matignon had turned green for pedestrians again. "Look," Lorenzo told her, "we've said everything we had to say to each other. There's a taxi stand over there. Perhaps we'll see each other again and perhaps not." He gestured goodbye with one hand. Milagros looked at him in astonishment, unable to understand the reasons for such a brutally sudden farewell. And Lorenzo added, with a slight touch of sadism, or perhaps of spitefulness when all was said and done: "If I were you, I wouldn't let myself have too many illusions. Xaviera is doubtless the brains of the Organization, but as a woman she's a dead loss. An absolute fright!" and he walked off, in great long strides, without even waiting to see Milagros's expression of utter horror at such sacrilege.

So after this unfortunate turn of events it was necessary to begin all over again.

He programmed the search of Xaviera's electronic memory again, as he had done before, adding just one supplementary requirement: "Must be white." And while he was at it, he added: "and blonde." The whole story would have had a tragi-comic end, of course, if this tiny germ had led to the proliferation of racial prejudices in Xaviera's transistorized circuits. Just in case, he promised himself to keep very careful watch on Xaviera's future conduct in this regard.

The second ideal companion located by the IBM computer was named Isabel. Isabel, then, was white. And blonde. And French. She spoke Spanish with a very slight accent leading one to suspect she had learned it in South America. More precisely: in Colombia. Lorenzo, at least, was prepared to wager that this was the origin of a certain number of her odd pronunciations, expressions, and turns of phrase. In any event, as was clear from the very first words they exchanged, Isabel had read The Autumn of the Patriarch and, moreover, had read it the right way, with great fervor and care. On the other hand, she had never even heard of Tirano Banderas, and all she knew of Valle-Inclán was his works for the theater, and that only indirectly through what she had heard about them at second hand. But then a person couldn't ask for too much. One couldn't be too *demanding. Moreover, as a sort of compensation, Isabel, in her gentle, reflective way, seemed quite ready to listen to him discourse on the remote influence of* Tirano Banderas *on South American novelists dealing with the same ancestral theme of the dictator or the populist caudillo sprung from the entrails of the epic history of Latin America.*

The weather was stifling that day in July on which Lorenzo interviewed Isabel for the first time. They had gone walking along the quay of the Seine, following the river upstream along the Left Bank. On arriving at the Pont-Neuf, the idea occurred to Lorenzo to invite her to dinner. It was already dark and a sudden coolness was mounting from the water. What was more, Lorenzo was eager to begin talking to Isabel about Tirano Banderas, *without wasting any more time.*

They crossed the river via the Pont-Neuf, which, as its name fails to indicate, is one of the oldest bridges in Paris, and headed toward the Vert Galant, the restaurant with a marvelous outdoor terrace in summer.

The first thing to greet Lorenzo's eye on entering the luxurious establishment was Santiago Carrillo. The secretary-general of the Spanish Communist Party was dining at a table with four other distinguished gentlemen. Or at least all of them looked like distinguished gentlemen. One of them was José Luis de Vilallonga. Easy to recognize, that one, no confusion possible. In fact, if he could not be immediately recognized from his film and serial roles as the quadrigenarian man about town whom young maidens inevitably fall head over heels in love with and from the recent television interviews in which he acted as spokesman of the Democratic Junta, Vilallonga had also recently been lending—or better put, selling—his elegant physiognomy for ads to promote the sale of sherry, which is what the English call what Spaniards call Xérès, whereas, the French baptize it Jerez. In all the magazines and weeklies of France there could be seen the rapt, aristocratic visage of Vilallonga, crowned with gray hair, beneath which were printed these unforgettable words: "Interviewed by Europe 1 [French radio station], José Luis de Vilalonga (and note that the printer's error—the inversion of the "ll" and the "l" in the illustrious patronymic—is not due to the transcriber or to the narrator but to the daily cited here, namely Le Figaro) *declares: "The first time sherry surprises you; the second time it pleases you; the third time you adore it." Words replete with meaning, or truly polysemic, or so some future student of the French philosopher Roland Barthes will say when a structural,historical study is made of these advertisements, in view of the fact that they are equally useful for speaking of sherry, xérès, or jerez, or of one's intimate relations with a woman for that matter, thus fulfilling a double function in the purest tradition of Spanish phallocratism. In a word, impossible to confuse José Luis de Vilallonga with anyone else in the world.*

Madame Bos, the proprietress of the restaurant, had seated Isabel and Lorenzo at the last free little table, not far from Carrillo's. As he sat down, Lorenzo was careful to place himself directly opposite Carrillo, face to face. Plump and jovial, the Great Pragmatist—that was what all Lorenzo's Spanish friends had nicknamed Carrillo some time ago—was explaining something or other to his table companions, obviously eager to convince them. The others were hanging on his every word.

Lorenzo guessed that one of them might be Rafael Calvo Serer. Or if it weren't, the gentlemen in question deserved to be, given his provincial air, his haughty manner, his self-conceit, typical of a social-climbing scion of the Levantine bourgeoisie. But perhaps Lorenzo was wrong. Perhaps it wasn't Calvo Serer, but some coadjutor bishop come incognito to gather information on the positions of the Democratic Junta, to establish contacts, thus applying the old precepts of "to each saint the offering due him," or "don't put all your eggs in one basket," or "light one candle to a saint and another to the devil." Or perhaps it was some notary from Logroño, the intermediary and spokesman for a financial group of the civilized right, the more powerful financially the more civilized, because civilization is not something the poor or parvenus should have anything to do with, damn it, that's all we need! But in any event, those distinguished gentlemen, Vilallonga, the putative Calvo Serer, and the other two, were lending Carrillo an attentive and sympathetic ear, that was plain to see.

"Have you seen who's here?" Isabel said the minute they were seated. Lorenzo nodded. He wondered who it was that Isabel had recognized, José Luis or Santiago. Most likely José Luis, he thought. "Carrillo and Vila-llonga," Isabel said, thus immediately dispelling his doubts. "C'est une soirée bien parisienne," she added in French. And turning to Lorenzo: "You'll have to offer me a dinner with champagne, in view of the circumstances." She raised her head, shook her short blonde hair, and laughed merrily. "All right," Lorenzo said, "no sooner said than done. Would you like Dom Pérignon or would you prefer a Cristal-Roederer?" Isabel chose without hesitating a second. She knew very well what she preferred.

Menus were brought each of them, hers with no prices indicated. It was taken for granted that she was his guest, as was indeed the case, but this merely proved that the notion of the equality of the woman had not yet made much headway in fancy restaurants.

Lorenzo raised his eyes briefly from the menu and met Carrillo's. It seemed to him, for the space of an instant, that Carrillo was scrutinizing him, as though his face were vaguely familiar to him, as though he were trying to place it. No, it was not possible. Too many years had gone by. However good a memory the Great Pragmatist may have had, and no doubt he had a very keen one, despite his calculated lapses when publicly *summoning up memories of his political life, as in* Dialogue on Spain *for instance, it was not very likely that he had recognized him. How many years had gone by? It was in the summer of 1962, so that made it thirteen years. And that was precisely how old he had been—Lorenzo, that is— when he had seen Carrillo in that "dacha" outside Moscow. Had Carrillo changed? of course. Thirteen years do not fail to make their mark, even on Great Pragmatists, Great Helmsmen, and Great Sharks who aspire to immortality. He was thinner, his features were sharper, the skin on his neck was wrinkled. But this inevitable aging was tempered by a greater freedom in his movements and gestures, a more noticeable self-assurance, a greater self-mastery. This was quite natural. Since Carrillo had abandoned the conquest of the masses or at least subordinated it to the conquest of the mass media, he had had considerable success in the area of public relations. Carrillo was news. Even Sulzberger had had an interview with him, published, coincidentally, in the* International Herald Tribune *the day before. It was true that Sulzberger had just written a book entitled* The Era of Mediocrity, *and of course Carrillo was right at home in this era, and even stood out, a one-eyed man in the kingdom of the blind.*

The title of Sulzberger's interview, "The Other Monsieur Giscard," had caught Lorenzo's eye, and he read the interview just the day before as he was eating breakfast. The fact was that thirteen years before, when he himself was thirteen, in that "dacha" on the outskirts of Moscow in which he and his parents were spending the last days of a vacation provided by the Spanish Communists (it so happened that François Larrea—that was his father's name—a Frenchman of remote Spanish origins, a university professor and distinguished Hispanist, and a member of the French Communist Party, had collaborated, without pay, for many long years with the clandestine apparatus of the Spanish Communist Party responsible for smuggling people over the border and for liaison), Lorenzo vividly remembered his father explaining to his mother and him ("You've reached the age of reason, Jean-Laurent, you can listen") the complex and moving situation of Señor and Señora Carrillo, who were living clandestinely in France and whose three sons were not only unaware, for reasons of security, that their father was a Communist leader, but did not even know that they were Spanish and were quite certain that their family name was Giscard, since that was the false identity under which they had been enrolled in school and the one they went by in French society. Lorenzo's father found this situation touching. To Lorenzo, despite his tender years, it seemed incomprehensible. How could those children, who had been born in France and gone to school along with all the other kids in the neighborhood, have believed that their father was French, with that accent of his? Well, they had been told that the family was of Spanish origin. And he,

Lorenzo, or rather Jean-Laurent, a stubborn youngster, went on asking questions. How could they be of Spanish origin with a name like Giscard? His father had lost his temper. What a shitty little Cartesian this kid who wants an answer for everything has turned out to be! But Eva, his mother, had burst out laughing. And Lorenzo kept chewing over what he was told and asking more questions. As far as I'm concerned, he finally concluded, it's either one thing or the other: either the kids are just plain dumb, though they don't seem to be, or else they know perfectly well what's going on and are pretending they don't so as not to worry papa and mama.

In any event, it never occurred to Lorenzo to tell anyone what Carrillo's false name was. Not even years later, when Carrillo could come and go as he pleased in France, once his real identity had been recovered and made legal, not even then did it occur to Lorenzo to comment on this secret long known to him, if only as an amusing little story told in the course of one of those evenings when people drink a lot and tongues begin to wag. He would not even have told Xaviera! Perhaps because it came naturally to him to respect the secrets of an organization, however insignificant they might be, and above all other people's secrets. And now this braggart comes along and tells the Yankee reporter Sulzberger that little folkloric secret to make himself seem like an interesting character. What a dumb-ass showoff! "The President of France," *Sulzberger wrote at the beginning of this interview,* "generally known by his countrymen as 'Giscard,' would be surprised to know that his capital is also inhabited by another ambitious political leader, who for most of the twenty-one years he has been a Parisian carried false identity papers with the alias 'Giscard.'" *The only interesting and pertinent remark in Sulzberger's interview is the comparison, or rather the equating, of the vastly similar ambitions of Giscard (d'Estaing) and Giscard (Carrillo) even though thus far the ambitions of the latter have not been crowned with similar success.*

But let's not be subjective, Lorenzo thinks to himself. Let's not succumb to polemics, however justified this might be. There are interesting things in the interview with Carrillo, Lorenzo thinks to himself, as he advises Isabel to try the homard à la nage *("now that you've decided to have champagne, we'll throw the house out the window," he tells her, but since she isn't familiar with the expression he has to explain that it means "going whole hog"), yes, he thinks, there are other interesting things in it. When Carrillo begins to talk about Portugal, for example.* "Cunhal is a narrow-minded man who does not see reality. Soares is softer and less combative, but he is wiser and sees the reality of what can be done in the present circumstances," *Carrillo says. And at the end of the interview, the Great Pragmatist says that* "Spain needs technological aid and capital from the United States," *a statement made to order to reassure the Anglo-Saxon* reader of the paper, but one that could not help but create certain problems when it came time to install a democratic regime in Spain.

Meanwhile Isabel had decided to choose the first and second course of her dinner. She would start with caviar and then have homard à la nage as the entrée. The charming blonde thus demonstrated that she had understood perfectly the meaning of the expression "to throw the house out the window." Lorenzo also ordered the famous homard à la nage as his entrée, and for a first course chose Parma ham, a San Daniele, to be more precise, always of excellent quality at the Vert Galant.

"What do you suppose the two of them talk about when they're alone?" Isabel mused. "Carrillo and Vilallonga?" The girl nodded. Lorenzo made a face. "Ever since Thermidor," he said, "all revolutionaries from the people have been fascinated by aristocrats." Isabel shrugged, sipping and savoring a swallow of champagne. "Well, yes, that's so. And the reverse is also true. But concretely, what about those two?" That word's come up again, Lorenzo sighed to himself. Concrete, concretely: magic words that dispel shadows, that shed light on perspectives. The concrete, the here and now: the concrete analysis of a concrete situation, as Lenin said. For some time now the concrete had seemed to Lorenzo to be as ponderous and boring a subject as cement—if one can permit and pardon this dubious play on words that came semantically from English. The concrete was almost always a pretext for delimiting a tiny operational area within reality in which to act pragmatically, isolating oneself from contexts, totalities, and other such confounded things. Instead of representing the multiple, polyvalent, and sometime contraditory aspects of reality, it had become a mere rhetorical figure, a mere handy device for confronting problems one by one, completely detached from any overall strategic vision. The concrete, in short, was living on impulses, on the turn of the cards, on come what may, on making the best of bad situations and a virtue of necessity. The concrete was, for example, the kind of nonsense typical of General Díez Alegría, totally aside from any serious analysis of the situation and the possible historical role that the army might reasonably be expected to play at this moment in the history of Spain. And in defense of the concrete, thus understood, or better put, misunderstood and deliberately ignored, pragmatists always had recourse, in addition to timely quotation of awkward little phrases of Lenin's on the soul of Marxism, to the words of Napoleon Bonaparte, as cited by none other than Lenin himself: "On s'engage et puis on voit": one commits oneself to action and then one sees. . . . Yes indeed, one sees. We've all seen. Seen altogether too much.

"Concretely, when they're alone," Lorenzo said, "those two no doubt talk about the Bourbons, as they've already done in their duo, their mano

a mano, *their interview in tandem in the magazine* Lui." *Isabel laughed.*
"*Do you think so?*" *Lorenzo shrugged.* "*What else would they talk about
besides the Bourbons, whether Franco's mythological cancer is affecting
his rectum or his right nut, or, who knows, Franco's Pazo de Meiras
bedroom secrets?! Or maybe you think Vilallonga is reporting to Carrillo
on the morale of Andalusian agricultural workers?*"

They had brought the first course. Isabel was absorbed in pleased contemplation of the copious serving of Iranian caviar, at its peak of freshness
and succulence.

There had also been heaps of caviar that long-ago night in that "dacha"
on the outskirts of Moscow. Lorenzo remembers it very well, despite all the
time that has gone by since: thirteen years, half his life. In mezzo del
camin. . . . Well, never mind the literary digressions. There had been heaps
of caviar, in any case, and different soups, some of them hot and thick and
another one, a cold one, more subtle than the usual ones with cabbage and
potatoes, a sort of gazpacho from Central Asia called "aknoshka," if he
remembered correctly, a name with a Basque ring to it; and all sorts of
smoked or pickled fish: herring, salmon, trout, eel (are eels fish?), and
others whose names he did not know, no doubt from the Baltic; and salads
and chicken croquettes and meat balls with hot sauces; and then the
taciturn peasant girls dressed like nurses in a charity hospital, or Little
Sisters of the Poor, with skirts of coarse faded gray or blue cotton cloth
and kerchiefs on their heads, who served the illustrious foreign guests'
dinner with ancestral slowness, began to bring the pièces de résistance,
the various courses of meat in juices and rich sauces; and the long table
was covered with bottles of vodka, with fat round flasks of harsh red wine
imported from Bulgaria, white wine from Chile, and another white produced in the Caucasus, and bottles of Armenian cognac; and from time
to time one could also hear the popping of a cork from a bottle of pink
champagne from the Caucasus, because there was no lack of champagne
either; and one of the Spanish leaders among those present, some of whom
were returning from vacation and on their way west again, others had just
arrived in the USSR and were on their way to the beaches of the Crimea,
the palm groves of Sochi—and the only other foreigners present were the
three of them, Monsieur and Madame Larrea and their son—one of the
leaders, pushing aside the glass of champagne that someone offered him,
proclaimed in a stentorian voice with an Andalusian accent: "I'm not in
the habit of drinking until the meal is half over," and the others hailed
this bon mot with great bursts of laughter, and Lorenzo noticed the
expression on La Pasionaria's face at that precise moment, because La
Pasionaria was also present at this dinner, with an expression of something
like irritation, or disgust, or infinite and bitter weariness, as she nervously

smoothed back a lock of her hair, a lock of white hair that had worked
itself loose from her severe coiffure; she was dressed in black, La Pasio-
naria, with an expresion of disgust, of irritation, or at least condescending,
distant reserve in the face of so much Iberian, Celtiberian laughter, so
much barracks-room male din and clamor (and today, years later, on this
July night in Paris, I, Juan-Lorenzo Larrea, age twenty-six, a lonely
bachelor, having traveled the road of despair to the very end, covered every
step of the way to the blinding certainty that the Revolution is a failure,
an orphan now of all our little tutelary gods that became bloody idols, how
much I should like to approach you again, Pasionaria, and ask you to tell
me the truths of so many years of faith betrayed, of cadaverous obedience
to the categorical and alienating imperatives of a solidarity that was no
longer that of a class but a clan; to ask you to tell me the dark truths that
you dare not tell even yourself, but that are necessarily crouching in your
memory, in the equivocal mourning of a life that has lost its mast, those
truths that have made of you the figurehead of a phantom vessel, whose
cargo is the corpses of comrades. . . .)

But I am in San Vicente de la Barquera, in a tavern on the docks,
facing the view of the bridge of my childhood, in the August sun, in 1975,
and I have just decided that Lorenzo and Isabel will come to have lunch
here in the next chapter of the novel I am writing and that I do not yet
know I will never finish, because the reality of Franco's death will come
and put a sudden end—and not to my regret—to this fiction of his
amazing assassination and his no less amazing resurrection.

A few weeks later, on September 27, five young anti-Fascists were
executed by a firing squad.

> We already know what death is,
> we know what its star shot full holes is like.
> We already know that when it came to see you
>
> it put roses of razor-sharp salt
> on the blind space of your forehead.
> But you are not dead, comrade. . . .

Of the hundreds of verses I wrote in a fervent, alienated, far-distant
youth, these are among the few I do not disavow. And I am not speaking
from a literary point of view, of course. From a literary point of view,
I could no longer write like that, if some day the urge to write poetry
chanced to come over me again. But I do not disavow them from the

point of view of feeling, of the anguish that overcomes one when comrades die after a long struggle, at dawn, face to face with the endless horizon of rifles of a firing squad.

In those last days of that bloody September, I went on frantically working on that novel I had entitled *Palacio de Ayete,* as though the description of the fictitious death of the dictator might somehow conjure away the specter of real death that his continued survival caused to hover over the heads of Spaniards.

And then in October of that bloody year, Javier Pradera telephoned me one afternoon from Madrid. Domingo González Lucas, "Dominguín," had committed suicide in Guayaquil.

Dominguito, "Petit-dimanche," as Ignacio Romero used to affectionately call him.

Guayaquil? The only thing I know about Guayaquil is that it is the birthplace of José Joaquín Olmedo, the poet and comrade of Bolívar. I can't imagine Domingo in Guayaquil, I don't know anything about Guayaquil. The last time I saw Domingo was on Principe, that street in Madrid where his mother, Doña Gracia, was still living. Domingo spoke to me of the fabulous Americas and invited me to join him there some day. Dominguito had aged but he still had the same vitality and enthusiasm as always, the same way of living life as though it were a dream

(but you will not speak about Domingo: you will not tell how you came to know him in 1956: when Javier introduced him to you: you will not speak about your first luncheon with him on Juan de Mena: a few steps away from the house in which you had lived your childhood in Madrid: you will not tell what Domingo's friendship and what friendship with Domingo was like through so many long years: you will not speak of number 12 Ferraz: you will not speak of the days in "La Companza": you will not speak of Canales: the old Communist from Quismondo who was a friend of Domingo's and the very incarnation of popular wisdom: and Domingo laughingly proposed that we exchange Marxism-Leninsim for Marxism-Canalism: "Just think how much easier everything would be," Domingo used to say: "Instead of having to consult the thirty-some volumes of Lenin's complete works all we'd have to do would be to go to Quismondo: just around the corner, that is: to know how to apply this imprecise science of Marxism to our situation: our fucked-up situation."

you will not speak of Domingo because you don't know if Domingo would have liked being in this book: you honestly don't know: and you don't want to force him to be in this book against his will: without having been able to talk the possibility over with him

you will merely say that Domingo's absence is something irremediable: something truly unthinkable: that some day you will go to

Guayaquil: to the place where Domingo is buried far from his homeland: you will go to Guayaquil before the bindweed of your death paralyzes your shoulders and your arms and cracks you heart that bears the imprint of his absence)

and a few days later you were in Madrid, talking with Simón Sánchez Montero, who was friend of Domingo's, and the dictator, Lord of the Flies and of death, was in his last long agony. And then, perhaps because this history that has been our Spanish history was ending, you remembered how it began.

You remembered Lekeitio.

The weather was splendid, I remember very well, during that month of July 1936.

In the first few days, it seemed as though that distant military uprising would introduce no fundamental change in the rhythm of this summer season. In the morning, we continued to go to the Carraspio beach. In the afternoon, after siesta-time, we continued to go to the Basque pelota games, or to the pine groves on the other side of the estuary, or on long walks to Mendeja, or in the other direction, to the lighthouse.

Then things began to go to pieces. The vacationers left. People from Bilbao went back home to Bilbao, or took off, like the people from Madrid, for Biarritz and San Juan de la Luz, in hopes of better times.

The Frenchwoman left too.

A legend, woven of gossip and rumors, had come to surround this woman ever since she had arrived in Lekeitio three years before, to spend the summer alone there, with her little girl. She was said to wear indecent bathing suits. She was said to go out at night with men in a boat and bathe naked far offshore. The fact that this took place at night doubtless made her crime more serious. The oral legend, in any case, stressed the perfidy of this foreign woman.

From the balcony of the House by the Bridge, where we were spending the summer, I could see the foreign woman walking by early every morning, heading for the beach, holding her daughter by the hand, as though by this maternal gesture that seemed so out of place on her part, so unworthy of her true hidden nature—which was surely evil and perverse—she were trying to further provoke the fierce, dark, jealous anger of the Lekeitio women. I could see the foreign woman walking in the direction of Carraspio, indifferent to the whispers behind her back, or perhaps unaware of them, her head held high and walking gracefully and unhurriedly, arousing in the men, one had every reason to suppose —and in me certainly—images of nocturnal nudity, in waters far off-shore.

From the balcony of the House by the Bridge I would see her walk by every morning at the same time. She would appear at the bend in the road that hid the palace of the Empress Zita from view, holding her daughter by the hand, with the morning sun glinting on her very short blonde hair and on the baroque necklace of pale gold set with blue stones that she usually wore, above a white dress that left her arms completely bare. I would see her coming round the bend in the road and then passing in front of the combined barracks and living quarters of the carabineers.

As she passed by the barracks every morning, the shouted conversations of the carabineers' wives between the geranium-filled windows would suddenly break off. A deep, almost threatening silence would ensue as the foreign woman walked past. But the moment she was beyond the barracks, heading for the bridge, the carabineers' wives would begin screaming excitedly again.

"Sisinia!" a shrill voice would shout, "did you notice how she's dressed?"

This daily indignation never ceased to surprise me, because the foreign woman was always dressed in the same way, immaculate white frocks with the baroque necklace of antique gold and blue stones gleaming at the neckline.

"What a hussy!" another voice, a hoarse one this time, possibly Sisinia's, would reply. "Her arms were bare naked!"

And then from the top floor a matron's voice, with an Andalusian accent, would proclaim self-righteously:

"Did you see that hypocrite, that harlot? The front of her dress was all right, a real ladylike dress, but did you see how low-cut it was in the back?"

And the evil-tongued chorus would comment on this cut of the foreign woman's dress, which bared the uniformly tanned skin of her back that contrasted with the snowy whiteness of the dress and showed not the slightest trace of chaste and innocent untanned patches, obvious proof that the foreign women sunbathed stark naked somewhere. And Sisinia's voice would habitually round off the comments with a resounding "What lewdness!" repeated each morning.

To me, enamored as I was in my child's way with this proud French-woman whose skin was smooth and soft and copper-colored, this word, only half understood, came to symbolize every possible unknown or forbidden pleasure.

But that year, the Frenchwoman went away before the summer had scarcely begun. The mechanisms of daily life began to fail. The mail didn't arrive, bread began to be in short supply, and its color and consistency were different. The most ordinary things began to involve problems.

At about this time my father took the American car we owned at the time, a Graham Page that he had put at the disposal of the Popular Front Committee of Lekeitio, and journeyed to Santander to give a speech over the radio, entitled "The North against the Rebels," which the daily press then reprinted.

The only cars on the roads then were ones covered with placards and full of armed men. And the entire length of the Carraspio beach, stretching from the mouth of the estuary to the rocky promontory, was practically deserted.

(yes, deserted, that is the way you remembered the Carraspio beach, as though the image in your memory were one of those faded postcards from the beginning of the century, in which the Cantabrian beaches are abandoned to the solitude of the sea, to the briny immensity, to the flight of seagulls skimming the waves, to two or three families scattered out over the vast sandy expanse, beneath the tutelary shadow of an aristocratic sun umbrella, but you have no photograph left of this period, no material trace, everything has been blotted out, obliterated by the Civil War, by exile, all you have left are the intermittent lightning flashes of a memory whose personages grow younger each day as you yourself approach the shadowy horizon of death

but you have just remembered an object dating from that period that you still have, not a photograph of course, or a postcard, or a letter, or even a flower pressed and dried between the pages of some book. It is, rather, a book, between the pages of which it is unlikely that a flower was ever pressed and dried, the only book you have that belonged to your father, and you go and get it down from the shelf in your library where you keep it, and open it; there on the first blank page, written in pencil, in that large angular hand of a former pupil of the Jesuits, is your father's full signature: *José Ma. de Semprún y Gurrea, June, 1932,* and you can't help smiling, because it is going to seem incredible, or contrived, or invented by you out of the whole cloth so as to make a point, but you haven't invented it, and you can prove it, that's the way life is, the chance happenings of life, the little ironies of your family history that are not without meaning, for the fact is that this one concrete testimonial you have left of that period, the only material proof that you have not dreamed the events and the images of that period, is a pocket book solidly bound in gray cloth, on which the author's name and the title are inscribed in red letters: Karl Marx: DAS KAPITAL, and you must confess you find it amusing that the only thing you have inherited from your father, who died in exile, apart from a certain number of atavisms that still cause you anxiety, and certain principles that, to save time, you will label moral ones, the only thing that you have inherited is a copy of Marx's *Capital,* published in Berlin in 1932 by Gustav Kiepenheuer, with a preface by Karl Korsch, without question a magnificent one, and with annotations in your father's handwriting, some of them in Spanish, others in German, which allow you to deduce that your father read Marx's work attentively and in a critical spirit, although nothing allows you to guess why your father had decided to read this book again in Lekeitio during the summer of 1936, which turned out to be the last one there, a decision that enabled this book to reach your hands

be that as it may, you remembered the Carraspio beach as almost deserted, until you came back one morning in August of 1975 and contemplated, in despair, the hundreds and hundreds of sun umbrellas, the hundreds of families, of potato omelettes, of Pepsi-Cola and orange drink bottles, the hundreds and hundreds of plump, screaming children, of women with big asses and bare breasts, of transistor radios blaring out the hits of the day, of bathers who had frightened off the seagulls, perhaps forever

well, what's gotten into you anyway? what's so surprising? this is progress, you said to yourself, laughing fit to kill and immensely sad, this is the result of the irresistible and praiseworthy, and perhaps even well-deserved, rise of the middle classes, of the long-suffering, insufferable middle classes, to levels of consumption comparable to those of the rest of Europe, this is the unmistakable sign of the massive spread of economic well-being in your country

and you laughed nervously, almost desperately, as you contemplated the amoebalike movements of the multitude on the Carraspio beach, as you tried to take refuge in the luxurious images of your privileged rich kid's memory, but it was impossible, the shock of reality made it impossible, because there is no way really to grasp reality, and poor Marcel—you are referring to Proust, of course—would have had his work cut out for him if he had had to undertake his search for lost time fifty years later; with the commercialization of social consumption ever expanding, it would have been a Herculean labor for him; because on the promontory that overlooks the beach they had built unspeakable apartment houses, and in Mendeja, which other maps call Celaya, the little village where you and Gonzalo and Ávaro, the three oldest brothers, used to stroll about, everything was unrecognizible, and though the old church with the Basque pelota court back to back with it still existed, it was merely the infinitely sad ghost of its former self, because they had reconstructed its humble and luminous stone facade by covering it over with a stupid and vulgar cement facing, and around this grayish ghost, or rather this corpse, of the old church, there was no sign now of the little houses of long ago, which had been replaced by charmless bungalows, and in Lekeitio itself the splendid open-air Basque pelota court no longer existed either, up there on the esplanade that overlooks the breakwater, where you had seen the aged but still redoubtable Mondragón play, and one or another of the Atano brothers, the seventh one, as you recall, and in its place there loomed up a building so modern it set your teeth on edge, a very functional one, no doubt, but utterly useless for your eager reconquest of time past, and what was worst of all, the biggest blow, the most unbearable thing was that the palace of the Empress Zita no longer existed in Lekeitio, and you reached the point of asking yourself at that moment if you hadn't perhaps dreamed all that, for the fact is that)

I have been dreaming all my life long of returning to Lekeitio.

And when I say dreaming, I mean real dreams, and not some sort of illusion, or vague hope. I am talking about the sort of meaningful dream one has at night, a pleasant or painful dream in which one's most intimate impulses are discharged or recharged. Ordinarily this type of dream vanishes the moment I have recovered my ever-vigilant waking consciousness. My inhibitions and defense mechanisms function very well. But the dream of Lekeitio has always contrived nicely to outwit the psychological devices of censorship and self-defense.

I have always remembered the dream of Lekeitio after waking up.

It was no trick at all to enter this dream. All the gates of dreams swung open, one after the other, softly, silently, and there one was, in the very heart of this dream, as though one were in the protected space of a courtyard with myrtle trees and quivering fountains. But one always entered this dream from the same direction: from right to left. Naturally, in order to understand this arrangement of space, one must imagine oneself facing the Cantabrian shore, standing perhaps on the promontory that overlooks the Carraspio beach, the mouth of the estuary, the bay. A seemingly arbitrary procedure, I grant, but the topography of the dream did reflect a secret desire.

When all is said and done, one entered this dream by way of the road from Ondárroa.

One entered this dream by way of the road from Ondárroa, which wound along the cliff face, amid steep groves of eucalyptus, spruce, and chestnut trees. One rounded a curve and there was the Carraspio beach. For an instant, one could see the entire panorama: the bay, the beach, the mouth of the estuary, the little island of San Nicholás, the fishing port. It used to rain on this panorama. In the dream, I mean. A warm, gentle rain usually. Or rather, a mist of rain, like a sort of aqueous veil that softened the contours of everything, as though the dream did not remember the summer vacation, as though it remembered only the last sad days of vacation, the days in September that preceded the return to Madrid.

But the dream was arriving now, via the itinerary of long ago, at the bridge over the estuary. To the left, before one crossed this bridge at the somnolent pace at which the dream was unfolding, the road leading up to Mendeja branched off. Then the dream crossed the bridge. And here was the House by the Bridge, the house of summer vacations of long ago. Then, on the left-hand side, built into the sloping hillside itself, the combined barracks and living quarters of the carabineers. And on the right-hand side of the dream, a short little footpath led down to the dockyard. There, when the sea was at high tide, when the estuary filled and widened, the dream remembered the launching of fishing boats. The dream has a perfect memory of the launching of the *Bisibedi Jesús.* Then the road turned to the left and there was the last straight stretch before entering Lekeitio. To the right, between the road and the bay, one could still see in the dream the walled grounds surrounding the summer palace of the Empress Zita.

The dream might end here, in front of the iron gate of the empress's palace. It might also go on for a bit, and sometimes it went on as far as the square in front of the church, as far as the public promenade for evening strolls, overlooking the fishing port.

But in either of the two cases, it was evident—however absurd this might appear at first glance—that the mysterious protagonist of this dream so often repeated, so often dreamed, image by image, without ever changing over the years, could only be the red Oldsmobile convertible, or the black Graham Page: one of my father's last two automobiles, both of which made the trip from Madrid to Lekeitio. It was evident, in any event, that it was not I who dreamed this dream, but the red Oldsmobile or the black Graham Page, as though we—my father, my brothers, and I—were only the silent, absorbed, invisible passengers of this dream being dreamed by an automobile.

It was evident that the dream reconstructed, at once anxiously and pleasurably, by objectifying it, the childhood memory of the arrival at Lekeitio, at the beginning of the summer vacation, by way of the itinerary of long ago.

That is why, when I finally returned to Lekeitio, in the middle of August 1975, I followed this itinerary: the road from Ondárroa. It wasn't the shortest way that morning, coming as we were from Bilbao after spending a few days in the province of Santander. We had to take a long way round—and we took advantage of it to go see the Tree of Guernika —so as to be able to come out at Ondárroa and from there follow the usual route of the dream.

A certain almost painful feverishness came over me as I approached this landscape of my childhood in that long-ago summer of 1936.

Not everything had changed however.

The House by the Bridge, recently whitewashed, was still the same. The church had not changed, nor had the altar-piece above the main altar. The public promenade had not changed.

But the summer palace of the Empress Zita no longer existed.

Why did this member of the dethroned imperial family of the Hapsburgs have a summer palace in Lekeitio? I have never been able to find out. But the fact is that she had a summer palace there at the entrance to the town, between the highway and the bay. I am prepared to swear to that, even though in August 1975 the building itself no longer existed, and there was now a public part where it had once stood. Even though it not only no longer existed, but what was more no one could explain to me just why it had disappeared.

When lunch was over in the restaurant where we ate, I asked the waitress, a very young girl, what had happened to the Empress's palace. She didn't understand my question. I repeated it, with more details and further explanations. It turned out that she was from Bermeo: she'd only been in Lekeitio a couple of years. She went to ask one of the other waitresses—one who'd been born in Lekeitio. They began talking together in Basque and nothing much in the way of solid facts was forthcoming from their conversation. The girl from Lekeitio didn't remember any palace of any Empress either. Then the first waitress asked me what year, more or less, I'd been talking about. I said the summer of 1936 and the summers before that. At that the girl from Bermeo and the girl from Lekeitio burst into uncontrollable fits of laughter. To them I was talking about prehistory, of course. They laughed and looked at each other and I told them I hadn't been back since 1936, since that war we'd had. Had they ever heard about that long-ago war we'd had? They turned very serious all of a sudden. They had a vague idea, perhaps, of what I was talking about. They turned serious and said yes, of course, they remembered that long-ago war. Or rather, they remembered the memories of their parents, filled to the brim with that long-ago war. Or maybe their grandparents' memories. They turned serious and perhaps they were thinking of the boys of ETA, the Basque separatist movement, who had died in Lekeitio, not so long ago, in the last battles of that old war. They turned serious, they vaguely understood my anguish, and said nothing.

In the bar where we had coffee, on the fishermen's wharf, I asked again about the palace of the Empress Zita. I was unable to locate anyone who remembered this palace, or at least remembered such a palace being destroyed.

The thought came to me that perhaps there had never existed in Lekeitio a summer palace of a former Austro-Hungarian empress of the dethroned Hapsburg dynasty. The thought came to me that I might have dreamed it.

But if that were so, had I also dreamed the field hospital?

In 1936, shortly after the beginning of the Civil War, the old deserted palace had been turned into a field hospital. One afternoon the first wounded arrived. Amid the silence of the villagers of Lekeitio who had congregated there, the first wounded of that long-ago war were carried inside on stretchers. Those slightly wounded and those seriously wounded. Those who would live to know defeat and those who would die without ever knowing that we would be defeated. Amid the deep silence of the men, women, and children congregated there, the first wounded of that long-ago war were brought into the field hospital.

But perhaps I had dreamed it, perhaps there had never been a field hospital in the lonely abandoned palace of the Empress Zita. Perhaps I had never been in Lekeitio, perhaps I had dreamed that summer of 1936.

And yet I have already spoken twice of that summer, I have written my memories of that summer twice. The first time in a play, *Soledad,* that not only was never published but disappeared from my memory for many long years. And then, much later, when I had long since forgotten *Soledad,* forgotten what one of the characters in this play said, I spoke once again, in almost the same words, as though it were a return of the repressed, of my memories of that summer, of "the house of the last vacations, at the foot of the pine grove, when the entire village began leaving in the panting silence, when the setting of the hills on fire and the arrival of the refugees from the closest town to the east [from Ondárroa, that is, I add today] were signs that Gambara's Italian troops were approaching, invading Basque soil. A few men erected a barricade of sandbags at the entrance of the bridge, brought hunting riffles, tin cans filled with dynamite, and I knew several of them, fishermen I had met down at the port during these summers, pelota players who would go up to Mendeja, to the open-air court standing back to back with the church, to begin yet another match in this sempiternal game between rival teams, the leather ball smacking into their bare hands or striking with a ripping, tearing sound the metal ribbon marking the lower limit of the playing area on the wall opposite: they looked at the hillsides that had been set on fire, they clasped their hunting rifles to their hearts and smoked in silence; to abandon them, to leave them there behind that useless barricade, face to face with Gambara's tanks, was to break the most essential bonds, to take the first step on the road to exile; we would have liked to be a few years older all of a sudden so as to stay with them, and we promised ourselves, in a confused way, in our terrible childish desperation, to make up some day for being so far behind, to recapture somehow or other this lost time. . . ."

That was what I said, years ago now, speaking of Lekeitio, remembering that last night in Lekeitio. No, to tell the truth, I didn't say it exactly like that, because I wrote this book, *The Long Voyage,* in a foreign language, French. It was Jacqueline and Rafael Conte who translated this book into Spanish for me not long ago. It will always seem strange to me to read myself translated into my own language, however well this is done, as it was in this case.

But I am not going to discuss here, with a certain narcissistic delight, the problems of the writer who is in exile and bilingual. Or rather, who is bilingual because he is in exile. I have referred to *The Long Voyage* for a very different reason. I have mentioned it because even though it was in French, this book was written at number 5 Concepción Bahamonde (on the second floor, the apartment on the right overlooking the street), the point around which the dizzying immobile spiral of my memory has unfolded, the sudden memory of which—as I look at La Pasionaria and the other comrades of the Executive Committee, as I note the absence of Simón Sanchez Montero, arrested on June 17, 1959 on the eve of the abortive *Aitch En Pee,* his absence in April 1964, at the meeting held in an ancient castle of Bohemian kings—has brought on this interminable digression. Simón Sáchez Montero, arrested on June 17, 1959 on the eve of the abortive *Aitch En Pee,* his absence in April 1964, at the meeting held in an ancient castle of Bohemian kings—has brought on this interminalbe digression.

8 LA PASIONARIA HAS ASKED FOR THE FLOOR

YOU'RE IN LUCK.

At the very moment La Pasionaria asked for the floor, smoothing back a rebellious lock of white hair and placing on the table before her the paper she was about to read to all of you, at that very moment the doors of the grand salon were flung open and several waiters in white jackets and immaculate gloves came in.

Silently and diligently, they walk over to the table and begin removing the ashtrays full of cigarette butts, the half-empty bottles of mineral water and orange juice. Diligently and silently, they place clean ashtrays, clean glasses, fresh bottles of mineral water, large pitchers of orange juice on the long table.

Looking displeased and impatient, La Pasionaria waits for them to finish before beginning to read her speech.

You have a few moment's respite left then.

So you raise your eyes from the papers, the notebook, the documents you have on the table in front of you. You contemplate the comrades of the Executive Committee at this decisive moment. You remember the phrase that Santiago Carrillo came out with the other day: "It is better to be wrong with the party, inside the party, than to be right outside of it or against it." And this phrase has not surprised you, because you yourself had uttered it, years before, when you were very sure of yourself and certain of your cause, like a Jesuit martyr in Japan.

In fact it is a phrase, an idea, that is typical of religion ("outside the Church there is no salvation"), that is to say, one linked to a totalizing and totalitarian conception of the world. In your years as a Stalinist, you defended this phrase ("it is better to be wrong with the party, inside the party, than to be right outside of it") against those who dared to cast doubt on it, or perhaps show surprise at its puritan rigor, by resorting to a pseudo-dialectical line of argument based on the negative aspect of the Hegelian tradition.

The premise of this argument consisted of affirming that the party—the Party Spirit—was the concrete incarnation of the victorious march of History toward its objectively progressive and Socialist goals. The party, its practical activity, its theory, thus incarnated the global Truth, Truth in its entirety. Outside the party, therefore, there were only partial, momentary, episodic, ephemeral truths, tiny shards of truth. To be right against the party meant only that one possessed a minute particle of truth, which on becoming detached from the global, concrete, historical Truth of the Party Spirit became dialectically transformed into global falsity.

An impeccable and aberrant line of reasoning that collapsed spontaneously like a house of cards the moment the Party Spirit ceased to be considered as the ultimate avatar of the Absolute Spirit, from the moment that History ceased to be something preordained, a process whose sole Subject is the Party Spirit—the concrete, concentrated, and incontrovertible expression of the Revolutionary Class, once and for all and *in saecula saeculorum,* amen—the sole aim of which is the establishment of a New Society, which is maturing in the breast of the Old Society and will emerge from this breast as Minerva sprang fully armed from the head of Jove. When one has convinced oneself that all the foregoing is false, that none of this corresponds to what is essential in the critical and practical exposition of Marxism by Marx, one has no difficulty confronting the Absolute Spirit, even in the concrete and sinister guise of the Party Spirit.

You contemplate your comrades on the Executive Committee, who today incarnate the Party Spirit, its severe but sacred rigor. You continue to contemplate them one by one. They are serious and silent as the waiters with the immaculate gloves and bureaucratic discretion change the ashtrays and the bottles of mineral water. Tongues of Pentecostal fire surround their heads. All the members of the Executive Committee are of working-class origins and this background sanctifies them and turns them into apostles, makes them worthy of proclaiming the virtues of the Party Spirit, of singings its praises and casting you into the hell of outer darkness. The only one who does not come from a working-class background—or a peasant one; naturally the two amount to the same thing so far as the effects of Pentecost are concerned—is poor Tomás García (Juan Gómez). That is why he is forever beating his breast in contrition and reciting his *mea culpas,* why he mortifies himself and torments himself by donning the hairshirt of permanent self-criticism, and although all this makes no one forget his nefarious origins, it does secure him a certain benevolent tolerance on the part of the others, on the part of those who may indeed be counted among the true apostles of the New Faith proclaimed by Irene Falcón.

You contemplate your comrades of working-class origins and see the tongues of Pentecostal fire that dance above their bald spots. In reality they haven't worked for decades and a goodly number of them have simply been of working-class origins without ever being real workers.

And even those who have been real workers for brief periods have been nothing more than bureaucratic managers for decades now, executive cadres of a political enterprise, with all the social privileges appertaining thereunto. And a few risks as well. But this is a truism. When have there ever been privileges without risks? Can there be anything that less resembles a worker than Manuel Delicado, a most delicate and refined sybarite, an Andalusian princeling till the day he's dead and buried. But this is beside the question here. The question has to do with something much more important: the question of Origins. And you might as well stop beating about the bush. They are of working-class origins and you are not. They are speaking in the name of Origins, condemning you in the name of Origins, casting you out into the hell of your own infamous Origins.

At this moment, your eyes meet Gregorio López Raimundo's.

When you arrived here a week ago—a century ago—the woman comrade of the Foreign Section of the Czech Central Committee who was taking care of arrangements for all of you wanted to put you up in the same room with Fernando Claudín. But one of the Spanish comrades of the technical apparatus seeing to it that the meeting went smoothly intervened immediately, no doubt obeying orders from above, and made sure that Fernando and you were separated. They put you and Gregorio López Raimundo in the same room, and put Claudín in with Eduardo García. It was as though you were in some Jesuit school and the reverend prefect had stepped in to separate two wayward pupils who might corrupt the others by their bad example and their wicked thoughts. As though separating you from Claudín could conjure away the complete agreement between the two of you with regard to the principal points of the debate.

In any event, you shared those days in the castle of Bohemian kings with Gregorio. You found yourself sharing his company every night in the same room. As the days went by, you could see that Gregorio was becoming more and more irritated. He could not understand how you could claim that you were right and the majority of the Executive Committee wrong. He could not understand your refusal to capitulate in the face of this majority. You explained to him at length that there are moments when it is a Communist obligation to stick to one's opinions even though they represent a minority view, when one is convinced that they are correct, when experience, if properly analyzed, without ideological blinders, would serve as ample demonstration of the truth of these divergent opinions. But even admitting as a sheer hypothesis that you might be right, López Raimundo was unable to admit that you were right to insist so unreasonably that you were right in the face of the majority of the Executive Committee. That is to say, in the face of the Party Spirit.

You have raised your eyes from your papers, and your gaze has met Gregorio's.

In a famous Catalan song, Raimon has described a chance encounter he had with Gregorio López Raimundo in a Barcelona street in the days when Gregorio was working underground.

T'he conegut sempre igual com ara,
els cabells blancs, la bondat a la cara,
els llavis fins dibuixant un somriure
d'amic, company, consciente del perill . . . .

[I have always known you as you are today,
with white hair, goodness on your face,
delicate lips forming a smile
of a friend, of a comrade, conscious of the peril. . . .]

Aside from the intrinsic beauty of the words and the music, aside from the fact that this song may be considered impersonally as a Brechtian "praise of work underground," and aside, finally, from the physical resemblance of this portrait to its subject, it is nonetheless true that it is an idealization—though doubtless understandable given the circumstances—of the real, the essential character of the leader of the PSUC. Above and beyond the "white hair," the "goodness" of the face, and the permanent cunning, artful "smile," the fact is that López Raimundo is one of the most deliberately forgetful, pragmatic, and implacable sectarians—the definition of a sectarian being "one who professes, follows, and stubbornly defends a given doctrine"—of the Party Spirit, one of the Communist leaders most capable of subordinating any sort of moral criterion to the immediate interests of the Party (and here the ritual capital letter must be employed).

But the waiters in their white jackets and immaculate gloves are picking up the last ashtrays, taking away the last empty bottles. You do not have much time left

I do not have much time left.

As soon as they have finished La Pasionaria will doubtless take the floor, as she asked to do a few minutes ago.

I turn my eyes toward her again.

Everything began in my memory a few minutes ago, as I remembered my first meeting with La Pasionaria in the offices on the Avenue Kléber. If I were writing a novel I would end it by telling about my last meeting with her. The very last one, doubtless, because I am never going to see her again. It was at the Belgrade airport, in 1970 or 1971, I don't remember the exact date. Colette and I had been in Belgrade, at Luis Miguel "Dominguín's" invitation, to attend something utterly absurd, at least in Belgrade, but which turned out to be marvelous, despite the fact that it took place in Belgrade: bullfights. It had no doubt been one of Domingo's fantastic ideas. We spent several days with him and Luis Miguel, having a wonderful time. Bullfights in Belgrade might be the story line of a screenplay by Rafael Azcona, it occurs to me, one of those stupendous screenplays of his, full of melancholy and healthy irony. But be that as it may, on the day that we were to return to Paris, Colette and I found ourselves in a departure lounge at the Belgrade airport. Suddenly someone shouted: "Federico!" It was Dolores Ibárruri, who was there with Irene Falcón and a group of Yugoslav comrades. La Pasionaria spoke with us for a few minutes, in a very natural way, as though nothing had happened, as though I were a party intellectual, or one of those faithful fellow travelers of the party. Did La Pasionaria even remember that she had cast me into outer darkness? It didn't seem like it that day at the Belgrade airport. Her cordiality appeared to be genuine enough. Then the loudspeakers announced the flight to Moscow, and La Pasionaria, accompanied by Irene Falcón and the little retinue of Yugoslav comrades, headed for the departure gate, giving us a hearty goodbye wave. And then one of the Yugoslav comrades halted in front of me. He was a tall, stout, middle-aged man, leaning on a cane as he walked because he had a slight limp. He halted in front of me and with a smile full of irony and cordiality and affection and intelligence, he said to me: "Comrade Federico, allow me to introduce myself: I'm Vlajo Vlajovich." It was a name I knew, naturally. Vlajovich had fought in the International Brigades and in the Yugoslav guerrilla campaign, and was one of Tito's lieutenants. At the time of the break between the Comintern and Tito and the violent campaign of calumnies that followed, Vlajo Vlajovich was one of the Yugoslav comrades who suffered most from these slanderous attacks, especially those mounted by the Spanish Communist Party. "The sinister one with the gimpy leg," was how Vlajo Vlajovich was referred to in the anti-Tito propaganda put out by the Spanish Communist Party. Vlajo Vlajovich had nonetheless come that day to see La Pasionaria off on the plane to Moscow, and had halted in front of me and introduced himself with a smile. And in order that there would be no doubt as to the meaning of his smile, he added: "When you see Fernando Claudín, say hello to him for me, and give him a big friendly embrace." And Vlajo Vlajovich went off.

But what I am writing is not a novel, or a screenplay with Rafael Azcona. I am simply telling, straight out with no fancy frills, what happened in that ancient castle of Bohemian kings.

I look at La Pasionaria again.

> And I wish to speak to you now in my own name,
> in my most intimate voice, from the depths of myself

That was what the long-ago poem of mine of 1947 had said, and that is what I say today, in April of 1964, today too I want to speak to you, in my own name, in my most intimate voice, from the depths of myself, to explain to you who I am, where I come from, tell you who Federico Sánchez was, to try to start, at last, a dialogue with you, to be able to hear, at last, from your own lips the hidden truths of your own life, to speak, finally, today, in the first days of a wet and cold April, in this Kafkaesque castle, speak, finally, after this long, monolithic monologue . . . .

But La Pasionaria is speaking.

As you were wandering about, lost in your memory, as you were imagining a genuine conversation with her that would never be, La Pasionaria has taken the floor. She is reading, in her splendid metallic voice, at once harsh and harmonious, the sheet of paper that she has all prepared. She is hurling the lightning-bolts of her wrath at you. She is speaking in the name of the Party Spirit, the sacrosanct Party Spirit. She is saying that Fernando and you are only "hare-brained intellectuals."

And this phrase spins dizzyingly in the sort of nauseated disgust that comes over you, it spins dizzyingly in the grand salon of the kings of Bohemia, it spins dizzyingly amid the bare leafless trees of the park,

hare-brained intellectuals, HARE-BRAINED intellectuals, HARE-BRAINED INTELLECTUALS . . . .

INDEX OF PRINCIPAL NAMES

ALBERTI, Rafael: Spanish poet and anti-Francoist driven into exile following the Civil War. Sympathizer, if not member, of the Spanish Communist Party (PCE).

ALEIXANDRE, Vicente: Spanish poet and Nobel Prize for Literature Winner in 1977.

ALVAREZ, Santiago: PCE Executive Committee member. Political commissar of the Spanish Republican army. Sentenced to death by Francoist tribunals in 1945, saved by an international campaign.

ANTON, Francisco: Communist party leader in the Civil War era and leading power in the secretariat at the beginning of the fifties. Criticized in 1952 for sectarianism and the abuse of power, he was removed from his leadership posts.

AUB, Max: Spanish writer. Died in exile. Andre Malraux's principal assistant in the making of the film, *Man's Hope.*

AZAÑA, Manuel: Spanish writer and politician. Leader of the Republican left from 1931–36. President of the Republic throughout the Civil War. Died in exile in 1940.

AZCARATE, Manuel: PCE Executive Committee member and foreign affairs specialist of the party.

BARDEM, Juan Antonio: Spanish film producer. Arrested in 1956 in Madrid while shooting *Calle Mayor.*

BÉCQUER, Gustavo Adolfo: Spanish romantic poet of the nineteenth century.

BERGAMIN, José: Spanish writer and left Catholic. Founder of the *Cruz y Raya* review during the thirties. Friend of Malraux's and model for Guernico in *Man's Hope.*

CALVO SERER, Rafael: member of the conservative-Catholic and pro-government Opus Dei. Moved into the monarchist opposition in the sixties. Participated in the ephemeral Junta Democratica, alongside Santiago Carrillo.

CARRILLO, Santiago: PCE secretary general.

CASTELLET, José Maria: literary critic, essayist, and Catalan publisher.

CERÓN, Julio: Spanish intellectual and one of the founders of the Popular Liberation Front (FLP) in the fifties.

CLAUDÍN, Fernando: rose from Communist Youth leader before the Civil War to the secretariat of the party in 1956. Expelled from the party in 1964 along with Federico Sánchez. Author of: *The Communist Movement: From Comintern to Cominform; Eurocommunism;* and *Marx and Engels and the Revolution of 1948.*

CLAUDÍN, Pilar: Fernando Claudín's sister. Clandestine militant against Franco.

COMORERA, Joan: secretary general of the PSUC from its foundation in 1936 until 1949, when he was condemned for "Titoism," slandered, and expelled. Died in a Francoist prison.

CONESA, Roberto: commissioner of the Political Police under Franco and to this day.

DELICADO, Manuel: early PCE leader, entering the Politburo in 1932.

DÍEZ ALEGRÍA, lieutenant general: chief of staff of the Spanish Armed Forces. Removed from office following a trip to Rumania, where he asserted that the military should remain neutral in any future settlement of Spanish political life. Considered to have been supported by the US as a "moderate" pro-NATO force in Spain.

EYMAR (colonel): president of the calle del Reloj military tribunal in Madrid.

FRAGA IRIBARNE, Manuel: at one time information minister under Franco. Currently leader of the non-fascist electoral right.

FRANQUI, Carlos: Cuban revolutionary and one of the first combatants in the Castroist July 26th Movement. Split with Castro in 1968 over the latter's defense of the Soviet invasion of Czechoslovakia, and left the country. Author of *Diary of the Cuban Revolution.*

IBARRURI, Dolores, "la Pasionaria": charismatic, historic figure of Spanish Communism. Member of the PCE Politburo since 1932. Secretary general from 1942, following the mysterious suicide of José Díaz in a Caucasian rest home, to 1960.

IZCARAY, Jesus: member of PCE Central Committee, journalist, and socialist-realist writer.

LÍSTER, Enrique: military chief of the Spanish Peoples' Army during the Civil War and PCE Executive Committee member for many years thereafter. Opposed the PCE's condemnation of the Soviet invasion of Czechoslovakia in 1968 and founded a pro-Soviet splinter group, the Spanish Communist Workers' Party.

LONDON, Artur: Czechoslovakian Communist Party leader purged in the Slansky trials of 1952. Author of *On Trial,* on which the Costa Gavras film, *The Confession,* was based.

LÓPEZ RAIMUNDO, Gregorio: PCE Executive Committee member and president of the PSUC.

MADRIAGA, Salvador de: internationally renown Spanish scholar and historian. Liberal Republican critic of the Franco regime, lived much of his life in exile. Author of *Spain: A Modern History.*

MIJE, Antonio: PCE leader since 1932. Died in exile.

MONZON, Jesus: PCE Central Committee member. Directed party work in France and Spain during the Second World War. After war, underground leader in Spain. Accused in 1947, by Carrillo from his exile in France, of being an "enemy agent."

NEGRÍN, Juan: leader of the Spanish Socialist Party (PSOE). Prime minister of the Republic from May 17, 1937 to the end of the Civil War. Died in exile.

PAJETTA, Giancarlo: leader of the Italian Communist Party.

PRIMO DE RIVERA, José Antonio: son of the military dictator. Founder of the Falange Española party. Executed by firing squad in Alicante at the beginning of the Civil War.

QUEREJETA, Elias: independent film producer.

ROMERO MARIN, Francisco: PCE Executive Committee member.

ROSSANDA, Rossana: Central Committee member of the Italian Communist Party. Expelled from the party after founding the left-communist review, *Il Manifesto.*

RIDRUEJO, Dionisio: former Falangist leader, died in June 1975. Having broken with the Franco regime in 1942, he became an important force behind the social-democratic opposition.

SÁNCHEZ FERLOSIO, Rafael: writer of the "realist generation" of the fifties. Son of a founder of the Falange, Sanchez Mazas. His most significant novel is entitled *The Waters of the Jarama.*

SÁNCHEZ MONTERO, Simon: PCE Executive Committee member.

TAMAMES, Ramón: member of the PCE Executive Committee, economist, and author of numerous books. Became active as an anti-Francoist in university in 1956.

TRENTIN, Bruno: Italian Communist Party leader. Secretary of the powerful Italian Metallurgy Union Federation.

TRILLA, Gabriel León: PCE underground leader accused of being an "enemy agent," executed in 1945 by order of the PCE leadership in exile.

URIBE, Vincente: historic PCE leader. Responsible for the PCE's central leadership cell from 1945 to 1956. Died in exile.

INDEX OF PERIODICALS

ABC: daily of the extreme monarchist right.

Action: Parisian weekly from the Liberation era. Run by Pierre Hervé, Pierre Courtade, and Victor Leduc.

Cuadernos de cultura: illegal PCE political and cultural agitation review.

Cuadernos para el dialogo: once monthly, now weekly, review. Of social-democratic tendency.

Cultura y Democracia: PCE cultural review published in France until 1950.

Independencia: political and cultural agitation review published under the control of the PCE in France before 1950.

Mundo Obrero: weekly of the PCE Central Committee, published legally in France until 1950, and then underground. Published today in Madrid as a daily.

Nuestra Bandera: theoretical and political review of the PCE Central Committee. Run by Fernando Claudín from 1956 to 1964.

Nuestras Ideas: PCE cultural review published in Belgium.

Objectivo: film review published in the fifties by Ricardo Muñoz Suay, Juan Antonio Bardem, and Eduardo Ducay.

Realidad: PCE cultural review published in Italy.

Triunfo: democratic weekly magazine published legally in the latter part of the Franco regime. Under the direction of Eduardo Haro Tecglen, it has been a center of free information and of formative training for Spanish left journalists.

INDEX OF ACRONYMS

ASU: University Socialist Association. Founded in 1956. Certain of its leaders can be found today in the executive organs of the PSOE.

CNS: National Confederation of Unions. Government-controlled "vertical" syndicalist trade unions under the Franco regime.

CNT: National Confederation of Labor. Anarcho-syndicalist movement and a predominant force among Spanish workers until 1939. Inactive under Franco, it has since been resurrected.

CPSU: Communist Party of the Soviet Union.

ETA: Basque Homeland and Liberty. Armed movement originating from a series of splits in the Basque Nationalist Left. The execution in 1973 of Carrero Blanco, Franco's right-hand man and presumed successor, undoubtedly constitutes this movement's most important action.

FLP: Popular Liberation Front. Anti-Francoist opposition movement created in the fifties. Radical, Christian-Marxist in inspiration.

FRAP: Revolutionary Anti-Fascist and Patriotic Front. Movement of armed struggle and urban terrorism, resulting from a series of Maoist splits from the PCE.

IDC: Christian-Democratic Left. Created in the fifties. Joaquin Ruiz Jimenez, education minister fired by Franco following the university troubles of 1956, has been one of its key leaders.

PCE: Communist Party of Spain.

POUM: Workers' Party of Marxist Unification. Created by the fusion of the Workers' and Peasants' Bloc with certain left-communist opposition groups. Influenced by Trotskyism.

PSAD: Social Party of Democratic Action. Social-democratic opposition group against Franco. Its principal leader was Dionisio Ridruejo.

PSOE: Spanish Socialist Workers' Party.

PSUC: United Socialist Party of Catalonia. The party of Catalan Communists, created in 1936 with the fusion of several Marxist-Leninist and left-socialist groups and parties.

SEU: Spanish University Syndicate. Official (government sponsored) nonrepresentative student union.

UGT: General Union of Workers. Socialist-inspired labor-union movement, organically tied to the PSOE.